Celebrating the Republic

Celebrating the Republic

Presidential Ceremony and
Popular Sovereignty,
from Washington to Monroe

Sandra Moats

NORTHERN ILLINOIS UNIVERSITY PRESS
DeKalb

© 2010 by Northern Illinois University Press
Published by the Northern Illinois University Press, DeKalb, Illinois 60115
Manufactured in the United States using postconsumer-recycled, acid-free paper.
All Rights Reserved
Design by Shaun Allshouse

Library of Congress Cataloging-in-Publication Data
Moats, Sandra.
  Celebrating the Republic: presidential ceremony and popular sovereignty, from Washington to Monroe / Sandra Moats.
    p. cm.
  Includes bibliographical references and index.
  ISBN 978-0-87580-411-8 (clothbound : alk. paper)
  1. Presidents—United States—History—18th century. 2. Presidents—United States—History—19th century. 3. Political customs and rites—United States—History—18th century. 4. Political customs and rites—United States—History—19th century. 5. Political culture—United States—History—18th century. 6. Political culture—United States—History—19th century. 7. Sovereignty—Social aspects—United States—History. 8. United States—Politics and government—1783–1809. 9. United States—Politics and government—1809–1817. 10. United States—Politics and government—1817–1825. I. Title.
  E176.1.M73 2010
  973.3—dc22
                     2009036600

For my parents

Contents

Illustrations ix

Acknowledgments xi

Introduction "Untrodden Ground"
Presidential Ceremony and Popular Sovereignty 3

1 "Ceremonies, Endless Ceremonies"
The People and Congress Inaugurate a President 10

2 "To Preserve the Dignity and Respect"
Washington's Republican Approach to Presidential Ceremony 35

3 "We Deal in Ink Only"
Jefferson's Rhetorical Opposition to Federalist Ceremony 63

4 Desperately Seeking "Good Feelings"
Monroe's Northern Tour of 1817 91

5 "The Success and Stability of Our Republican Institutions"
Monroe's Southern Tour of 1819 135

Conclusion Celebrations, Parties, and Antebellum Politics 170

Notes 179

Bibliography 219

Index 233

Illustrations

1. Charles Willson Peale's drawing of his wreath-dropping machine   18
2. Triumphal Arch erected by the ladies of Trenton   19
3. George Washington being greeted by the ladies of Trenton   20
4. Washington being transported from Elizabethtown, N.J.   21
5. Washington's arrival in New York City at the end of his preinaugural journey   23
6. Washington receiving the oath of office at Federal Hall   26
7. Portrait of George Washington commissioned by Harvard University   53
8. Thomas Jefferson portrait by Charles Willson Peale   67
9. Dolley Madison, circa 1805   87
10. Map of the route of James Monroe's northern tour   93
11a & b. Christopher Gore and Jeremiah Mason   99
12. Harrison Gray Otis, a younger Federalist   102
13. A tactile souvenir of the northern tour   120
14. Daniel Webster, another younger Federalist   123
15. Map of the route of James Monroe's southern tour   136
16. John Calhoun, Monroe's secretary of war   145

17. Portrait of James Monroe by Samuel F. B. Morse   152
18. William H. Crawford, Monroe's secretary of the treasury   155
19. Major General Andrew Jackson   159
20. Henry Clay, speaker of the house   162
21. Andrew Jackson's 1829 inauguration   172

Acknowledgments

I have lived with this project longer than I had expected, and now that it is finally done, there are many people I need to thank.

The section of this book dealing with James Monroe's two tours originally comprised my doctoral dissertation. I am grateful to Joyce Appleby, who provided excellent guidance and support while I worked on it at UCLA. Her advice that I select a topic that I could live with for ten years proved to be right on the mark, since exactly ten years has elapsed since I embarked on this topic.

My dissertation research took me to the American Antiquarian Society, the Huntington Library, the Library of Congress, the Massachusetts Historical Society, the New-York Historical Society, and the New York Public Library. I have also benefited from the generous universal borrowing system that exists at the University of Wisconsin. The staffs and resources of these institutions were tremendously helpful as I conducted my research. Some of the material in Chapter 4 appeared in an article I published recently, "Partisan Healing and Political Futures during James Monroe's Boston Visit of 1817," in the *Proceedings of the American Antiquarian Society*, vol. 118, pt. I (2009).

As I made the slow transition from dissertation to book, I stubbornly believed that this project had the makings of a book. I appreciate the input and suggestions of professors Scott Casper, Jason Frank, Betsy Glade, Andrew Robertson, and Ed Schmitt as I pondered the "what's next" of my dissertation. An NEH summer seminar on Governance in the Early Republic, led by professors John Larson and Mike Morrison, proved extremely helpful as I tackled the larger theoretical and intellectual issues surrounding presidential ceremony, popular sovereignty, and the U.S. Constitution.

The history department at the University of Wisconsin, Parkside, is a model of collegiality and intellectual talent. I enjoy the ongoing support and friendship of Jeff Alexander, Nat Godley, Ed Schmitt, and Daryl Webb. David Bruce provided valuable assistance with early American newspapers. Our chair, Laura Gellott, deserves particular recognition for building and mentoring such a strong department. I have received generous financial support for research and conferences from the Provost's Fund and the Committee on Research and Creative Activity at the university. The history department also has supported this project by covering the cost of permissions. I am grateful to Don Littner and his staff for their assistance in producing the images used in this book; to Jeannie Walker for her assistance with permission requests; and to Katie Gray, Abbie Schnaare, and Diane Weyker for their research help.

Northern Illinois University Press originally expressed interest in this project while I was still a graduate student. About ten years and three acquisition editors later, I greatly appreciate their ongoing interest and patience. I thank Martin Johnson for his initial interest, Melody Herr for her encouragement and advice as the dissertation slowly became a book, and finally, Sara Hoerdeman for her efforts in bringing about its ultimate publication. I would also like to thank the outside reviewers whose comments greatly strengthened the finished product.

Finally, I want to thank (in no particular order) my friends and family. In addition to my history department colleagues, I would like to thank Dana Oswald, Mary Lenard, Maria Martinez, Anna Stadick, Laurie Moats, Henry Moats, Icky Moats, Catherine and Dale Stephens, Charlie Sleigh, Margaret Foley, and Gail Gonzalez for their friendship and support during this and other endeavors. My parents, Drs. William and Sheila Moats, are scientists who always seemed a little unclear as to what their historian daughter was researching. This book is dedicated to them, with love, in an attempt to answer that question.

Celebrating the Republic

Introduction

"Untrodden Ground"

Presidential Ceremony and Popular Sovereignty

On January 20, 1977, Jimmy Carter famously abandoned his inaugural limousine and walked down Pennsylvania Avenue to signal the beginnings of a more accessible and accountable administration than had existed in recent years. Unbeknownst to many Americans, Carter was borrowing a page from Thomas Jefferson, who had undertaken an equally famous stroll to his own inauguration in 1801. Throughout our nation's history, we have grown accustomed to our presidents employing symbols to convey their political priorities and governing philosophies to the nation's sovereign citizens. This book tells the story of how our first presidents invented the American political culture that endures today by employing the symbols and rituals they believed best illustrated republican principles to an American citizenry who now possessed sovereign authority over this new national government.

As the nation's first republican president, George Washington acknowledged the enormous challenges he faced, writing, "I walk on untrodden ground." He then explained the importance of establishing appropriate presidential conduct: "There is scarcely any action, whose motives may not be subject to a double interpretation. There is scarcely any part of my conduct which may not hereafter be drawn into precedent." Washington concluded, "Under such a view of the duties inherent to my arduous office, I could not but feel a diffidence in myself on the one hand; and an anxiety for the Community that every new arrangement should be made in the best possible manner on the other."[1] A year into his presidency, Washington understood that for the new Constitution to succeed, rituals and practices would need to be developed that made republican government relevant and tangible to those Americans who possessed sovereign authority over it.

A republican political culture would require symbols, rituals, and practices that animated and illustrated abstract principles such as the government's authority, legitimacy, and scope. Successful governments needed a vibrant ceremonial culture to bring dry constitutional ideas to life, and such a governing culture would be particularly imperative in the uncharted waters of American republican government. A political culture offered more than just lively street theater or colorful iconography.[2] Instead, these symbolic presentations of republican government provided a dramatic (and therefore, tactile) interpretation of the U.S. Constitution for the approval or disapproval of the nation's citizens.[3] Seemingly mundane matters such as titles, accessibility, protocol, tours, and inaugurations spoke volumes on how the nation's early political leaders chose to interpret the Constitution.

While all forms of government benefit from symbolic forms to promote their legitimacy and authority, the new American government faced the additional challenges of fostering a new and potentially fragile form of government amidst a people distrustful of centralized authority. Since monarchical pomp and ceremony defined most forms of late 18th-century government, the nation's early leaders struggled to invent signs and rituals compatible with republican ideas. This book concerns the efforts of the first five presidents, along with the contributions of the nation's citizens and its newspapers, to construct a political culture that would ensure the successful launching and longevity of the new republican government.[4]

Despite the primacy of the legislative branch in republican government, the unique characteristics of the presidency permitted the executive branch to play an unusually large role in defining republican ceremony. First, this office paralleled the singular head of state associated with monarchy, an office that was both familiar to many Americans and offered a rich tradition of ceremonial precedents. Second, it was easier to follow the activities of one person rather than the entire House and Senate. Third, the president possessed a national constituency since he had been selected by the entire nation, albeit indirectly, unlike the other branches. Finally, Washington's election as the first president gave this office a commanding presence that built on his long service and leadership to the nation.

While the first five presidents shared the common goal of launching an effective national government, they disagreed sharply on the form a republican culture should take. Each president experimented with a variety of symbols and practices that ran the gamut from formal to informal, polished to pompous, accessible to invisible.[5] Eventually two competing philosophical approaches emerged, both of which had the potential to strengthen or destroy republican government. George Washington, building upon the monarchical rituals instituted by the public and Congress during his first inauguration, introduced additional royal practices such as tours and formal receptions to energize the new government.[6] Twelve years later, Thomas Jefferson famously rejected Washington's example as too monarchical and unrepublican. Instead, Jefferson adopted an informal presidential style within the nation's capital and strengthened popular sovereignty outside its confines, employing rhetorical tools such as letters and editorials to promote a nascent political organization.[7] Among the other early presidents, John Adams and James Madison struggled, without much success, to find presidential styles that suited them. Instead, their wives, Abigail Adams and Dolley Madison, filled the ceremonial vacuum with varying degrees of success by using the feminine realm of entertaining as a political tool. James Monroe, the last of the founding presidents, embarked on a more democratized version of Washington's presidential tours to renew the sovereign bond between government and citizen while also welcoming a new generation of politicians to the national scene.

What the presidential styles of Washington and Jefferson neatly summarized were competing interpretations of the Constitution, particularly in the areas of federal authority, the president's constitutional role, and the nature of popular sovereignty. Washington believed a strong centralized government should take the lead in setting the nation's agenda, and he worked to establish a viable connection between the federal government and the nation's sovereign citizens through a ceremonial repertoire of tours and receptions.[8] Jefferson favored a more decentralized form of government where the citizenry defined the federal government's role, and his informal style encouraged citizens to exercise their sovereign authority through participation in local political organizations.[9]

The ultimate test for these presidential styles was whether the interpretation of the Constitution they were promoting met with the approval of the sovereign citizens who imbued the government with its authority. Tours, receptions, levees, and party organizations triggered a lively discussion among citizens, newspaper editors, and politicians concerning the best way to implement the Constitution's republican mandate.[10] Whether serving on an organizing committee, watching a presidential procession, marching in a welcoming parade, delivering an address or a poem, displaying a banner, constructing a triumphal arch, or rejecting all of these activities, Americans had ample opportunities to engage with the nation's government and to exercise their authority over the government to bring the notion of "we the people" to life.[11] Presidential ceremonies and political parties provided venues for the exercise of popular sovereignty, the crucial republican idea that separated the young nation's government from European monarchies. Presidential symbolism did more than mirror the new political landscape; it effected political change as these forms initiated a new generation of citizens into the rituals of republican government. Although some historians have dismissed popular sovereignty as a "fiction," this governing principle had to be activated for the new government to succeed.[12] Thanks to presidential efforts to establish a republican political culture, popular sovereignty became a vigorous and viable concept in the early republic as Americans participated in their own governance.

Newspapers proved to be a particularly rich outlet for Americans to discuss the meanings of republican government, and highly partisan editors did not hesitate to offer their opinions on the appropriateness of presidential tours. As Washington and Monroe passed through a city or town during their respective tours, the local editors reported on these visits, freely inserting favorable and unfavorable comments within their coverage. These accounts were then widely distributed through the U.S. mails, and were reprinted in other newspapers throughout the northern, southern, and western states.[13] Because of the widespread sharing of newspapers at that time, the presidential tours of Washington and Monroe engaged a much wider audience than just the citizens who participated in these events. The *New-York Daily Gazette*'s enthusiastic embrace of Washington during his preinaugural tour neatly captured the sovereign bond being affirmed for many Americans: "Our beloved Magistrate delights to show, upon all occasions, that he is a man—and instead of assuming the pomp of master, acts as if he considered himself the father—the friend—the servant of the People."¹⁴ Not everyone was convinced that such an enthusiastic outpouring was compatible with republican ideas. A Boston correspondent wrote to the *New-Jersey Journal*, "I am sorry to differ in sentiment with you, respecting the mode we adopted to show our respects to our illustrious visitant," the implication being that Boston had been excessive in its welcoming reception of Washington during his eastern tour.¹⁵ Newspapers not only offered a crucial forum for the debate over republican ceremony and popular sovereignty, but the editors' strong regional biases and open partisanship ensured that a wide range of opinions were present in these discussions.¹⁶

Beginning in 1789, the nation's presidents experimented with a variety of symbolic forms that they hoped would engage the nation's citizens and bring the republican concept of popular sovereignty to life. In particular, Washington, Jefferson, and Monroe employed signs and rituals that illustrated their understandings of republicanism to the American people. Although these presidential efforts did not yield a consensus on republican culture, they produced something even more vital. These ceremonial presentations stimulated a vigorous discussion among the nation's citizens and provided them with a tangible opportunity to exercise their sovereign authority over the government through their embrace or rejection of these presidential interpretations of republicanism. The availability of symbols and events to enliven the relationship between citizen and republic created communities of nationally engaged citizens and contributed to the new government's successful establishment. During the nation's first thirty years, the debates over a political culture played a critical yet overlooked role in energizing the new government's underlying principles to ensure the relevance of republican ideas and institutions for the American people.¹⁷

During the 1790s, presidential ceremony and partisan organizations emerged as two leading ways for the nation's early leaders to convey and invigorate the government's republican principles. Although these forms represented opposing viewpoints along the political spectrum, they shared many similar attributes because of their ability to express substantive messages through symbols and icons. Despite their positive qualities, ceremony and parties also posed significant risks for republican government. While George Washington's understanding of republican government provided the ideological basis for his presidency's ceremonial culture, his tours and receptions also borrowed heavily from monarchical traditions. The opponents of presidential ceremony believed that the excesses and corruption associated with the rejected monarchy could easily overpower the more modest republican values of virtue and simplicity, and destroy this system of government. Similarly, political parties or factions posed a threat to republican virtue because of their ability to subvert the public will. During the ratification of the Constitution, James Madison had warned in *Federalist #10* that the deleterious effect of special interests, whether organizational or ideological, needed to be managed within republican government. Symbols and rituals were needed to enliven the new government; determining which ones would vitalize rather than attenuate republican ideas provoked a vigorous discussion that went to the heart of how best to interpret the Constitution.

Symbols and ceremony also proved to be surprisingly useful to the politicians of the early republic, who needed to find ways to promote their careers and agendas without appearing ambitious and selfish. Republican principles prized virtuous and disinterested leaders, while self-interested officials were considered unseemly and inappropriate. To succeed under these conditions, many politicians employed ceremonies or partisan organizations in order to downplay their aspirations while remaining politically engaged and effective. In an environment in which overt campaigning was tantamount to disqualification, particularly at the presidential level, public events such as receptions or tours afforded an officeholder with ways to promote himself while also advancing the common good. In addition, public rituals and partisan surrogates provided camouflage for politicians to engage in disputes and rivalries with one another, while appearing to respect the rules of republican decorum. As the nation's early leaders debated the best way to exercise power under the Constitution's mandate, they discovered that symbolic forms not only promoted republican government but advanced their plans and programs as well.[18]

In 1789, the first generation of American leaders faced the daunting yet exciting challenge of launching the new government and bringing its constitutional ideas to life. Paramount among these republican ideas was the concept of popular sovereignty: the idea that the government derived its authority from the people. The nation's first five presidents, particularly Washington, Jefferson, and Monroe, worked to develop a republican political culture that incorporated their understandings of the Constitution's mandate and would ultimately engage the citizenry with the government. The failure of our leaders, citizens, and newspaper editors to reach a consensus on ceremonial forms was exactly what the new government needed to succeed. In the discussions, debates, and reactions to presidential ceremony and non-ceremony that resulted, popular sovereignty came to life as Americans interacted with their leaders to define the meanings and parameters of republican government.

Thirteen years had passed since the American colonists had declared their independence from Britain, and the Constitution of 1787 offered an opportunity to complete the nation's philosophical and political separation. Venturing into the uncharted territory of popular sovereignty and republican ideas, the nation's leaders turned to symbols and rituals for guidance. Thirty years of presidential experimentation in ceremonial forms produced a dynamic relationship between the government and its citizenry that ensured the government's successful launching. Celebrations and parties mattered, because they defined republican government for the founding generation and for all the ones that followed.

1

"Ceremonies, Endless Ceremonies"

The People and Congress Inaugurate a President

A month into his first term as president, George Washington candidly addressed the high expectations that accompanied his new responsibilities. Writing to Edward Rutledge, Washington declared, "I greatly apprehend that my countrymen will expect too much from me," adding that public opinion would quickly swing from "extravagant (and may I say undue) praises" to "equally extravagant censures" as his policies failed to satisfy these diverse expectations.[1]

Washington accurately read both the enormous challenges and contradictory instructions facing the new government and his role as its first president. First, the government needed to establish its authority and legitimacy in a manner that was acceptable to the nation's sovereign citizens. Second, the government needed to demonstrate its authority over the vast territory that extended to the Mississippi River, as well as over the thirteen states that had grown accustomed to a relatively ineffectual national government. Rhode Island and North Carolina, which had not ratified the Constitution by the spring of 1789, illustrated the difficulty the federal government faced in asserting itself among the several states.[2] Republican government also offered its own historical and institutional problems. Despite its ability to counter the capricious, tyrannical qualities of monarchies, republican government nonetheless possessed the seeds of its own destruction. The difficulties in cultivating a virtuous, engaged citizenry capable of responsibly exercising their sovereign authority over this government stood as one of the greatest obstacles confronting the government's launching. Lastly, Washington wanted to affirm that the president was a popularly elected national figure who held limited and defined terms, like other political officials, and who served the nation on behalf of the people, not the other way around. At the same time he wanted to assert that this uncharted office was viewed as something more than a county clerk but certainly less than a monarch.

While the success of the new government would depend heavily on Washington's performance, the constitutional procedures for electing the president made him a relative latecomer to it. A respect for the electoral rules established in the Constitution quickly emerged as a republican value with universal support, both to ensure the government's successful launching and to demonstrate that republican government, unlike monarchies, functioned in a world of publicly sanctioned rules. This constitutional lag allowed the Congress and the public to take the initial lead in defining a republican culture, a process that seemed to reduce Washington into a passive figure during the preinaugural planning and festivities. The first ceremonial acts of the new government centered on the election of the new Congress, their arrival in the temporary capital, and their certification of the presidential and vice presidential election results. Congress also organized Washington's inauguration and later participated in a vigorous debate on what title should be used to address him. At the same time, many American citizens explored ways to exercise their sovereign responsibilities by participating in Washington's preinaugural journey from Mount Vernon to New York City, attending his inauguration, and welcoming the president during his northern and southern tours of 1789 and 1791.

The ceremonial culture that characterized Washington's presidency was always defined by a generous use of monarchical rituals.[3] It is important to note that royal practices had already played a prominent role in the nation's political theater even before Washington officially became president. The preinaugural tour of 1789 resembled a royal progress, complete with triumphal arches and ceremonial entries, reminiscent of Elizabeth I, while his inauguration included the unlikely pronouncement "Long live the President," borrowed from the Hanoverians.[4] Despite the three thousand miles separating the colonies from the motherland, British newspapers, royal officials, and trans-Atlantic travelers provided detailed reports of the king's comings and goings. Prior to 1776, many colonists had celebrated royal births and coronations, and had gathered publicly to mourn the monarch's passing.[5] Knowledge of royal history, traditions, and practices actually increased during the 1770s as many Americans took to the streets to express their unhappiness with King George III's failure to fulfill his obligations to them.[6]

By 1789, many Americans saw the rituals of the repudiated monarchy in a different light and used these familiar practices to help energize the Constitution's abstract ideas. The inaugural festivities included a liberal quoting of monarchical practices from a variety of sources, including those of Tudor, Stuart, Hanoverian, or Habsburg origin that would both lend dignity to the proceedings and permit accessibility to the new president. Not everyone was thrilled with the appearance of royal or any other ceremonial forms in republican government, as Pennsylvania senator William Maclay's sarcastic observation, "Ceremonies, Endless Ceremonies," made clear.[7] But for the time being, the dissenters were in the minority as people in the streets and in the Congress saw the usefulness of adopting and adapting monarchical forms to launch republican government and promote popular sovereignty. For his part, Washington wisely waited to be inaugurated before asserting his preferences on ceremonial matters, and in true republican fashion, his suggestions merely fine-tuned the monarchical rituals that Congress and the public had already sanctioned.[8]

As the Congress and public excitedly prepared for Washington's arrival in New York City, there seemed to be an unspoken understanding that the new national government was incomplete unless its star attraction had appeared to lend it legitimacy and authenticity. Washington's emergence as the nation's number one republican served as the culmination of his long service to the young nation, and despite the liberal borrowing of monarchical practices during the preinaugural and inaugural festivities, most Americans understood that Washington was a popularly elected president and not a king.[9] Since the Revolution, Washington had been acting as the de facto national leader, and many Americans felt comfortable deferring to his judgment and wisdom in defining the Constitution.[10] Washington's participation in the new government (like his involvement in the Constitutional Convention of 1787) provided both credibility and reassurance to this otherwise risky experiment.[11] Although the legislature functioned as the leading branch in republican government, many Americans had grown accustomed to a single head of state in the form of a monarch because it was easier to follow and emulate the activities of one person rather than those of the entire House and Senate. Lastly, the presidency possessed a representative quality that the other branches lacked—this was the only office that all American voters played a part in choosing, albeit indirectly. These factors converged to provide Washington (and to a lesser degree, his presidential successors) with unusually wide latitude in defining the nation's republican culture.

While Washington's unique position as the nation's preeminent republican would allow him to assume a leading role in defining America's political values and to institute his vision of what republican government should be, the constitutional procedures for electing the president also meant that Washington would have to wait his turn. The initial discussions on republican ceremony rightfully belonged to the House of Representatives, the Senate, and the public as they explored ways to perform their constitutional and sovereign responsibilities.[12] What better way to institute republican government than have its leading branch, the Congress, begin to define republican ceremony, while the public found ways to express their sovereign authority through their participation in the festivities surrounding the inauguration. This chapter concerns the protean efforts of Congress and the public to create a republican ceremonial culture, based largely around George Washington, in order to animate the new government.

The establishment of a republican political culture began almost immediately after the newly elected federal government opened for business on March 4, 1789, a date the Continental Congress had established.[13] The ratification of the Constitution in July 1788 permitted most of the states to hold elections for the House of Representatives and to appoint U.S. senators by the fall of 1788.[14] The election of the president and vice president occurred concurrently, with each state appointing or electing a slate of president electors by January 7, 1789, who would meet on February 4, 1789, to cast their votes. These deadlines were agreed to by the outgoing Continental Congress.[15] With Congress possessing the sole constitutional authority to affirm the results of the Electoral College, a president and vice president could not be chosen until the Congress had been elected and a quorum had been established.

As the new Congress slowly gathered in New York City, George Washington remained wisely noncommittal about the results of the pending presidential election. As the unofficial state results became known, job seekers sent premature letters of congratulations to his Mount Vernon home. Washington understood that these leaked results meant nothing until the Congress officially certified them.[16] In his silence, Washington was affirming two important principles of republican government: a respect for elections and the constitutional process, and a desire to downplay his ambitions, particularly for the nation's highest office, in order to demonstrate his worthiness to hold this office.[17] John Adams, the putative frontrunner for vice president, maintained a similar reticence as he awaited the official election results from his Braintree, Massachusetts home.[18]

Despite an official opening date of March 4, 1789, Congress could not begin work until a quorum had been achieved. A variety of factors, including slowness on the part of the states in electing and appointing members, difficult travel conditions due to a severe winter, and a general feeling of ennui about the national government, conspired to delay the legislative branch's work.[19] Senators who had managed to arrive in New York in a timely manner grew so impatient with their dilatory colleagues that they sent two reminder notes, one on March 11 and another on March 18. The later missive illustrates the challenge they faced: "We addressed a letter to you the 11th instant, since which no Senator has arrived. . . . We therefore again earnestly request your immediate attendance, and are confident you will not suffer our, and the public anxious expectations to be disappointed."[20] As members trickled into the temporary capital, they presented their credentials, including certification of their election to the House or their appointment to the Senate, and then took their seat in the appropriate chamber.[21] Almost a month after its official opening, on April 1, the House of Representatives achieved a sufficient number of congressmen, and five days later the Senate reached a similar milestone.[22]

The attainment of a quorum in both houses allowed the Congress to meet in a historic joint session on April 6 to certify the results of the presidential and vice presidential elections. George Washington had received a unanimous sixty-nine electoral votes from the states while John Adams had competed against a field of ten candidates to earn thirty-four votes.[23] With the outcome of these momentous elections finally resolved, the Congress debated the best way to inform the victors of the result and then appointed several officials to travel to Mount Vernon and Braintree to deliver certificates that conveyed the news.[24] John Adams learned from Sylvanus Bourn that he had become the first vice president of the United States on April 12, while George Washington received news of his election on April 14, when Charles Thomson, secretary to the Continental Congress, arrived at Mount Vernon.[25] Washington responded to Thomson and the nation with a signature mixture of humility and preparedness: "I believe I cannot give a greater evidence of my sensibility for the honor they have done me than by accepting the appointment," and then added, "I shall therefore be in readiness to set out the day after to morrow" to travel to New York City.[26] Years in the making, Washington was once again ready to lead the nation, this time in its fragile experiment in republican government. Newspapers completed the notification process by reporting the news to their readers and then providing regular coverage of the two men's journeys to New York City.[27]

With the national election resolved, the newly formed government turned its attention to a new round of ceremonial considerations. Washington and Adams prepared for their respective journeys to New York City, and the House and Senate put the constitutionally established legislative process to work as they debated, planned, and resolved the ceremonial procedures for inaugurating the president. While both congressmen and senators would participate equally in Washington's inaugural festivities, the Senate gained the upper hand in defining this event, in large part due to John Adams. On April 9 and April 13, respectively, the Senate and House each appointed committees consisting of three members to make decisions, in the words of the House of Representatives, "respecting the ceremonial of receiving the president."[28] On April 15, the two committees offered some initial plans, including the appointment of three senators and five congressmen to greet Washington upon his arrival in New Jersey and escort him to lower Manhattan.[29] The two committees also agreed to contact Mr. Osgood, who had previously housed the president of Congress, to prepare and furnish this house for the new president.[30]

The widely anticipated elections of Washington and Adams stood as enormous personal achievements for both men as they prepared for the physical and intellectual transformation from private citizens to becoming the first and second republicans of the United States. John Adams began the journey first, leaving his Braintree home on April 13, 1789, to travel to New York City. The *Boston Independent Chronicle* reported, "at 10 o'clock, the Vice-President of the United States, John Adams, Esq., set out from his seat in Braintree, on his departure from the commonwealth for the seat of the federal government."[31] Newspapers tracked Adams's progress through Worcester, Hartford, and New Haven, where well-wishers greeted him with cannon salutes, processions, and speeches praising his service to the young nation.[32] In Hartford, he was given a "bolt of locally manufactured brown broadcloth considered worthy for an inaugural suit."[33] After this emotional send-off from his New England supporters, Adams reached the temporary capital on April 20, where citizens, cavalry, and members of Congress welcomed the vice president-elect and escorted him to his temporary lodgings at John Jay's home.[34] The next day, April 21, John Adams entered the Senate chamber, and the president pro tempore, John Langdon of New Hampshire, congratulated Adams on his "appointment to the Office of Vice President of the United States of America."[35] The new vice president officially accepted this position by addressing the Senate, a body he also now headed, and then joined in the preparations for welcoming and inaugurating George Washington.[36]

On April 16, several days after Adams had departed from Braintree, Washington began his own emotional weeklong journey as he traveled from his home in Mount Vernon, Virginia, through Maryland, Pennsylvania, and New Jersey to assume the presidency of the United States in New York City. On the eve of his departure, Washington wrote in his diary, "I bade adieu to Mount Vernon, to private life, and to domestic felicity . . . and with the best dispositions to render service to my country in obedience to its calls, but with less hope of answering its expectations."[37] What began, in Washington's mind, as a solemn journey quickly became an emotion-filled republican progress as cities large and small honored the nation and their new leader.

Four themes emerged during the weeklong preinaugural procession: a celebration of the nation's revolutionary heritage, including Washington's exemplary service and heroism; Washington's reluctant willingness to be the star of the theatrical performance as long as the public and Congress had written the play; the widespread appropriation of classical and monarchical symbols to imbue republican government with legitimacy and authority;[38] and, most importantly, the rituals of the preinaugural journey—processions, speeches, dinners, toasts, and receptions in Washington's honor—anticipated the upcoming inaugural ceremony by providing citizens outside the capital with an opportunity to celebrate the new government and establish their sovereign bond with it.[39] During Washington's 1789 tour to New England and his 1791 journey to the South, well-wishers would repeat these patriotic rituals as they joined their countrymen in becoming American citizens.[40]

The city of Alexandria, Virginia, located near Washington's Mount Vernon home, launched the first celebrations of his preinaugural journey. On the evening of April 16, Washington's friends and neighbors gathered at Wise's Tavern to offer both thirteen toasts and an address to honor his past and future service to the nation. Alexandria's mayor, Dennis Ramsay, declared: "Farewell! Go, and make a grateful People happy; a People who will be doubly grateful when they contemplate this recent sacrifice for their interest." Mayor Ramsay also praised the "spontaneous and unanimous suffrage of three millions of free men" who elected Washington, a republican theme that newspaper commentators emphasized because it distinguished the preinaugural tour from a monarchical progress.[41] In his response, Washington emphasized the twin themes of duty and service to his Virginia friends: "Those who have known me best . . . know better than any others my love of retirement is so great, that no earthly consideration, short of a conviction of duty, could have prevailed upon me to depart from my resolution."[42] The sentiments expressed in Alexandria would be repeated throughout his weeklong journey as the public expressed their high expectations for Washington's leadership, and he responded with his commitment to serve the nation's citizens. Using a monarchical progress to initiate a republican concept, Washington and the participating public began to establish the sovereign bond between government and governed through these addresses.[43]

As he continued northward, Washington received a hero's welcome from crowds gathered along his route who saluted his past revolutionary glories while symbolically imparting their hopes for the new government he was elected to lead. Local dignitaries from Baltimore to New York expressed their support by hosting dinners in his honor, replete with an endless succession of speeches and toasts. As he passed through Philadelphia, Americans expressed their support for the president and the new government: "The raptures of a grateful people broke forth in such emphatical expressions, as, long live George Washington, the father of the people."[44] Several cities constructed triumphal arches for this journey, a monarchical symbol of power and legitimacy intended to elevate both the new government and Washington's presidency.[45] Outside Philadelphia on the Schuylkill River Bridge, the artist and inventor Charles Willson Peale erected an arch that included a mechanism for placing a laurel wreath on Washington's head as he rode under it.[46] This wreath invoked classical images of heroism as well as the virtuous origins of republican government.[47] An embarrassed Washington brushed the wreath off, but

Charles Willson Peale's drawing of his wreath-dropping machine, employed during George Washington's preinaugural journey, April 1789. Source: *George Washington and the New Nation (1783–1793)*, vol. 3, by James Thomas Flexner. Copyright ©1970. By permission of Little, Brown and Company.

expressed his gratitude to Peale by greeting his 15-year-old daughter, Angelica, with a kiss.[48] The women of Trenton, New Jersey prepared a triumphal arch, supported by thirteen pillars, which made explicit the connection between Washington's reputation and his exemplary conduct in the Revolutionary War. Mixing feminine support with masculine exploits, the arch spelled out the dates of the revolutionary battle in flowers, December 26, 1776, to January 2, 1777, and contained the following phrase, also written in flowers: "The Defender of the Mothers will be the Protector of the Daughters."[49] As Washington passed through the arch, the young women of Trenton, dressed in white and holding flowers, sang a sonata that began, "Welcome mighty Chief! Once more, welcome to the grateful shore."[50] The two generations of Trenton women made their expectations clear: Washington, the revolutionary hero of 1776, would now become the republican hero of 1789.

After this emotion-filled visit, Washington proceeded north to Elizabeth, New Jersey, where a specially constructed barge carried the president-elect and local dignitaries, including the delegation of

Triumphal Arch erected by the ladies of Trenton during George Washington's preinaugural journey, April 1789. Source: American Philosophical Society.

congressmen and senators, on a fifteen-mile journey to Battery Park in New York City.[51] In honor of the thirteen original states that participated in the American Revolution, even though only eleven had approved the Constitution, the forty-seven-foot barge was rowed by thirteen oarsmen, and during the procession Washington was honored with a thirteen-gun salute.[52] The cacophonous and multifaceted outpouring moved Washington to write in his diary on April 23 of the "pleasing" sights of "boats which attended and joined us on this occasion, some with vocal and some with instrumental music on board; the decorations of the ships, the roar of cannon, and the loud acclamations of the people which rent the skies, as I passed along the wharves."[53]

As Washington drew closer to the temporary capital and his inauguration, monarchical practices became more pronounced as the nation's elected leaders employed recognizable rituals of power to legitimate the new government.[54] Washington's barge had barely left New Jersey when a sloop containing a chorus of two men and two women serenaded the presidential entourage with new words to the familiar tune of "God save the King": "Joy to our Native Land, Let every heart expand, For Washington's at hand, With glory crowned."[55] Marking the

A more elaborate imagining of George Washington being greeted by the ladies of Trenton during his preinaugural journey, April 1789, printed in 1845. Source: *Day of Jubilee: The Great Age of Public Celebrations in New York, 1788–1909*, by Brooks McNamara. Copyright ©1997 by Brooks McNamara. Reprinted by permission of Rutgers University Press.

Washington being transported from Elizabethtown, New Jersey, to New York City during his preinaugural journey, April 1789. Source: *Day of Jubilee: The Great Age of Public Celebrations in New York, 1788–1909*, by Brooks McNamara. Copyright ©1997 by Brooks McNamara. Reprinted by permission of Rutgers University Press.

completion of Washington's preinaugural journey, New York governor George Clinton welcomed him to Manhattan and offered a carriage for his use, but Washington remembered his republican roots and opted to walk the half mile to his new house escorted by a well-ordered procession of military units, government officials, and fellow citizens.[56] The *Pennsylvania Mercury* summarized the elaborate outpouring that greeted Washington: "The bells were rung, and colors were displayed from the fort—from the vessels in the harbor, and from several buildings in the city; the streets were crowded with citizens, and the windows decorated with the fair daughters of Columbia."[57] Upon reaching his residence, Washington concluded his preinaugural journey by saluting the enthusiastic crowds as he "frequently bowed to the multitude, and took off his hat to the ladies at the windows, who waved their handkerchiefs, and threw flowers before him."[58]

The preinaugural journey of 1789 permitted the nation's citizens (including women and children) to make their contributions to a republican political culture that emphasized the nation's heroic past and hopeful future under the steady leadership of George Washington. In turn, a stunned Washington embraced this outpouring by acknowledging the crowds and delaying his journey in order to receive and respond to their accolades. Washington's decision to connect directly with the public symbolically reinforced a fundamental principle of republican government—that the American government derived its sovereignty and legitimacy from the people and that this bond needed to be maintained and nurtured in order to ensure the government's survival. In this extemporaneous display of good will, the president and the gathered spectators established a precedent for the public's regular participation in the new government. Although the public invoked monarchical rituals to honor and elevate their new president, the public demanded an access and familiarity that was more in keeping with the republican values of their new government. By transcending the monarch-subject model, Washington and his admirers invigorated the new government by celebrating the concept of sovereignty that defined it.

Newspaper editors and correspondents contributed to the formation of the new political culture by highlighting what they considered to be essential aspects of republican government both leading to the inauguration and afterwards. Several newspapers commented upon the significance of the presidential election results. One said: "The unanimous vote of three millions of free citizens, in favor of this distinguished Farmer, Hero, and Statesman; and the unspeakable joy with which he has been welcomed by all classes of people, on his way to New-York, are not only the greatest honors that ever were conferred on man, but the happiest presages of the future greatness and respectability of our country."[59] Other newspapers warned readers of the dangers of too much public enthusiasm for Washington and praised the new president's republican demeanor amidst the outpouring. A Boston correspondent wrote: "Although the human mind is frequently intoxicated with exalted praises, our President has demonstrated that he is superior to its pernicious influence. His answers to the various addresses . . . discover the best signs of virtue and moderation; and lead us to expect great happiness under his administration."[60] Washington's preinaugural tour demonstrated that the press and the public intended to play an active and enthusiastic role in honoring their new government and its leaders.

"Ceremonies, Endless Ceremonies" 23

Washington's arrival in New York City at the end of his preinaugural journey. Source: *Day of Jubilee: The Great Age of Public Celebrations in New York, 1788–1909*, by Brooks McNamara. Copyright ©1997 by Brooks McNamara. Reprinted by permission of Rutgers University Press.

What remained to be resolved was how the government and its leaders should accommodate this popular outpouring on a regular basis.

With Washington's arrival in New York City on Thursday, April 23, the House and Senate committees could begin to contemplate an actual date for the inauguration. In characteristic fashion, Washington deferred to the Congress to set the date, reflecting his status as president-elect and his respect for the Constitution. The two planning committees reported Washington's response to their respective chambers: "That the President hath been pleased to signify to them that any time or place which both Houses may think proper to appoint, and any manner which shall appear most eligible to them, will be acceptable to him," and then concluded that the earliest day the inauguration could occur was a week later, on April 30.[61] Meanwhile, the president-elect kept busy in the week before his inauguration paying courtesy calls to senators and congressmen. Senator William Maclay of Pennsylvania, who despised all ceremonial forms, sought to bring a little perspective to the overblown reaction by sarcastically describing a visit with "General George Washington the greatest Man in the World."[62]

Several days before the scheduled inauguration, a turf war developed between the two committees concerning the precise location for the oath.[63] The House members proposed that the president be "formally received by both Houses in the Senate chamber," but added that the "representatives-chamber being capable of receiving the greater number of persons, that therefore the president do take the oath in that place, in the presence of both Houses."[64] The Senate, unwilling to yield such an honor to the lower house of Congress, sought a geographical and philosophical middle ground between the two chambers, and John Adams took the lead in formulating an alternative site.[65] On April 27, the House received a letter from the vice president proposing, "The oath should be administered to the President in the outer gallery adjoining the senate-chamber, than in the representatives-chamber."[66] The House of Representatives, less invested in the inaugural planning than Adams, agreed to the Senate proposal on April 29, allowing the inauguration to take place the next day, and permitting the lower house to turn its attention back to a discussion on import duties.[67]

Among Congress's less controversial arrangements were the selection of Robert R. Livingston, the Chancellor of New York state, to administer the oath and a post-inaugural church service at St. Paul's Church.[68] With these intricate details resolved, it would seem that the Congress had successfully tackled the ceremonial rules involved in inaugurating a republican president. Thanks to John Adams, this was not to be the case. On April 23, a bill was introduced in the Senate asking "What styles or titles it will be proper to annex to the Offices of President and Of Vice President of the United States—if any other than those given in the Constitution."[69] Both the House and Senate appointed committees to address this issue, after the president's inauguration, in a debate that would expose the widely divergent ideas that existed concerning ceremony and republicanism.

After much congressional planning and public fanfare, the day to inaugurate the president finally arrived on Thursday, April 30. The cacophony that had marked his arrival in New York City resounded once again as thirteen cannon shots, church bells, and a gathering crowd announced the arrival of the momentous day.[70] At noon, a joint committee of congressmen and senators arrived at Washington's temporary lodgings to escort him,[71] this time by carriage, to Federal Hall, the national government's new home. This escort transformed itself into a parade, consisting of local militias, the delegation of senators, Washington and his secretaries, members of the House of Representatives, various governmental officials (including Chancellor Livingston), and finally, a group of citizens, as an enthusiastic throng of spectators watched the procession.[72]

Upon reaching Federal Hall, Vice President Adams welcomed Washington to the Senate chamber, and Washington acknowledged the assembled dignitaries by bowing to the "senators and to the envoys of foreign powers who stood on his right," and "to the members of the House of Representatives on his left."[73] Adams then addressed Washington, "Sir, the Senate and House of Representatives are ready to attend you to take the oath required by the Constitution. It will be administered by the Chancellor of the State of New York." Washington responded, "I am ready to proceed."[74] The oath of office occurred on a second floor balcony attached to the Senate chamber, in full public view, so that the gathered crowd could offer its approval of the new president and the new government.[75] Washington placed his right hand on a Bible, and Chancellor Livingston administered the constitutionally prescribed oath. Upon its completion, Livingston turned to the crowd and said, "It is done. Long live George Washington, President of the United States."[76] Thirteen cannons were fired, and the crowd responded boisterously and enthusiastically to this pronouncement. Washington bowed repeatedly to acknowledge their outpouring.[77] While the cheering continued unabated, Washington and the other dignitaries returned inside the Senate chamber, where Washington delivered his inaugural address to both houses of Congress and other invited guests.[78]

The pronouncement, "Long live George Washington, President of the United States," originating in the monarchy's "The King is dead; Long live the King," seems woefully out of place in a republican inauguration. At its most basic level, this expression is incongruous because republican government represents a direct repudiation of monarchy and everything associated with it. On a practical level, this phrase does not make sense because presidential elections occur every four years, so a particular president's life expectancy does not seem to matter. In the absence of existing republican forms, Americans made use of monarchical practices (during this occasion and others) because they provided a familiar means to legitimate the new government. During Washington's inauguration, this salute conveyed the hope that the presidency (and the constitutional

Washington receiving the oath of office at Federal Hall in New York City, April 30, 1789. Source: *George Washington and the New Nation (1783–1793),* vol. 3, by James Thomas Flexner. Copyright ©1970. By permission of Little, Brown and Company.

system) rather than the president would endure for a long time. It also elevated the newly created government by placing it on the same level as the well-established and powerful British monarchy. Borrowing monarchical rituals seemed to be permissible as long as the integrity of republican government was maintained and even strengthened by the appropriation. Determining which regal practices were permissible and whether they belonged in republican government still remained to be resolved.

While the administering of the presidential oath mixed monarchical phrases and democratic outpourings as the public witnessed and cheered Washington's swearing in, the delivery of the inaugural address assumed a strictly republican cast as Washington returned indoors to the Senate chamber where an audience consisting of the House, Senate, and invited dignitaries heard his specific plans for leading the government. As Washington stood to speak, his audience rose as well and remained standing during the twenty-minute oration.[79] His respectful audience must have been relieved that he had heeded the advice of James Madison and dispensed with the seventy-three-page address he had originally drafted.[80] During his much briefer speech, Washington touched on three familiar themes that reaffirmed his understanding of republican government and his role as its first president: his duty to answer the nation's call to service, coupled with his doubts regarding his abilities; the providential nature of the nation's journey to that point; and his deferral to Congress to initiate policy because they have the best understanding of the public will.[81] In a gesture intended to underscore his belief that the presidency should be about service and not personal gain (unlike the rule of European monarchs who enriched themselves at their subject's expense), Washington concluded his speech with a sacrifice that had characterized his previous public service: he would refuse a salary as president, with the exception of specific expenses required for the public good.[82] Washington's service-oriented understanding of republican government left most of his audience deeply moved, even reducing some to tears. Amidst this emotional outpouring, William Maclay maintained his firm opposition to ceremonial forms, beginning his April 30 diary entry with a sarcastic comment: "This is the great important day. Goddess of etiquette assist me while I describe it."[83]

With the oath and the speech completed, the president and the assembled dignitaries walked from Federal Hall amidst a throng of well-wishers to St. Paul's Church to attend church services and bring the festivities to a close.[84] Within the church, Washington sat in a square pen specifically designed for the occasion that separated him from the other worshippers. Afterwards, the president returned to his lodgings, where he dined alone and recuperated from the day's excitement, while the House and Senate returned to their respective chambers to contemplate an appropriate response to the president's address.[85] In the evening, Washington and the rest of New York City enjoyed a fireworks display that illuminated the skyline and brought the nation's first presidential inauguration to a successful conclusion.[86]

As the Congress contemplated appropriate responses to the president's inaugural address, the House and Senate returned to a familiar pattern insofar as republican ceremony was concerned. The House quickly dispensed with the matter, appointing James Madison to prepare a response that the House members delivered to the president in a room adjoining the House chamber on May 8.[87] In the more style-conscious Senate, the discussion launched a highly contentious debate that went to the heart of what role, if any, ceremony should play in republican government. What bothered many senators, particularly William Maclay of Pennsylvania, was that any congressional response would seem to mirror the House of Commons's reply to the English monarch's address. In the May 1 discussion, Maclay objected to Vice President Adams's description of the speech as "his most gracious speech," because of its association with the discredited monarchy. Maclay declared, "Everything related to that species of government is odious to the people. The words prefixed to the President's speech are the same that are usually placed before the speech of his Britannic majesty. I know they will give offense. I consider them as improper."[88]

The Senate debate quickly turned into a debate on the English monarchy rather than a formulation of the Senate's response. Adams "rose in his chair and expressed the greatest surprise, that any thing should be objected to on account of its being taken from the practice of that Government under which we had lived so long and so happily formerly."[89]

Maclay bristled at Adams's defense of a governmental system that Americans had fought so hard to overcome. He commented, "That Mr. Adams should however so unequivocally avow this motive at a time when a republican form of government is secured to every State in the Union, appears to me a mark of extreme folly."[90] A week later, the Senate adopted more neutral language that praised the president's "excellent speech." The entire Senate presented their response in person to Washington at his home on May 18 and received a gracious reply in return.[91] With the procedures on presidential addresses satisfactorily resolved, the House and Senate turned their attention to other pressing matters, most notably revising the president's title. The May 1 colloquy between Adams and Maclay provided a preview of the issues that would inform the Senate's more extensive debate on the president's title.

During the month leading to and culminating in the presidential inauguration, George Washington might appear to have been a passive figure, as the Congress and the public took the leading role in planning and defining these events. His role as a vehicle for Congress's and the public's understanding of republican ceremony might convey the impression that Washington did not recognize the importance or need for public rituals in government. To the contrary, he was deeply conscious, if not self-conscious, about his public demeanor and actions as president.[92] Washington's conduct prior to and during his inauguration demonstrated his understanding that symbols and rituals were needed to launch the new government, and he worked strenuously to strike an appropriate balance between ceremony and republicanism prior to and during his presidency.

In the opening act of his performance as the nation's first republican, Washington deferred to Congress as they planned the inauguration, out of respect to the representative nature of this branch and out of respect to the Constitution—Washington did not officially become the president until April 30, so it would have been inappropriate for him to exercise authority he did not possess. During his preinaugural tour, he allowed the nation's citizens to define the parameters of their interaction with him as an exercise in the development of ideas of citizenship and, ultimately, popular sovereignty. In his penultimate preinaugural performance, he conducted himself with restraint and dignity, respectfully bowing to admirers of all stations and ranks. In appearance, Washington also embodied republican values, dressed simply in a "dark brown suit with silver buttons, white stockings, black shoes with square silver buckles, and a sword."[93] Washington's choices in clothing and accessories were fraught with meaning. The suit had been manufactured at the Hartford Manufactory, which had also given John Adams a bolt of domestic broadcloth during his journey to New York City for his own inaugural suit.[94] The sword served as a quiet reminder of Washington's heroic military service to America, and the role his military leadership played in elevating him to the presidency in the first place.[95]

Contemporaries who witnessed Washington's inauguration believed that his inaugural conduct exemplified republican values and demonstrated to the nation's citizens and the world that these desirable, albeit abstract, political ideas were attainable. Congressman Fisher Ames of Massachusetts wrote, "His aspect grave, almost to sadness; his modesty, actually shaking; his deep voice, a little tremulous, and so low as to call for close attention . . . I sat entranced." Ames continued, "It seemed to me an allegory in which virtue was personified."[96] Washington conveyed republican simplicity and ceremonial dignity in a manner that no other

American could. While thoughtful congressional planning ensured a successful and appropriate inauguration, the day's tableau would have been incomplete and unsatisfactory if Washington had not been there to play the role of America's first republican. Now that he was officially president, Washington intended to assert himself on presidential ceremony, beginning, not with a pronouncement or a proclamation, but with a query that solicited opinions on how he should conduct himself.[97]

With Washington poised to take an increasingly assertive role in defining republican ceremony, the title debate represented one of Congress's last occasions to unilaterally influence presidential protocol. The title debate began in earnest on May 5 when the House committee appointed to consider the Senate's proposition quickly dispensed with the matter by reporting that "it is not proper to annex any style or title to the respective styles or titles of office expressed in the Constitution."[98] Preempted by the House's hasty dismissal, the Senate proponents brought the issue to the floor in an effort to rally support for their cause. On May 8 and 9, a lively debate on titles dominated the Senate's business. Senator Richard Henry Lee of Virginia initiated the discussion by arguing that "All the world civilized and savage called for titles."[99] Senator Oliver Ellsworth of Connecticut supported this view by adding that "president" was too commonplace and undignified because "there were presidents of fire companies and of a cricket club."[100] Senator Lee then suggested that certain state constitutions permitted titles, a claim that led Senator Maclay to declare that the "spirit of the [Constitution] was against not only granting titles by Congress but against the permission of foreign potentates granting *any titles whatever.*"[101] On a practical level, Maclay added that given the House's opposition to this business, "the gentlemen seemed to court a rupture with the other House."[102]

Although a group of senators believed in principle that the president's title should be embellished, they had yet to present any specific suggestions. The House's rejection of the broadly conceived proposal forced these senators to formulate clear-cut alternatives in order to salvage this initiative. During the May 8 debate the Senate Committee on Titles proposed "his excellency," while other senators suggested "his highness" be combined with "elective" to produce the more democratic-sounding "elective highness."[103] The justification for this embellishment was that "such a dignified title would add greatly to the weight and authority of the Government both at home and abroad."[104] Maclay objected that "it was impossible to add to the respect entertained for General Washington," and that "elective highness" smacked of European dukes and princes.[105] Unable to reach a consensus, the Senate rejected the proposed titles and appointed a new committee in the hopes of achieving a more satisfactory proposal.

On May 9, the newly appointed Committee on Titles reported the following: "His Highness the President of the United States of America and Protector of the Rights of the Same."[106] Not surprisingly, this recommendation did little to resolve the dispute and merely fueled the firestorm that existed in the Senate. Although there was support for changing the title, the coalition in favor of this began to unravel when its supporters were unable to find an alternative that succeeded in enhancing presidential dignity but was also consistent with republican values. A motion to adopt the committee's report was not seconded, and the issue's supporters began to contemplate postponing the report.[107] An exasperated Adams entered the debate, delivering what Maclay described as a forty-minute harangue in an attempt to reinvigorate support for his initiative. Drawing on his experience as American minister to Great Britain, Adams returned to America's reputation abroad, declaring, "What will the common people of foreign countries, what will the sailors and the soldiers say, 'George Washington, President of the United States?'" Adams continued, "They will despise him *to all eternity*."[108] Adams saw the president's title as a way to strengthen a young, untested political system against foreign encroachments. In Adams's mind, unless the Congress made the needed changes, they were inviting the world to look down upon the American government and its president.[109] Rather than ending the impasse, Adams's speech produced the same points of opposition that had stalled the previous day's debate. The Senate opted to postpone consideration of the issue and moved to appoint a conference committee in the hope of resolving its differences with the House.[110]

On May 11 the House of Representatives began consideration of the Senate's proposal for a conference committee on titles.[111] Demonstrating the strong opposition that existed on ceremonial matters in general, Representative John Page of Virginia opened the debate by objecting to the use of "honorable gentleman" on the House floor "because it added neither to the honor nor the dignity of the House." Representative Thomas Tucker of South Carolina expressed dismay that the Senate had proposed a conference committee. Instead, he suggested that America "establish tranquility and good order at home, and wealth, strength, and national dignity will be the infallible result." Representative James Madison (who seemed to be single-handedly running the American government in 1789) offered the most comprehensive and eloquent rebuttal of the Senate's position by explaining why this proposal was fundamentally incompatible with republican government.[112] He began his speech by saying that he did not fear titles *per se*, because they were a superficial designation and as such did not threaten our liberties or our constitution. He stated, "We have seen superb and august titles given, without conferring power and influence, or without even obtaining respect." Instead Madison opposed titles "because they are not very reconcilable with the nature of our Government or the genius of the people," because "instead of increasing, they diminish the true dignity and importance of a republic." Expanding upon the sentiments of Representative Tucker, Madison declared that dignity and strength in a republican government came from its commitment to simplicity and its rejection of ostentation. Madison argued, "The more truly honorable shall we be, by showing a total neglect and disregard to things of this nature; the more simple, the more republican we are in our manners, the more rational dignity we shall acquire."[113] Madison concluded his remarks by reiterating his support for the original House position, but also recommended the appointment of conferees to meet with the Senate "to cement that harmony which has hitherto been preserved between the Senate and this House."[114]

Despite the appointment of House conferees, the exposition of republican principles by the Father of the Constitution delivered a fatal blow to Adams's efforts to embellish the president's constitutionally designated title. The Senate's response on May 14 made it clear that Madison's statement against titles had carried the day. Senator Lee of Virginia defended the Senate's interest in titles, stating: "To keep up a proper respect for our Chief Magistrate attention should be paid to the customs of civilized nations. That the appearance of the affectation of simplicity, would be injurious, that the Senate had decided in favor of titles from these motives."[115] Having justified the time and energy devoted to this issue, the Senate then acquiesced to the House position, citing the need to maintain harmony between the two bodies. The Senate concluded its consideration by issuing the following resolution: "For the present they resolved to address the President without title." This brought this contentious debate to a close.[116]

Although the Senate had prevailed over the House in the earlier ceremonial matters, their failure to embellish the president's titles demonstrated that limits existed in the use of monarchical practices in republican government. First, the Senate's proposal would have repudiated the Constitution, which had already titled the president, and which explicitly forbade the granting of additional titles. Second, unlike other royal practices during the inauguration, which brought the people and Congress closer to the president and affirmed republican principles, the enhanced title would have made the president a more remote and exalted figure in a government that emphasized the House of Representatives, not the executive. Republican ceremonial practices were welcomed in the new government, even if they were imported from European monarchies, as long as they affirmed the Constitution and strengthened the connection between the government and the governed. The Senate proposal on titles demonstrated the gamut of opinions, ranging from Adams to Maclay, that existed on republican ceremony inside Congress. And outside of Congress, a "citizen of the United States" warned, "As republicans, we should be careful not to introduce any distinctions, which might lead the people to suppose that there was a design to establish an aristocracy."[117] Among some Americans an excess of ceremony could destroy the new government, while for others the lack of rituals to illuminate the Constitution might render it irrelevant.

When the first republican Congress opened for business in 1789, presidential ceremony quickly emerged as one of its top priorities, as it devoted as much time to establishing the ceremonial aspects of the executive branch as it did to setting up the remaining two branches of the government. During its first few months, Congress debated the best ways to elect, welcome, inaugurate, title, and pay the president, while also passing legislation to set up congressional rules and offices, to codify federal oaths, to establish the judicial branch and the departments of war, state and treasury, and to define the protocol that would govern interactions between the houses of Congress and with the president. While the Congress, particularly the Senate, lavished enormous attention on planning and executing the president's dramatic inaugural festivities, both houses were sworn in with little fanfare or public acclaim. The House wasted no time in administering its oath on April 8 and then did so again on June 2nd to accommodate late arrivals. The style-conscious Senate, including Vice President Adams, received theirs on June 3, after establishing rules for administering oaths.[118]

The best explanation for this ceremonial gap in the conduct of the presidency and the Congress centers on the singular nature of the executive branch. Many members of Congress understood that the presidency, particularly when occupied by George Washington, would epitomize the American government, both at home and abroad. As America's head of state and its first republican, the new president's conduct and interaction would go a long way in explaining the crucial tenets of republican government such as its legitimacy, authority, and sovereignty. In its first debates, Congress devoted an enormous amount of attention to matters of presidential ceremony, particularly the inauguration, because of the symbolic importance of this office to the government's successful launching. While everyone knew that Washington would be the star attraction of the new government, Congress and the public made sure their constitutional responsibilities were not forgotten or ignored, and Washington wisely deferred to their plans, at least initially. Although there was not universal agreement on the need for ceremonial forms in republican government, there was enough early consensus to support the use of symbols and rituals, even monarchical forms, to energize the Constitution's principles. While Washington (and his successors) would make lasting contributions to presidential ceremony that would define republican government, the contributions of Congress and the American public in initiating these discussions should not be overlooked or underestimated.

"To Preserve the Dignity and Respect"

Washington's Republican Approach to Presidential Ceremony

Immediately after Washington's inauguration, newspapers published a tentative schedule of meeting times he had established to deal with the onslaught of office seekers and well-wishers: "We are informed that the President has assigned every Tuesday, and Friday, between the hours of two and three, for receiving visits; and that visits of compliments on other days, and particularly Sundays, will not be agreeable to him." The reports added that because of "the various and important business imposed upon him by the Constitution, that he will find himself constrained to omit returning visits, or accepting invitations to Entertainments."[1] While this widely publicized announcement offered an initial hint of Washington's approach to presidential ceremony, it was by no means the final word on the subject. Instead, this notice was intended to provide a temporary solution to accommodate the eager citizens who hoped to gain a moment of their republican president's time.

A few days later, on May 10, 1789, George Washington formally joined the ceremonial discussion already begun by Congress and the public when he issued a comprehensive questionnaire to leading political officials that offered his suggestions on presidential conduct. In this query he stressed the importance of seemingly trivial matters such as entertaining and furnishings, writing: "Many things which appear of little importance in themselves and at the beginning, may have great and durable consequences from their having been established at the commencement of a new general Government."[2]

Washington recognized the importance of symbols and rituals in animating the abstract republican principle of popular sovereignty. He also understood that for these forms to benefit the new government, their substance must be grounded in the Constitution's ideas, even if the practices themselves came from European monarchs. In the aftermath of his successful inauguration, Washington responded to the tremendous (and growing) expectations that greeted him as president by suggesting an array of public events designed to bring citizens into contact with their government. Before proceeding with the levees, receptions, and tours that would characterize his presidency, Washington solicited political approval for these rituals in order to affirm and strengthen the risky experiment known as republican government.

As the nation's first president, Washington placed republican ideas at the center of his ceremonial repertoire by circulating his preferences to prominent officials inside and outside of Congress for their approval, disapproval, and comments. By issuing a document concerning presidential protocol, Washington demonstrated that republican ceremony, like republican government itself, functioned in a world of publicly sanctioned rules and procedures. This questionnaire affirmed the precedents established before and during the inauguration as Congress and the president-elect abided by the explicit procedures laid out in the Constitution for the election of the new government. Illustrating the importance of these ceremonial forms, Washington established a consultative process that encouraged the input of leading figures within the three branches of government. He also understood the need to act judiciously and carefully before embarking on any policies, ceremonial or otherwise, because of the newness and fragility of republican government. Finally, he solicited input for his ceremonial proposals because symbolic representations of a Constitution that began "We the People" would need popular support in order to have resonance.

Washington's enormous stature in 1789 would have permitted him to unilaterally develop ceremonial practices and still enjoy public support. But over the long term, he understood that for the new government to thrive, its symbolic presentation needed to be based in republican ideas, not in his popularity, because he would not live forever and the American system was not a hereditary monarchy. Perhaps better than anyone, Washington knew the difficulties the nation had faced during the Revolutionary War when it had lacked an effective central government. Washington's careful attention to these ceremonial matters reflected his continuing service to America, this time to ensure the successful launching of the Constitution. While some of the resulting rituals might be reminiscent of a monarchy, Washington made sure that these practices emerged, not from autocratic fiat, but from a consultative process that celebrated the ideas of republican government.

In his May 10 query, Washington proposed a variety of ceremonial forms that he believed would bolster republican government, define the role and responsibilities of the president, present his political priorities to the American people, and most importantly, institute the sovereign bond between the government and citizenry. After receiving written feedback on his proposals, Washington developed a ceremonial schedule that included levees and dinners for officials in New York and Philadelphia (cohosted with his wife, Martha), as well as open visiting hours and frequent walks through the two temporary capitals to stay in touch with the public. Washington also concerned himself with seemingly prosaic matters such as carriage design, appropriate housing and furnishings, and dress because he understood that these familiar domestic items proclaimed volumes about what republican government meant, both for people at home and in Europe. His ceremonial efforts culminated with his two presidential tours in 1789 (to New England) and 1791 (to the southern states), where he explicitly embraced the practice of royal progresses to bring republican government to the nation's citizens.[3]

While the letter of May 10 may seem like routine presidential business, this query had a profound impact on his presidency and on the elaboration of republican government itself. The questionnaire functioned as both the first ceremonial act of his presidency as well as the ceremonial blueprint for his two terms in office. True to republican principles, Washington never deviated from the program of levees, receptions, dinners, and tours he had proposed and that had been blessed by influential politicians such as John Adams and Alexander Hamilton.[4] During his first term, Washington carefully and successfully adopted monarchical rituals infused with republican ideas to activate the government's legitimacy and authority, and most importantly, to establish the sovereign bond between the nation and its citizens. Washington's ceremonial efforts illustrated an understanding of republican government that favored a vigorous executive, a broad interpretation of the Constitution's powers, and the primacy of the federal government over the states. While Washington's use of monarchical rituals engendered some criticism during his first term, the real backlash came during his second term and during John Adams's presidency as competing interpretations of the Constitution challenged his vision. The celebration of republicanism came to a complete and abrupt halt during Thomas Jefferson's presidency, who repudiated this monarchical culture in favor of a more unadorned and decentralized republican culture. Nonetheless, Washington's ceremonial approach permitted the young nation to make a surprisingly smooth transition, from the rejected but familiar trappings of monarchy to a new set of governing principles known as republicanism, so as to ensure the successful launching of the new Constitution.

Less than two weeks into his presidency, Washington made a quiet but momentous contribution to republican government when he issued a questionnaire to prominent political leaders concerning presidential conduct and accessibility. His successful inauguration on April 30 permitted him to assume his constitutional responsibilities and to assert his ceremonial preferences, an issue he had remained silent on until he officially became president. On May 10, as the Senate and House continued to debate the president's title, Washington offered his own suggestions concerning presidential protocol in a questionnaire he submitted to John Adams, a leading proponent of republican ceremony.[5] On May 12, Washington wrote to James Madison, the putative father of the Constitution, seeking his input on a similar set of questions.[6] As top officials in the new government, the vice president and Virginia congressman were obvious choices to offer their comments. Prior to his May 10 letter, Washington had also solicited the views, in person, of three people who possessed strong opinions on the conduct of republican government: Alexander Hamilton, an advocate for a vigorous executive branch and the future secretary of the treasury; John Jay, a coauthor of the *Federalists Papers* who had been active in foreign affairs and would become the first chief justice of the Supreme Court; and Robert R. Livingston, chancellor of New York state and the presiding official at Washington's inauguration.[7] (In Jay's case, Washington also submitted a letter because a "gentleman coming in put an end to the conversation.")[8]

While Washington had clearly initiated these discussions, he also wisely chose three respondents who believed in the necessity of presidential ceremony and whose input and support would guarantee the success of his proposals.[9]

In laying out his nine-point ceremonial program, Washington devoted the first four questions to what had emerged as a pressing concern since his inauguration: how to handle a continual stream of well-wishers and job seekers eager to meet with the president. Aware of the political importance of maintaining a connection to the public, Washington also desired to limit these visits in order to maintain the dignity of the presidency and to have sufficient time to govern the country. In the query, Washington sought a way to strike a balance between "all kinds of company on the one hand and from a total seclusion on the other." He asked his recipients whether there should be a weekly time for visitors to pay "compliments," and a daily "8 o'clock in the morning" meeting time "to give audience to persons who may have business with him."[10] Washington also proposed hosting "four great entertainments a year on such great occasions as— the Anniversary of the Declaration of Independence, the Alliance with France, the Peace with Great Britain, and the Organization of the general government" as additional opportunities to interact with the public.[11]

Washington's next set of concerns centered on entertaining members of Congress and other public officials. Drawing a distinction between the limited presidential role under the Articles of Confederation and the separate branch of government established in the Constitution, Washington clarified that "the President is not to give general entertainment in the manner the Presidents of Congress have formerly done."[12] Nonetheless, he recognized the need to host a regular rotation of dinners for congressmen and senators. He also asked whether "making informal visits—that is to say, in his calling upon his Acquaintances or public Characters for the purposes of sociability or civility" was appropriate for a president.[13]

Washington did not see his constitutional or ceremonial role as limited to the environs of the temporary capital in New York City. In his final question, he proposed expanding the government's authority into the several states by undertaking a presidential tour, asking:

> Whether, during the recess of Congress, it would not be advantageous to the interests of the Union for the President to make the tour of the United States, in order to become better acquainted with their principal

Characters and internal Circumstances, as well as to be more accessible to numbers of well-informed persons, who might give him useful information and advice on political subjects?[14]

Given Washington's propensity for retaining receipts, it is not surprising that the final point of his query noted that these proposed entertainments and tours did not come cheaply, and that, if they were adopted, Congress would have to "make a permanent provision for the support of the Executive."[15]

In concluding his query, Washington stressed the importance of these seemingly mundane ceremonial matters: "It will be much easier to commence the administration, upon a well adjusted system, built on tenable grounds, than to correct errors or alter inconveniences after they shall have been confirmed by habit." In addition to their impact on the new government, Washington added that they were also of great personal concern to him. He wrote, "The President in all matters of business and etiquette, can have no object but to demean himself in his public character, in such a manner as to maintain the dignity of Office."[16]

Through this carefully crafted document, presented as a questionnaire, Washington made clear his beliefs regarding the best way for a republican president to conduct himself. By soliciting the written comments of leading public officials, Washington was establishing a public record and a consensus on the potentially controversial issue of presidential protocol. This process also illustrated that his ceremonial preferences were by no means the final word. Washington understood that for republican government to succeed, the opinions of other elected officials and the citizens themselves mattered as much as the president's, if not more so. Washington's query on presidential ceremony illustrated the consultative nature of republican government as he shared his proposals, circulated them for comment, and then incorporated the suggestions before proceeding. Having disseminated his own ideas concerning presidential conduct, Washington now awaited the verbal and written responses that revealed the strong and competing opinions that existed on republican ceremony.

The overriding theme that emerges from the extant responses to Washington's query was that his respondents—Livingston, Hamilton, and Adams—each envisioned a much less accessible president than Washington did, and each based their recommendations on the practices of European monarchs, the preeminent example at the time of how a head of state should behave. (John Jay also offered written comments to Washington, but his letter has not survived.)[17] Their suggestions seemed to assume that the president would be able to maintain a sharp distinction between his public and private realms. Washington wisely understood that all of his time and activities would be public, and his behavior would serve as a living, tangible presentation of republican government. Not surprisingly, all three men laced their comments with their own priorities for what the president should emphasize, whether political information, European precedents, or foreign affairs. Notably absent from this collection of detailed, opinionated, and, most importantly, written recommendations was a response from James Madison who, unlike Washington's other correspondents, was not an advocate for republican ceremony in the new government, a position he had made clear during the recent congressional title debate.[18]

The first response came on May 2, 1789, from Robert R. Livingston, who had received Washington's questions in person. Despite the access to Washington that Livingston enjoyed, he recommended that the new president adopt a detached and almost invisible public role in order to promote and maintain the dignity of the office. Livingston wrote that "the utmost distance should be maintained by the President and that he should avoid all social and free intercourse with the people." He also encouraged Washington to maintain "more reserve and distance" than he had in the Continental Army in order to exalt the government's principles.[19] Livingston then proceeded to reject Washington's specific proposals, writing that the "president should (except on some great festival) give no formal dinners, that he should accept no formal invitation, that he should return no visits."[20] The social role Livingston did envision for the president consisted of a personal social life as well as a network of young advisors who could keep Washington informed of the pressing political issues in the capital. Livingston's blatant advocacy of a presidential court as the best way to launch republican government probably did not come as a big surprise to Washington. As chancellor of New York, Livingston had already introduced monarchical practices into republican government when he declared to the assembled crowd at Washington's inauguration: "It is done. Long live George Washington. The President of the United States."[21] Representing one voice in the sea of political opinion, Livingston believed formality, detachment, and, most of all, tried and true monarchical practices offered the best model for presidential behavior.[22]

Further down the ceremonial spectrum, although not by much, were the recommendations of Alexander Hamilton. On May 5 Hamilton offered written comments stemming from a conversation Washington had initiated. Affirming the importance of presidential protocol to republican government, Hamilton wrote, "The public good requires as a primary object that the dignity of the office should be supported," and then he proceeded to offer specific comments on Washington's plans.[23] Hamilton agreed that the president should host a weekly, hour-long levee for visitors, but thought he should limit his time and his access at such events. Hamilton wrote, "The President to remain half an hour, in which time he may converse cursorily on indifferent subjects with such persons as shall strike his attention, and at the end of that half hour disappear."[24] Hamilton supported the idea of the president's hosting two to four formal entertainments such as Independence Day, but also added that the president should not accept any invitations. Finally, Hamilton believed that dinner parties for six to eight members of Congress and other public officials were appropriate, but again wanted to limit the president's time at these events.[25] Hamilton did not mention the possibility of tours or other direct interactions with the nation's citizens, perhaps because Washington did not mention these ideas to him. Hamilton's vision of presidential ceremony would have resulted in a less accessible president than Washington intended. It relied heavily on the examples of European Courts and the English and French governments (precedents Washington never mentioned in his May 10 query).[26]

John Adams, a leading advocate of republican ceremony, must have relished the opportunity to share his views on presidential conduct, a desire Washington shrewdly capitalized on by addressing the May 10 query to the vice president. In his May 17 response, Adams affirmed Washington's goal of striking a balance between total presidential isolation and total access, writing that "an association with all kinds of company, and a total seclusion from society, are extremes, which, in actual circumstances of this country, and under our form of government, may be properly avoided."[27] On Washington's specific proposals, Adams believed that two days a week, rather than five, offered sufficient time to deal with visitors, but he also wondered whether a "chamberlain or gentlemen in waiting" should act as a filter between visitors and the president.[28] Adams also supported Washington's proposed dinner parties for members of Congress, but he did not think the president should accept social invitations, except those of a private nature. He opposed the president hosting large public entertainments, believing that a cabinet minister or even the vice president should handle this responsibility instead. Finally, Adams supported a presidential tour, with the caveat "if the time can be spared," adding that "foreign affairs arrive every day, and the business of the executive and judicial departments will require constant attention."[29] Adams's advocacy of a strong ceremonial component in republican government derived, in part, from his experience in foreign affairs and his desire to project the image of a strong republic to the rest of the world. Adams concluded: "Neither dignity nor authority can be supported in human minds, collected into nations or any great numbers, without a splendor and majesty in some degree proportioned to them."[30] His ceremonial recommendations, while the closest to Washington's own, ultimately reflected a greater concern with the president's (and America's) reputation in foreign affairs and less concern with public opinion at home.

While the May 10th query seemed to be a routine presidential inquiry, this letter solicited a variety of opinions on presidential ceremony, created a republican political process consisting of consultation and consensus, and legitimized the ceremonial rituals that emerged from the discussion. Awash in a sea of competing opinions on what a republican government should look like and how a president should behave, Washington sought political cover by encouraging the loudest voices on presidential ceremony to offer their opinions in order to produce an agreement. By seeking written comments, Washington produced a ceremonial culture based in compromise rather than one emanating from unilateral executive fiat. The ceremonial program that emerged from these discussions was more accessible than Livingston, Hamilton, or even Adams had recommended, and consisted of a weekly levee; open visiting hours twice a week (down from five days); a regular rotation of small dinners for members of Congress and other officials; the hosting of public entertainments; and finally, two presidential tours.[31] Although many found even these compromises excessive, from Washington's perspective, these rules offered practical guidelines on how a republican president should behave and permitted him to get to work.

With the general parameters of presidential conduct established and blessed, Washington sent word to Mount Vernon that his wife Martha should join him.[32] Accompanied by two of her grandchildren, Martha Washington left Mount Vernon on May 16.[33] As she was already a familiar presence in her husband's career, adoring crowds celebrated her reentry into public life as she journeyed north, just as they had done with Washington a month earlier.[34] The president confirmed his wife's new status by meeting her in northern New Jersey and escorting her to New York City on the same specially made barge that had recently carried him.[35] Upon her arrival in New York City on May 28, she received a thirteen-gun salute and the crowd shouted, "Long live Lady Washington."[36] The appearance of the president's wife triggered a brief title debate as Americans confronted the familiar dilemma of conveying respect while honoring republican values. Among the suggestions were Marquise Washington or Lady Washington, a holdover from her service during the Revolutionary War. Martha Washington chose the unadorned Mrs. Washington, which endured through other presidencies until the advent of the title "First Lady" in the early twentieth century.[37]

Once in New York City, Mrs. Washington joined the president at the rented home Congress had arranged for them on Cherry Street.[38] Although presidential housing appeared to be a relatively mundane concern, the numerous private invitations Washington had received prior to his arrival in New York City transformed this issue into something more significant.[39] Once again, seeking a way to be accessible yet dignified without showing favoritism to the wealthy and well-connected, Washington had crafted a standard response to these invitations: while flattered by the offer, he knew that such a stay would "give so much trouble to a private family" because of "the party that may possibly attend me, the crowd that always gather on novel occasions, and the compliment of visiting ... all contribute to render a public house the fittest place for scenes of bustle and trouble."[40] These refusals meant that he would still need to find a place to stay in New York, so Washington turned to James Madison for help in finding either a home, or temporary space in the "most decent tavern, till a house can be provided for the more permanent reception of the President."[41] Madison and other members of Congress arranged for the president to rent a house that had previously served as the residence of the president of the Confederation Congress.[42] The resolution of the Washingtons' housing needs permitted the launching of their social calendar, at least for the time being. Finding, furnishing, and staffing a home, as well as hosting entertainments, would become an even greater concern when the nation's capital moved to Philadelphia in August 1790.[43]

Martha Washington's arrival in New York City permitted the inauguration of the social schedule that Washington had worked so diligently to craft. In response to the tremendous excitement and curiosity swirling around her, Mrs. Washington immediately stepped into her official role, hosting her first Friday evening "drawing room" on May 30, two days after arriving in New York.[44] Her weekly drawing rooms (or open houses) emerged as the most festive and informal event of the Washingtons' social calendar. The guests, who did not require an invitation as long as they wore "full dress," included elected officials and men and women of prominent social standing.[45] The president signaled a more relaxed, convivial atmosphere by eschewing a hat or a sword and circulated among the guests, while Mrs. Washington played a more formal role as hostess, remaining seated to receive well-wishers. The refreshments served included tea, coffee, cakes, and ice cream.[46] To bring the party to a close, Mrs. Washington stood up and announced, "The General always retires at nine, and I usually precede him."[47] In 1790, her drawing room coincided with New Year's Day, transforming this occasion into another opportunity for the president and his wife to entertain the public. The Washingtons also hosted an annual Fourth of July party for invited guests.[48]

In addition to the drawing rooms and their annual public entertainments, both Washingtons offered social events aimed at a variety of constituencies, all of which originated from his May 10 query. The most accessible part of Washington's calendar was announced in the New York–based *Gazette of the United States* and offered two opportunities for the general public to meet with the president.[49] Those wishing to pay compliments could come on Tuesdays and Fridays between 9:00 a.m. and 3:00 p.m. without appointment, as long as they were appropriately dressed, while those with business could visit any day, except Sunday.[50] Washington also promoted an image of openness by embarking upon regularly scheduled walks in the capital and by taking early morning horseback rides that combined his presidential duties with physical activity.[51] While the Washingtons eschewed personal invitations, they hosted a regular rotation of dinners for congressmen, senators, and state and civic officials every Thursday at 4:00 p.m.[52] The first couple also regularly attended the theater and extended invitations to others such as the Adamses and the Jays to join them.[53] These theater outings, along with occasional appearances at balls, were widely reported in newspapers.[54] The last item on Washington's social calendar proved to be the most formal and the most controversial. Every Tuesday afternoon from 3:00 to 4:00 p.m., Washington hosted a weekly levee for male guests.[55] Intended to complement Mrs. Washington's lively and popular drawing rooms, the levees were characterized by their extreme formality bordering on discomfort, due in large part to Washington's desire to maintain a dignified presence. John F. Watson, an observer of Philadelphia life, described a typical gathering:

> At 3 o'clock the visitor was introduced to this dining room, from which all seats had been removed for the time. On entering, he saw the tall manly figure of Washington, clad in black silk velvet, his hair in full dress; powdered and gathered behind in a large silk bag; yellow gloves on his hands, holding a cocked hat with a black cockade in it. . . . He wore knee and shoe buckles, and a long sword. He stood always in front of the fireplace, with his face towards the door of entrance. The visitor was conducted to him, and his name distinctly announced. He received his visitor with a dignified bow, in a manner avoiding to shake hands, even with his best friends. As visitors came they formed a circle around the room; and at quarter past three the door was closed, and the circle was formed for that day. He then began on the right, and spoke to each visitor, calling him by name, and exchanging a few words. When he had completed his circuit, he resumed his first position, and the visitors approaching him in succession, bowed and retired. By 4 o'clock this ceremony was over.[56]

When political criticism of Washington increased during his second term, the levees epitomized for many the president's aristocratic pretensions, despite his efforts to devise a well-rounded and accessible social calendar.[57]

In their entertainment schedule, the Washingtons worked diligently to strike a balance between formality and graciousness while avoiding any hint of ostentation. They regarded their social obligations as a duty to be endured rather than enjoyed. After a few months in New York, Martha Washington complained to her niece, "I am more like a state prisoner than anything else."[58] To cope with her unhappiness, she sought solace in her family and her close friends, counting the days until she could return to the "fireside at Mount Vernon."[59] Nonetheless, as a team, the Washingtons successfully managed the various constituencies who desired access to their national government via its president, and with the assistance of his wife, Washington reached a wider audience than he could have alone. Washington considered presidential accessibility and dignity to be critical to the survival of the new government. To achieve these dual goals, the Washingtons established a politically effective social calendar that accommodated the various constituencies who desired access to the president: prominent men and women, elected and governmental officials, and the general public. Despite the variety of opportunities to meet with the president, many saw the hierarchical social structure as antithetical to republican principles.[60]

The relocation of the nation's capital to Philadelphia in August 1790 for a ten-year stint revived and expanded issues of presidential housing and entertaining that seemed to have been largely resolved.[61] Although the Washingtons had carefully crafted their New York social calendar, their entry into the well-established Philadelphia social scene required additional attention.[62] Martha Washington would need to establish her social presence in a milieu where the "dazzling" Mrs. William Bingham, the wife of a wealthy merchant, already hosted lively drawing rooms for other fashionable and prosperous Philadelphians.[63] Unfortunately for the Washingtons, the need to offer more sparkling social events coincided with a growing political opposition who regarded these occasions as unrepublican. Moving to Philadelphia also revived the issue of housing. Finding, furnishing, renovating, and staffing a new presidential home took on additional importance since the temporary capital would be situated in a somewhat more permanent location. No detail was too minor for presidential consideration as domestic concerns assumed a public significance in Washington's ongoing efforts to strike an appropriate balance between republican accessibility and presidential dignity.[64]

Even before the relocation to Philadelphia, the domestic management of the president's household had attracted the attention and approval of the nation's citizens. On May 4, 1789, Samuel Fraunces, Washington's household steward, issued a widely reprinted advertisement concerning the payment of presidential bills. The announcement stated: "Whereas, all servants and others, employed to procure provisions or supplies, for the household of the President of the United States, will be furnished with monies for those purposes. Notice is therefore given, that no accounts . . . are to be opened with any of them."[65] In other words, in order to avoid the incurrence of high bills, the president's staff was not authorized to establish accounts with merchants. Instead, the household servants would pay cash for an item or service, permitting careful control over presidential finances. This seemingly routine announcement struck a chord with many who took it as further evidence (along with Washington's refusal to collect a paycheck) of the president's republican virtue and selfless devotion to the nation. The *New-York Daily Gazette,* in a widely reprinted commentary, observed that the "President is determined to pursue that system of regularity and economy in his household, which has always marked his public and private life." The *Gazette* added that this careful attention to expenditures will "guard against any waste or extravagance, that might be committed by the servants of the family."[66] Clearly, the nation's citizenry approved of republican simplicity and transparency in all aspects of presidential conduct, an approach Washington willingly embraced.

The president's Philadelphia housing needs seemed to be quickly resolved with the acquisition of Robert Morris's capacious mansion at 190 High Street.[67] While Washington considered it "the best single house in the city," he expressed concern to his private secretary, Tobias Lear, that it was "inadequate to the commodious accommodation of my family" unless renovations occurred.[68] (Washington's ample family included his wife, her two grandchildren, their maids, the steward and his wife, his private secretary Lear and his wife, the coachmen, and other servants and slaves.)[69] Between August 30, 1790, when he left New York City for good, and November 27, 1790, when he returned to Philadelphia for Congress's first session in the new capital, Washington supervised the renovations, staffing, and furnishing of his new home from his beloved Mount Vernon.[70] In a letter to Tobias Lear, Washington neatly captured the role housing played in his overall philosophy on presidential appearance and conduct: "The additions and alterations which are about to be made; presumably in a plain and neat manner, not by any means in an extravagant style; because the latter is not only contrary to my wishes, but would, in reality, be repugnant to my interest and convenience."[71] Despite his vigilance and specific instructions, Washington arrived in Philadelphia in late November only to discover that the housing renovations had not been completed and would be continuing as he prepared for the new session of Congress.[72] When rumors circulated throughout Philadelphia that the president did not like the Morris house, the normally reserved and cautious Washington exploded in a letter to Lear: "I have no scruple in declaring to those Gentlemen or any others, that no one has a right to publish sentiments as mine that were never uttered, or conceived, by me."[73] Matters of presidential housing, a seemingly prosaic concern, preoccupied Washington's time and energy as he struggled to reconcile personal needs with republican principles in his choice of a residence.

Furnishing and staffing the presidential home also engaged the president as he vacationed at Mount Vernon. With an eye to his entertaining, Washington wrote to American ministers in Europe for help in obtaining domestic furnishings such as lamps, a tea service, china settings, and large serving platters.[74] Since he became president, finding suitable and reliable people to work in the presidential mansion was an ongoing challenge given the high rate of turnover of the white servants. At a minimum, the president's home required a steward to manage the household and supervise the staff, as well as a cook "who can provide genteel dinners," a coachman, a washerwoman, maids, and general laborers.[75] Initially, the Washingtons' New York household consisted of fourteen white servants, as well as seven slaves from Mount Vernon, including Molly and Ona, Martha's personal maids.[76] Although it may seem incongruous to have a staff consisting of free, indentured, and slave workers, slavery was not illegal in New York until 1799, when a gradual emancipation law was passed.[77] Amidst a staff of strangers, the presence of the Mount Vernon slaves must have comforted both the Washingtons, who had relied on slaves their entire lives.[78]

The staffing situation became more complicated with the capital's relocation to Philadelphia. Pennsylvania had passed a gradual emancipation law in 1780 that included a provision freeing any slave who resided in the state for six months.[79] In April 1791, three of Washington's slaves, Hercules, Austin, and Moll, were eligible for liberation under this law, triggering a household crisis with enormous national significance.[80] Washington, alarmed at the prospect of losing his slaves, arranged with Lear that Hercules and Austin be sent back to Mount Vernon to avoid their manumission, while Moll, a female slave, had not demanded her freedom.[81] Once again, domestic concerns forced the publicly aloof Washington to exhibit an unusual degree of passion as he personally confronted the explosive public contradiction that could destroy the fragile Constitution.[82]

With the entertaining and housing portions of his ceremonial program largely resolved, Washington turned his attention to fulfilling the last proposal of his May 10 query: touring the United States. Between October 1789 and June 1791, Washington would undertake two long tours and a short one that would permit him to bring republican government to all thirteen states.[83] Washington carefully scheduled his tours to include only those states that had ratified the Constitution. When he visited New England in 1789, he avoided Rhode Island, making a separate visit there in August 1790, after it had officially joined the union. Similarly, he delayed his southern tour until 1791, awaiting North Carolina's approval of the Constitution.[84] Not wishing to show favoritism to any state or region, Washington avoided those states he had already visited during his preinaugural journey (New Jersey and Delaware), did not linger in those that were unavoidable as he toured (Maryland and Virginia), and did not tour those that housed the temporary capitals (New York and Pennsylvania) because their citizens already enjoyed access to the national government. The goals of these tours were twofold: to establish the national government's authority in the places he visited, and more importantly, to forge the crucial sovereign bond between the government and its citizens that would ensure the successful launching of republican government.

As word of Washington's impending tour spread through New England's newspapers, towns and cities along the proposed route began to make preparations based on the following reports: "We are informed the President of the United States will set out on a tour to the eastward tomorrow morning: We are further informed, that he proposes to go as far as Portsmouth, New Hampshire."[85] Hoping to offer both the dramatic spectacle and the widespread public participation that had characterized the preinaugural receptions, organizers throughout New England debated the best way to welcome the president. The Boston Committee of Arrangements reported: "We are not able to say what mode will be adopted to respect the President upon his arrival." Among the suggestions they had received from their correspondents: "one proposes a general illumination—another, a partial one such as, the Main Street from the Fortification to the Market—together with three Bonfires, one on Fort Hill, one on Cops Hill, and one in the Common."[86] Another correspondent agreed that there should be a "general illumination" but with a "public subscription for the purpose of supplying those persons with candles, whose circumstances will not permit such an expense" in order to ensure large crowds and a memorable display upon Washington's arrival.[87]

While New Englanders discussed eye-popping logistics, newspapers in Philadelphia and New York, who had already participated in rituals of citizenship during the preinaugural tour, offered their insights concerning the meaning of the impending presidential visit. John

Fenno, the nationalist editor of the *Gazette of the United States*, declared: "The ocular demonstration which this opportunity will afford, of the peace and harmony of the people under the new Constitution . . . and especially of the warm and unparalleled attachment of the people to the first of citizens . . . will serve to animate the ruler of our rising country."[88] During the president's visit, the citizens of Connecticut, Massachusetts, and New Hampshire would get a chance to pledge allegiance to the new Constitution and officially join the national fold.

Before embarking on his "eastern" tour, Washington emphasized the republican character of his efforts by once again seeking approval from James Madison and John Jay, as well as Henry Knox and Alexander Hamilton, who were now members of his newly installed cabinet.[89] In his diary, Washington wrote of polling these men concerning the "propriety" of his proposed tour. Hamilton thought it "very desirable," as did Knox. Madison "saw no impropriety in my proposed trip," while Jay offered his high approval, "but observed a similar visit would be expected by those of the Southern."[90] Offering their political consent verbally and visually, Jay, Hamilton, and Knox escorted Washington to the New York City limits on October 15, 1789, when he took advantage of the congressional recess to begin his trip.[91]

Washington's month-long tour through towns in Connecticut, Massachusetts, and New Hampshire replicated the protocol that had characterized his preinaugural journey: processions of citizens and militia companies accompanying him into towns; welcoming receptions consisting of speeches to and from Washington; and evening dinners, toasts, and balls hosted by the town's leading citizens.[92] Where time and resources permitted, particularly in Boston, odes and oratorios were written in Washington's honor, triumphal arches erected attesting to his status as the nation's hero, and of course, fireworks and illuminations displayed to match those during the inauguration.[93] Now that he was officially president, Washington seemed more comfortable with the enormous outpouring than he had been during the preinaugural journey. His public responses to welcoming speeches sounded a familiar note: love of country, fulfillment of duty, and the blessings of Providence the young nation enjoyed.[94]

A malady nicknamed "Washington's influenza" or the "president's cough" offered a measurement of the enormous public outpouring that greeted the president. Although this respiratory ailment had already spread through the lower states, it reached New England at the same time as Washington.[95] As crowds of spectators gathered to welcome and cheer the president, they were inadvertently infecting one another, including Washington himself.[96] The tour's dubious association with "Washington's influenza" did little to dampen the enthusiasm of those eager to see the president.[97] Two more memorable souvenirs were the presidential portraits initiated during the New England tour. The Boston selectmen asked Washington "to sit for his portrait to satisfy Boston's ladies 'who are ambitious of transmitting to their Children a perfect likeness of their justly Beloved President at the moment he blessed them with his presence.'"[98] Harvard University also commissioned a portrait to commemorate the presidential visit of October 29, 1789.[99] These requests resulted in portraits painted by Christian Gullager and Edward Savage, respectively.[100]

During Washington's stay in Boston, an unexpected power struggle with Massachusetts governor John Hancock afforded the quick-thinking and shrewd Washington an invaluable opportunity to demonstrate the primacy of the federal government (and its leader) over the states (and their leaders). At the time appointed for Hancock to call on Washington, Hancock declared himself too ill with gout to journey to the president's lodgings and requested that Washington pay a visit to him instead. Recognizing Hancock's blatant challenge to the president's stature, Washington refused Hancock's invitation, and the governor eventually acquiesced by allowing servants to carry him into the president's drawing room.[101] With this competition over honor satisfactorily resolved, Washington received a lavish reception in Boston that represented the pinnacle of this journey.[102] After leaving Boston, Washington traveled north to New Hampshire, visiting Portsmouth and Exeter. Washington returned to New York City on November 13, 1789, where his arrival "was announced by a federal salute from the Battery," which informed the residents of New York that its leading citizen had returned.[103]

In August 1790, Washington undertook a tour of Rhode Island in his ongoing campaign to bring the national government to all thirteen states. This small and recalcitrant state had finally mustered enough Federalist support to call a state convention in January 1790, and on May 29, 1790, it voted to ratify the Constitution by a slim majority of two votes.[104] In recognition of this achievement, Washington boarded a packet on August 15, along with Secretary of State Thomas Jefferson and New York governor George Clinton, to tour the state.[105] In addition to the coastal city of Newport, the president and his party visited the state

"To Preserve the Dignity and Respect" 53

Portrait of George Washington, commissioned by Harvard University during his visit to Massachusetts when he toured the eastern states in the fall of 1789. The portrait was completed by Edward Savage in 1790. Source: Harvard Art Museum, Fogg Art Museum, Harvard University Portrait Collection, Gift of Edward Savage to Harvard College, 1791, H49.

capital of Providence, where Washington and the national government were saluted in welcoming speeches, processions, dinners and toasts, and balls.[106] Thirteen-gun salutes greeted the president's packet upon its arrival and departure from Newport and Providence.[107] The welcoming reception in Providence contained many of the same rituals of citizenship that had appeared during the earlier tours: "The general Attendance of almost every inhabitant of the Town in the Procession, together with the brilliant appearance of the Ladies at the windows and doors of the Houses, evinced in the most sensible manner their pleasure on this happy occasion." In the city's welcoming remarks, the citizens of Providence pledged their support to the national government: "From our most excellent Constitution, and the benign influence of those virtues which characterize your administration, we entertain the most pleasing hopes of the extension of commerce, the encouragement of agriculture and manufactures, . . . and that the Liberties of America will be transmitted to very late posterity."[108] To bring the day's festivities to a close, and not to be outdone by their Boston neighbors: "In the evening the College Edifice was splendidly illuminated."[109] Less than a week later, Washington returned to New York City on August 21, having brought Rhode Island into the national fold during a tour marked by logistical ease and popular support.[110] Before he could contemplate a tour of the southern states, Washington's immediate task in late August 1790 concerned relocating the capital to Philadelphia.

In the spring of 1791, Washington completed his proposed itinerary by traveling to North Carolina, South Carolina, and Georgia, beginning his journey on March 21 to avoid the "dangerous heat" associated with southern summers.[111] If his Rhode Island trip represented the easiest of his four presidential journeys, then the southern tour was easily the most difficult. In contrast with his month-long tour of New England, this trip lasted three months, covering greater distances through the more primitive roads that separated southern population centers.[112] Further complicating his progress was the president's lack of familiarity with southern geography. Despite hailing from Virginia, Washington had never traveled farther south than northern North Carolina.[113] Additionally, fewer towns meant a dearth of newspapers and inns.[114] Without newspaper coverage tracking the president's progress, many communities did not realize Washington was expected until he arrived.[115] Even relatively short jaunts such as Washington's journey from his Mount Vernon home to Fredericksburg, Virginia, took people by surprise: "The citizens not being apprised of his approach, were disappointed in the opportunity of evincing their respect to this illustrious character."[116] The lack of inns forced Washington on a few occasions to stay in private homes, despite his previously stated policy of eschewing personal accommodations.[117] In one embarrassing incident, Washington stayed with Colonel Allen's family in Newbern, North Carolina, believing the lodgings were public. Washington only discovered his mistake the next morning when he tried to settle his bill.[118] These barriers of infrastructure resulted in less fanfare and more anonymity for Washington as he slowly completed his 1,887-mile journey through the southern states.[119]

Despite these geographical limitations, the towns and cities that Washington visited throughout the south, particularly Charleston, South Carolina, participated in the rituals of citizenship that had occurred during the previous three tours. The familiar pattern of welcoming processions; speeches to and from Washington; dinners, toasts, and balls in the president's honor; and tours of a town's highlights was repeated throughout his three-month journey, although less frequently than during the northern tour. As he had done during the preinaugural and the New England tours, Washington continued his pattern of traveling by horse-drawn chariot and then riding a white horse to accompany the town's mounted escort.[120] This theatrical flourish simultaneously made Washington the hero on a white steed, while also putting him on the same level as his escorts and making him more accessible and visible to the assembled crowds.[121] Not wishing to be outdone by New York's preinaugural ferrying of Washington (and later Mrs. Washington), both Charleston and Savannah transported the president by barge. Charleston offered the requisite twelve captains and a thirteenth coxswain to symbolize the nation's original thirteen states. The rowers on Savannah's barge wore "round hats with black ribbons, having the words 'Long Live the President' in letters of gold" linking Savannah, Georgia, if not the entire south, to the president's 1789 inauguration.[122] Charleston assumed the role that Boston had during the 1789 tour, offering the most lavish entertainments and the longest visit of the southern tour, with the president staying for a week. And as in Boston, the Charleston city council commissioned a portrait of Washington to be painted by John Trumbull and hung in the city hall to remind citizens of the president's historic visit and symbolic presence.[123] According to the city council's May 7 resolution, this portrait was intended "as the most lasting testimony of their attachment to his person, to commemorate his arrival in the metropolis of this state, and to hand down to posterity the resemblance of the Man, to whom they are so much indebted for the blessings of peace, liberty and independence."[124] In order words, this painting of Washington would symbolize the national citizenship and federal presence that the southern tour was meant to engender. When an exhausted Washington reached his Mount Vernon home on June 12, 1791, he had accomplished his goal of bringing the national republican government to all thirteen states, despite the enormous strain of the journeys.[125]

Superficially, Washington's tours resembled a monarchical progress, but more than an ocean separated these ceremonial forms. As Washington traveled the northern and southern states, local residents greeted him with speeches and dinners that affirmed their support for republican government. But unlike royal progresses, in which the king or queen was the object of celebration, Washington worked to ensure that republican government was the star attraction. Also, the governmental relationship being celebrated was one of equals, with citizens directly addressing the president, unlike that in a progress, in which subjects offered their acquiescence by kneeling before the monarch.[126] Washington believed the new government would not succeed without the establishment of the crucial sovereign bond between the new republican government and the nation's inexperienced citizenry. Washington's tours simultaneously created a memorable event in people's lives while providing an opportunity for them to exercise their political role through the repetition of welcoming rituals that affirmed their support for the Constitution.[127]

Two years into his presidency, Washington had successfully launched the ceremonial program he had originally proposed in his May 10 query. Wishing to bring his efforts to a conclusion, particularly after his northern and southern tours, he wrote to correspondents in Europe and America to announce the successful launching of the republican government. In a series of letters to the British historian, Catherine Macaulay Graham, Washington described the positive state of political affairs in America.[128] A few months after returning from his northern tour, Washington wrote to Macaulay Graham: "That the Government, though not absolutely perfect, is one of the best in the World, I have little doubt."[129] With the completion of his southern tour, Washington offered an almost cocky assessment of life under republican government: "the United States enjoy a scene of prosperity and tranquility under the new government that could hardly have been hoped for under the old." Contrasting the turbulence of the French Revolution with American peace and prosperity, Washington added that "while you in Europe are troubled with war and rumors of war, every one here may sit under his own vine and none to molest or make him afraid."[130] Washington's correspondence to Macaulay Graham announced to a skeptical European intellectual community that republican government was not only succeeding in modern times, it was thriving as well.

Washington's campaign to promote the successful launching of republican government occurred on the domestic front as well. Writing to his personal secretary, David Humphreys, Washington enthused: "Each day's experience of the government of the United States seems to confirm its establishment, and to render it more popular." He added, "A ready acquiescence in the laws made under it shows in a strong light the confidence which the people have in their representatives and in the upright views of those who administer the government."[131] This letter, serving as a written record for both the American public and posterity, offered a hopeful assessment of the state of the new government and a model for how Americans should exercise their citizenship.

While Washington publicly celebrated the successful launching of republican government, privately he expressed dismay at the growing partisan criticism of his ceremonial efforts. By 1791, a tangible political opposition had emerged in response to Alexander Hamilton's proposals on credit, banking, and manufacturing. For Thomas Jefferson and James Madison, Hamilton's policies represented an unnecessary and dangerous expansion of federal power, particularly that of the executive branch, in violation of the Constitution's explicit powers. While these political rivalries had formed slowly, in part, because the national government had taken shape incrementally, the election of 1792 announced the organizational existence of two fundamentally different interpretations of the Constitution that each saw the other as a threat to the survival of republican government.[132] Washington's carefully crafted ceremonial program, which had borrowed liberally, yet superficially, from monarchical rituals symbolized for many Democratic-Republicans the Federalists' destructive violation of republican principles.

While Alexander Hamilton's ambitious policies and haughty personality made him an easy target for the Republican opposition, increasingly unvarnished charges of monarchism were directed at Washington himself.[133] An editorial published by the pro-Jeffersonian editor, Philip Freneau, offered an extreme illustration of the political effectiveness and acceptability of attacking Washington for his "kingly" pretensions: "We have given him [Washington] the powers and prerogatives of a King.

He holds levees like a King, receives congratulations on his birthday like a King, receives ambassadors like a King, makes treaties like a King, answers petitions like a King . . . swallows adulation like a King and vomits offensive truths in your face."[134] In the face of such overheated criticism, Washington offered a systematic explanation of his ceremonial intentions in a series of letters to his confidant David Stuart.[135] In 1789, Washington explained that his overall goal in ceremonial matters had been "to preserve the dignity and respect" of republican government and to avoid "an ostentatious imitation, or mimickry of Royalty."[136] A year later, Washington defended his carefully constructed ceremonial program, reminding Stuart and others that he was "*compelled . . . to allot a day for the reception of idle and ceremonious visits*" because he "was unable to attend to any business whatsoever."[137] Washington then answered his critics: "If it is supposed that ostentation, or the fashion of courts . . . gave rise to this custom, I will boldly affirm that no supposition was ever more erroneous."[138] By 1795, political attacks on the Federalists had grown so prolific that even Washington had lost his exalted status and had been dragged into the partisan muck.[139] Although Washington tried to explain his ceremonial program, his efforts fell on deaf ears as the Democratic-Republican press continued to exploit the threat his monarchical aspirations posed to republican government.

Despite Washington's vigorous defense of his ceremonial program, the criticisms nonetheless affected him, causing him to modify some of his public conduct. At his second inauguration he scaled back the public grandeur, while more effusive outpourings were limited to increasingly partisan events such as the annual birthday celebrations his Federalist supporters hosted in his honor. At noon on March 4, 1793, Washington went to the Senate chamber to be inaugurated for a second term. While members of Congress and foreign dignitaries were present, as well as an eager public, the ceremony lacked the processions and outpourings that had characterized his first inauguration. According to widely reprinted reports, "After taking the oath, the President retired, as he had come, without pomp or ceremony." The crowd broke the solemnity of the occasion by "saluting him with three cheers" as Washington departed.[140] By the mid-1790s, the celebration of Washington's birthday had become increasingly partisan, as Federalists used this occasion to promote their superiority over their Democratic-Republic opponents, who had appropriated the Fourth of July for similar purposes.[141] Washington's birthday celebrations, usually held in his absence, contained the toasts and speeches to the president and the nation that had once been a nonpartisan ritual of citizenship during his presidential tours.[142] The partisan debate over ceremony had tainted these rituals so that they no longer possessed the broad national appeal that they once had had and now were employed purely as political statements.

While Washington believed that a well-constructed ceremonial program was the best way to engage the nation's citizenry and launch republican government, his political opponents adopted a more grassroots approach that engaged the nation's citizenry through newspaper editorials, fiery political rhetoric, and local party organizations. The competing ceremonial styles of the two parties captured their governing philosophies, with the Federalists favoring a more centralized, top-down approach and the Democratic-Republicans emphasizing a more decentralized national government that drew its inspiration from the citizens at the state and local levels. Although monarchical rituals helped Washington to launch republican government, these practices also became his political Achilles' heel. The Democratic-Republicans accurately pointed out that the American Revolution had disposed of monarchy and that this rejected system of government posed the greatest threat to republican ideas.[143] Although Washington had no desire to be America's first king, many Federalists were comfortable with a more aristocratic approach to governing, a political style that made them vulnerable to Democratic-Republican criticism.[144] The presidential election of 1800 would permit Jefferson and his supporters to introduce a grassroots political culture as the best way to foster republican citizenship and strengthen the Constitution. Until then, Washington completed his two terms following the politically sanctioned schedule of levees, dinners, public celebrations, and visiting hours that he believed successfully promoted republican accessibility and presidential dignity.[145]

Into this overheated partisan environment stepped Washington's vice president and ideological successor, John Adams, whose failure to develop an effective ceremonial style pointed to the political obstacles he could not overcome as president. Given Adams's earlier enthusiasm for majesty and titles, one might have expected his presidential legacy to include a ceremonial renaissance that emulated and even rivaled the practices found in European courts. Several factors, including Adams himself, conspired to curtail his ceremonial ambitions. The partisan rancor that had begun during Washington's presidency had now become institutionalized into political organizations, with the 1796 election pitting Adams's Federalist

Party against Jefferson's Republican coalition.[146] This bitter campaign resulted in Adams's being elected president and Jefferson's becoming both vice president and the administration's chief antagonist as the leader of the political opposition.[147] In this hostile environment, Adams lacked the popular support or the political clout to develop a ceremonial culture to support his presidential goals. Adams also had the misfortune of succeeding the larger-than-life Washington.[148] Lacking Washington's popularity and authority, particularly amidst vigorous critics within and outside his administration, Adams faced very few ceremonial options as president.

In sharp contrast to Washington's first inauguration, Adams's presidency began with a ceremonial blankness that would characterize his entire term. Adams refused to allow an official procession to escort him to Congress Hall, and he rode to the ceremony in a modest two-horse carriage.[149] As he took the oath of office he wore a plain gray suit that suggested a newfound republican simplicity but not much else.[150] One newspaper account praised the constitutional principles that produced the day's events, but did not offer much enthusiasm for Adams: "According to the principles laid down in our Federal Constitution, the period of service of George Washington in the office of President of the United States, terminated with yesterday, and this morning commenced the term of four years for which John Adams is elected to same important and honorable station."[151] The real star of the day's events was Washington, who was taking his final bow from the national stage. One newspaper, forgetting that Adams was about to become the new president, gushed: "At an early hour, a great number of citizens had assembled around Congress Hall, to witness the retirement of our late worthy President Washington from public life." The weeks preceding Adams's inauguration had been filled with farewell dinners for Washington hosted by Philadelphia's clergy and merchants, among others.[152]

The Adamses hosted the presidential requisite levees, drawing rooms, and dinners that the Washingtons had instituted. But the Adamses offered these events more out of social obligation than as a complement to a coherent political program. With John Adams's failure to develop a ceremonial agenda, Abigail Adams assumed most of the responsibility for presidential entertaining, a role she regarded as a "splendid misery."[153]

An incident that occurred in 1798 illustrates how the volatile combination of a hostile partisan environment and a tone-deaf leader conspired to destroy the open-air discourse that might have strengthened

Adams's presidency and republican government. A Federalist-led Congress had passed the four-part Alien and Sedition Acts to limit the Republican press and to attenuate the political rights of foreigners.[154] The sedition law, which curtailed free speech, produced a public embarrassment in what might have been a celebratory moment during the Adams presidency.

In late July 1798, President and Mrs. Adams left the Philadelphia capital for their Quincy, Massachusetts home. As was customary, crowds gathered to cheer and salute the president as he traveled north. Among the entourages accompanying the president in Newark, New Jersey. was an artillery company called "The Association of Young Men." During his July 27 passage through Newark, a cacophony of sounds saluted the Adamses as the artillery fired rounds, church bells rang, and a group of young men chanted, "Behold the Chief who now commands."[155] Noting that the cannon was firing after the president had passed, an inebriated spectator named Brown Clark commented to the equally inebriated Luther Baldwin, "There goes the president and they are firing at his ass." Baldwin responded that "he did not care if they fired thro' his ass," a seemingly innocent, albeit candid, comment that led the Federalist tavern owner to accuse Clark and Baldwin of defaming the president.[156] Clark and Baldwin, along with a third man named Lespendard, were charged with sedition and stood trial in 1799 in the United States Circuit Court in New Jersey. Found guilty, Clark was fined $50, Baldwin $150, and Lespendard $40.[157] Because of the absurdity of this incident, the Republican papers in and around Newark and Philadelphia made sure that the details of this case were widely known in order to inflict the maximum damage upon the Federalist administration's attempts at political censorship. In his desire to control the political debate, Adams unintentionally shot himself in the foot (or perhaps a bit higher) by undercutting the spontaneous expression of public support and adulation that was integral to republican government. Adams's one term as president represented the decline of the public celebrations Washington had introduced, while Jefferson's election two years later would mark a dramatic departure in the type of political symbols used to energize popular sovereignty and strengthen republican government.

When George Washington became president on April 30, 1789, the public and Congress had initiated a ceremonial culture before and during the inauguration that included a generous borrowing of monarchical rituals to bring the abstract proceedings to life. Two weeks into his presidency, Washington also found himself tapping into the treasure trove of royal precedents in order to define the president's responsibilities and to illustrate the nascent concept of popular sovereignty. While much has been written about the monarchical aspects of his presidency, Washington, like the Congress and public before him, worked to separate the symbols from the substance. Washington circulated his ceremonial program for political approval, consistent with republican government, and then followed its provisions to the letter. During his two terms as president, Washington toured all thirteen states; held open visiting hours; hosted levees, receptions, dinners, and public celebrations; and took walks and rode his horse through the two temporary capitals. While the practice of tours and levees had originated in European courts, Washington undertook these activities, as well as all of the others, to promote political accessibility and to establish the critical sovereign bond between citizen and government.

Despite the care Washington took to place republican ideas at the center of his ceremonial repertoire, an increasingly vocal partisan opposition believed any hint of monarchy, even superficially, was inconsistent with republican government. Their politically effective newspaper campaign ignored the republican substance beneath the monarchical patina, an approach that overlooked Washington's successful efforts to establish the new government among the nation's citizenry. Although many in the Federalist Party, including Adams and Hamilton, favored more aristocratic trappings in the new government, Washington's ceremonial approach was more accessible and public than many of his ideological colleagues had envisioned. Washington's presidential style reflected an interpretation of the Constitution that favored a strong central government led by a vigorous executive, while his Republican opponents preferred a more decentralized understanding of the Constitution that emphasized the participation of local newspapers and party organizations. While the 1800 presidential election would allow Jefferson and his supporters to promote their vision of republican government, there can be no denying the role that Washington's ceremonial efforts played in defining, fostering, and energizing republican government among the nation's citizens in its crucial early years.

3

"We Deal in Ink Only"

Jefferson's Rhetorical Opposition to Federalist Ceremony

On March 4, 1801, Thomas Jefferson famously walked from his Washington, D.C. boarding house to the U.S. Capitol to be inaugurated as the third president of the United States. In this single act, Jefferson announced that the presidential election of 1800 had brought a sharp departure from the ceremonial trappings and political ideas of his Federalist predecessors. This walk neatly summarized his interpretation of the Constitution based in the Spirit of '76, the legislative branch, personal liberty, and the rejection of anything monarchical. The ease and simplicity of this gesture disguised the more complex story of what had brought Jefferson to his inauguration in the first place. For the previous eight years, Jefferson had steadily and tirelessly built a political opposition, not through performance, but through words, rhetoric, and reaction to the Federalist policies he considered a threat to republican government. While Washington's ceremonial style had emphasized the president's starring role as the nation's first republican, Jefferson's political approach favored a behind-the-scenes philosophical opposition that built a partisan following in Republican newspapers, among political allies, and within nascent local organizations. At the heart of the difference between Washington's and Jefferson's styles were their views of the best way to enliven popular sovereignty in order to strengthen republican government.

While the Jeffersonian opposition to Federalist policies and their triumphant presidential victory in 1800 has been a frequently told tale, a lesser-known story was how opposing interpreters of the Constitution brought republican government to life using rituals that mirrored their philosophical understandings.[1] Both Washington and Jefferson possessed strong opinions concerning what republican government should look like, and neither was shy about promoting his point of view for the approval of the nation's sovereign citizens. Washington, who favored a strong centralized government headed by a vigorous leader, introduced a series of monarchy-inspired rituals that made the president the preeminent figure in republican government and allowed the nation's citizens to interact with him directly. Jefferson, favoring a more decentralized national government in which the legislative branch and the states held equal influence, developed a philosophical program that opposed Federalist policies and offered a Republican alternative in its place. By disseminating this program to his political surrogates, to nascent organizations, and through Republican newspapers, Jefferson let the citizens exercise their sovereignty when they decided whether to adopt his platform, to organize a political coalition based on his ideas, and to support political candidates through voting.

Both of these approaches possessed risks: monarchy, of course, was the type of government the Constitution was intended to replace, not replicate, while party organizations raised the corrupting (and destructive) influence of factions. Despite the Achilles' heels inherent in both of these approaches, Washington and Jefferson believed that as long as the strengthening of republican government was their ultimate concern, the benefits associated with these rituals outweighed their weaknesses. More was at stake here than just legitimate political disagreements; both sides fundamentally believed that the policies of their opponents were an illegitimate interpretation of the Constitution and if left unchecked, these policies would destroy republican government.

Unlike George Washington, who developed his ceremonial repertoire as president in the public eye, Thomas Jefferson developed his partisan rituals in a more clandestine fashion: as an outsider, as an opponent, and as a letter writer. In building his opposition to the Federalists, Jefferson adopted a closely related two-pronged approach. First, Jefferson practiced a thrust-and-parry style of political combat that simultaneously promoted Republican ideas and eviscerated those of his Federalist opponents. Second, Jefferson encouraged the formation of sympathetic venues such as newspapers, nascent organizations, and political surrogates to disseminate his larger message: Federalist policies and the men who promoted them, Alexander Hamilton, John Adams, and even Washington, threatened republican government, while the Republican approach offered a more faithful interpretation of the Constitution. Just as monarchy and factions posed a threat to republican government, so did personal ambition. In conducting his rhetorical campaign, Jefferson made every effort to disguise his negative attacks and partisan activities, sometimes more successfully than others. As president, Washington had been vulnerable to charges that he wanted to be king; as the putative leader of the Republican opposition, Jefferson was equally vulnerable to criticisms that his political machinations were self-interested and would destroy republican government.[2] In both cases, each man defended his efforts as the best way to interpret the Constitution. Jefferson's seemingly spontaneous and effortless walk of March 4, 1801, was actually the result of eight years of careful planning, writing, and organizing, with Jefferson serving as the Republican Party's philosopher-in-chief.

Thomas Jefferson's opposition to Federalist ideas emerged from an unlikely perch: his membership within the Federalist administrations he was criticizing. Because the political and constitutional rules of the new government were still being ironed out in its early days, Jefferson inadvertently (or opportunistically) became a Trojan horse in the administrations of George Washington and John Adams. When Washington appointed Jefferson and Hamilton to his cabinet in 1789, the competing interpretations of the Constitution that would divide his administration by 1792 had not yet formed.[3] While serving as Washington's secretary of state and Hamilton's cabinet colleague, Jefferson developed his initial opposition to Federalist policies, particularly the secretary of treasury's financial program. Between 1797 and 1801, Jefferson owed his service as Adams's vice president to a quirk in the original Constitution that permitted the second place presidential finisher to become vice president, even though the two men had been adversaries.[4] Even in the period from 1793 to 1797, when Jefferson did not hold political office and professed to be "happier at home than I can be anywhere else," he remained engaged in political affairs, paying particular attention to Hamilton's activities during Washington's second term.[5] Jefferson's twelve-year involvement with Federalist administrations, both as a participant and as an observer, provided the opportunity to oppose Federalist policies and to formulate the Republican alternative.

By the time Thomas Jefferson arrived in New York City on March 21, 1790, to join Washington's cabinet as secretary of state, the first presidential inauguration had already occurred and the other cabinet officers, most notably Secretary of Treasury Alexander Hamilton, had already taken their places.[6] Jefferson had served as minister to France during the entire period of the drafting and ratification of the Constitution and did not begin his return to America until September 28, 1789.[7] Although he relied heavily on Madison's reports and officially supported the finished product, his personal opposition to strong governments combined with his geographical distance made him a detached and even hostile observer of the Constitution that was ratified in 1788.[8] Because Jefferson had been absent during the Constitutional Convention, Hamilton's proposals on the public debt provided him with the first opportunity to express his concerns about the powers and responsibilities of the new government. During this debate, Jefferson adopted two arguments that would epitomize his oppositional strategy: to invoke his outsider status to suggest there was either a cabal or corruption at work, and to denounce the encroachment of a strong national government on the states and on individual liberties.[9]

In January 1790, Alexander Hamilton submitted a proposal to Congress recommending that the U.S. government assume the Revolutionary War debts incurred not only by the national government, but by the state governments as well. Both Madison and Jefferson initially opposed this program as an unnecessary power grab by the federal government as well as a measure that unduly benefited northern creditors, who would receive the full value of their shares, and northern states, who had been slow to pay off their debts. Eventually, Hamilton, Jefferson, and Madison ironed out a compromise that permitted the public debt or "assumption" plan to proceed in exchange for placing the permanent national capital in a halfway point between the northern and southern states.[10] Despite agreeing to a compromise that seemed to balance northern financial interests with southern regional concerns, this compromise became the opening act in Jefferson's attacks against Hamilton and his emerging Federalist coalition.

Simultaneously invoking images of naiveté and corruption, Jefferson defended his opposition to Hamilton by declaring in a letter to George

Portrait of Thomas Jefferson painted by Charles Willson Peale in 1791, when Jefferson was serving as Washington's secretary of state. Jefferson began to formulate his opposition to Hamilton's Federalist policies while serving in this post. Source: Independence National Historic Park.

Washington that he had been "duped... by the Secretary of the Treasury, and made a tool for forwarding his schemes, not then sufficiently understood by me." Jefferson added that this compromise with Hamilton "occasioned me the deepest regret" as the greatest error in his political life.[11] Jefferson then promoted his own interpretation of republican government based in liberty and the legislative branch, as he continued to critique Hamilton's approach: "His system flowed from principles averse to liberty, and was calculated to undermine and demolish the republic, by creating an influence of his department over the members of the legislature."[12] While this attack on Hamilton's reputation, and the defense of his own, occurred in a publicly acknowledged letter to George Washington, Jefferson continued his two-pronged philosophical campaign in a furtive manner through newspapers, letters, and legislative action.

During the summer of 1792, Jefferson translated his philosophical opposition into practical tactics by launching an anticorruption campaign that focused on Alexander Hamilton and his pet project, the Bank of the United States. First, Jefferson spread word of Hamilton's corruption to his close associates and then telescoped these charges into pro-Republican newspapers and into punitive legislation directed at Hamilton personally. On June 4, 1792, Jefferson wrote to Madison requesting the list of names of members of Congress who held public securities or public stock in the Bank of the United States.[13] Jefferson also repeated his charges through official channels, particularly in several meetings he held with George Washington, where he reported in his notes that he had concerns about financial improprieties in the treasury department, and added that "My wish was to see both houses of Congress cleansed of all persons interested in the bank or public stocks; and that a pure legislature being given us."[14] Jefferson, with Madison's help, then expanded his campaign to the pro-Republican *National Gazette,* based in Philadelphia and edited by Philip Freneau, which broadcast the charges of Hamilton's financial misdeeds. (Hamilton responded to these charges in the pro-administration *Gazette of the United States,* employing the pen name, "An American.")[15]

The final portion of the anti-Hamilton campaign occurred in the U.S. Congress, where Jefferson encouraged his congressional supporters to pursue legislation to reform the treasury department and to censure Hamilton for corruption in office. Although Jefferson denied all involvement in these activities, consistent with the rules of republican politics, his correspondence in this period tells a different story. In June 1792, Jefferson prepared a list of proposals for scaling back the treasury department such as "divide the treasury department; abolish the bank; repeal the Excise law and let states raise the money; lower impost; treasurer to pay and receive cash not bills; and exclude paper holders."[16] In early 1793, days before Washington's second inauguration, Jefferson drafted resolutions intended to censure the secretary of treasury and force his resignation from the cabinet. Introduced by one of Jefferson's political surrogates, Congressman William Branch Giles of Virginia, the resolutions did not pass, but the damage had been done.[17] The anti-Hamilton corruption debate of 1792–1793 signaled two important changes in the practice of politics. First was the effectiveness of corruption charges to discredit opponents and to question their worthiness to serve in republican government, a tactic that would be trained on Jefferson as well. Second was the arrival of two distinctive ideological coalitions, if not quite party organizations, both of which were willing to employ whatever tools were available to promote their interpretation of the Constitution and to oppose that of their opponents.[18]

Emboldened by his experiences in attacking Hamilton and his financial program, Jefferson turned his pen to another aspect of the Federalist program he found offensive: the presence of monarchical rituals in republican government. Unlike the corruption charges, about which Jefferson tried to remain behind the scenes, although very much in charge, Jefferson was more open in his opposition to monarchy as he positioned his coalition as the legitimate interpreters of republican government. His denunciation of monarchy, beginning in 1792 and intensifying as the decade progressed, followed a familiar strategy: to provide his allies at home and abroad with the language to attack the Federalists by labeling the party as "Monocrats" and "Anglomen"; to establish the philosophical differences between himself and Washington by gently chastising him for using monarchical rituals; and to promote the view, whether substantiated or not, that Hamilton had always wanted a monarchical government. Writing to allies in France who were witnessing the demise of monarchy, Jefferson complained to the Revolutionary War hero Marquis de Lafayette that "while you are exterminating the monster aristocracy . . . a contrary tendency is discovered in some here," and added to French traveler Brissot de Warville, "we too have our aristocrats and monocrats."[19] In several letters to his son-in-law (and political confidant), Thomas Mann Randolph, Jefferson described the threat the "Monocrats" and their ostentatious "tassels and baubles of monarchy" posed to republican government.[20]

Jefferson engaged in a revealing colloquy with Washington concerning the presence of monarchy in republican government. In one exchange, reported in Jefferson's notes of May 23, 1793, Washington told Jefferson that what he feared was not monarchy, because only a few individuals in America would support that, but anarchy, the prospect that the American political system would spin out of control. In his notes from this meeting, Jefferson stressed to Washington the importance of a free press in order to keep the Monocrats in check, while expressing concern that Washington did not appreciate either the threat caused by the Monocrats or the good produced by the opposition press.[21] In a second exchange concerning monarchy and the Constitution, Washington declared that if "there was a party disposed to change it into a monarchical form . . . there was not a man in the United States who would set his face more decidedly against it than [him]self." Jefferson responded to Washington that no one expected Washington to support a monarchical government, but there were less rational people who might, an ongoing concern of Jefferson's.[22] In 1792 and 1793, Washington and Jefferson enjoyed several civil exchanges, both in person and in writing, in which they discussed the political disagreements developing within the cabinet and elsewhere. Despite Washington's best effort, this harmony and their friendship would not survive the partisan turmoil of the 1790s.

Jefferson saved his most devastating and irresponsible comments regarding monarchy for his nemesis, Alexander Hamilton, whom he blamed for promoting these rituals, and for preferring this system of government over a constitutional republic. The content of these accusations was as significant as the form in which Jefferson presented them: usually notes of conversations with his political supporters, where the attribution was unclear but the dissemination was guaranteed.[23] On June 7, 1793, Jefferson wrote of a conversation in which John Beckley, secretary of the House of Representatives and a Jefferson supporter, had reported that prior to the Constitutional Convention of 1787, "Hamilton conceived a plan for establishing a monarchical government in the United States."[24] Not surprisingly, this information would make an appearance during the 1804 New York state gubernatorial campaign, despite a lack of evidence to support such an accusation.[25] Jefferson reported a similar conversation in 1797, this time with Tench Coxe, a Republican Party operative who specialized in anonymous pamphlets accusing leading

Federalists of being monarchists.²⁶ Coxe claimed that in his last days as secretary of treasury, Hamilton finally admitted that "'for my part . . . I avow myself a Monarchist.'"²⁷ In 1798, Jefferson made notes of a conversation with three men named Abraham Baldwin, John Brown, and John Hunter, in which Brown described Hamilton referring to the federal government and exclaiming, "'Say the federal monarchy. Let us call things by their right names, for a monarchy it is.'"²⁸ From 1792 onward, Jefferson waged a determined campaign against monarchy among his political supporters that exposed the dangers these ideas and their alleged proponents posed to republican government.

The congressional elections of 1792 signaled the beginning of two ideological coalitions in American politics, thanks in large part to the campaign Jefferson had waged against Federalist polices.²⁹ In the aftermath of these elections, Jefferson began to pay closer attention to the electoral results and the organizational efforts springing up locally as a result of his ideological efforts. In 1793, Jefferson observed in a letter to his son-in-law Thomas Mann Randolph that "the elections have been favorable to the republican candidates every where south of Connecticut."³⁰ While these comments may seem innocuous by our modern political standards, this level of engagement was uncharacteristic and actively discouraged for a person of Jefferson's stature, according to the rules of early republic politics.³¹ As the 1790s progressed, Jefferson would increasingly add practical political concerns to his ongoing ideological activities to cement his role as the Republican Party's putative leader.

The attacks on the locally based Democratic-Republican societies proved pivotal to Jefferson's ideological development and his tenure as secretary of state, as he witnessed the administration's infringement on their First Amendment rights and its aggressive use of force against these groups during the Whiskey Rebellion of 1794. Democratic-Republican societies began to appear in rural and urban areas as early as 1790 to oppose Federalist policies. These splinter groups gained greater prominence in 1793 due to their visible and vocal support for the controversial revolutionary French minister to the United States, Edmond Genet.³² Upon Genet's arrival, he attempted to undercut American neutrality and disrupt trading relations between the U.S. and Britain, forcing Washington to ask that Genet be recalled after only four months.³³ Genet's outrageous conduct played right into the hands of Federalist politicians who had always favored Britain over

France and had doubts concerning the revolutionary similarities between the United States and France, particularly in light of the recent "Reign of Terror."[34]

The activities of both Citizen Genet and the Democratic-Republican societies placed Jefferson in an awkward position. On the one hand, he had always been a strong supporter of the French Revolution, and his Republican ideas had certainly influenced these societies in their formation of a Federalist opposition. On the other hand, as a member of Washington's cabinet, Jefferson had no choice but to support Genet's recall and to distance himself from the pro-Genet and pro-French activities of the Democratic-Republican societies.[35] Privately, though, he expressed alarm at the administration's encroachment on the First Amendment rights of these political organizations. In a letter to James Madison, Jefferson specifically targeted Hamilton and Secretary of War Henry Knox as the chief architects of the administration's campaign against these groups, writing that Hamilton and Knox "made the establishment of the democratic society here the ground for sounding an alarm that this society (which they considered as the *antifederal and discontented faction*) was put into motion by Mr. Genet."[36]

After resigning from Washington's cabinet in 1793, Jefferson continued to privately criticize the administration's conduct toward these societies, while formulating a Republican response. In a letter to Madison, Jefferson contrasted the popularly based Democratic-Republican societies with the Society of Cincinnati, an organization of Revolutionary War officers that counted Hamilton and Knox among its members and that Jefferson considered aristocratic and unrepublican.[37] Jefferson wrote: "What line their ingenuity would draw between democratic societies, whose avowed object is the nourishment of the republican principles of our Constitution, and the society of the Cincinnati, a *self-created* one, carving out for itself hereditary distinctions."[38] In addition to the contrast between aristocracy and democracy, Jefferson disseminated an ideological platform to his supporters that presented the Federalists as opponents of liberty and the Republicans as its defender. Writing to one of his reliable lieutenants, William Branch Giles, Jefferson declared: "The attempt has been made to restrain the liberty of our citizens meeting together, interchanging sentiments."[39] Although the Genet episode provided Jefferson with potent ideological ammunition to use against the Federalists, the immediate political ramifications of these events proved far more damaging to the Republican cause. During the Whiskey Rebellion of 1794, Washington and Hamilton succeeded in blaming the western Pennsylvania societies for stirring up local opposition to the federal tax on whiskey, even questioning the legitimacy of these organizations.[40] Despite Jefferson's efforts to publicly distance himself from these groups and from the Genet controversy, the political pressure was so great that he was forced to leave the cabinet on December 31, 1793, opening a new chapter in his partisan career.[41]

The year 1796 proved to be pivotal in the ascent of partisan politics and in Jefferson's development as party leader. With Washington's retirement from the presidency, the 1796 contest pitted two philosophical opponents, Adams and Jefferson, against each other, and resulted in their subsequent election as president and vice president.[42] Adams, seeking a way to make his new administration a success, proposed a bipartisan arrangement with Jefferson in which republican ideas would trump partisan disagreements.[43] Jefferson initially warmed to this proposal, telling James Madison under what circumstances he would be willing to join Adams's administration: "If Mr. Adams can be induced to administer the government on its true principles, and to relinquish his bias to an English constitution, it is to be considered whether it would not be on the whole for the public good to come to a good understanding with him as to his future elections."[44]

Within a few weeks, though, Jefferson had concluded that the philosophical chasm between the two men was too wide to permit such a coalition. Writing again to Madison, Jefferson explained: "As to my participating in the administration, if by that be meant the executive cabinet, both duty and inclination will shut that door to me. I cannot have a wish to see the scenes of '93 revived as to myself, and to descend daily into the arena like a gladiator to suffer martyrdom in every conflict."[45] In the same letter, Jefferson proposed a constitutional reconfiguration that would permit him to serve as vice president, but not as a member of Adams's cabinet: "As to duty, the constitution will know me only as the member of the legislative body. . . . If this principle be not expressed in direct terms, yet it is clearly the spirit of the constitution."[46] Jefferson repeated this constitutional interpretation to others, writing to his son-in-law, Thomas Mann Randolph, "The constitution makes me the member of a legislative house, and forbids the confusion of legislative and executive functions except in the person of the president," and even requesting parliamentary rules of procedure from his former law teacher, George Wythe, since he would be presiding over the debates in the Senate chamber.[47]

In this reconfiguration (that employed a broad interpretation of the Constitution), Jefferson could oppose Federalist policies as the putative leader of the Republicans because he did not regard himself a member of Adams's cabinet. As the oppositional vice president from 1797 to 1801, Jefferson pursued a multifaceted campaign as party leader that involved generating extensive political promotion through newspapers and other public writings; tracking electoral politics, including encouraging candidates to run for office; and attacking Washington in the ultimate assault on the Federalists, with the final goal being Republican control of the presidency and even the Congress by the 1800 election.

Since the birth of the Republican opposition in the early 1790s, Jefferson believed the press offered the most effective venue to counter the growing Federalists' influence in the executive branch and to build a popular following for the Republican alternative.[48] Until the Republican Party gained control of either house of Congress or the executive branch, Jefferson and his supporters would need sympathetic newspapers to serve as the fourth branch of government in order to check the excesses of Federalist policies and to offer a more palatable alternative to potential Republican voters. Jefferson explained his philosophy to one of his supporters, Archibald Stuart: "As long as the presses can be protected, we may trust to them for light."[49] The use of newspapers represented a symbiotic marriage of Jefferson's ideas and his tactics, as freedom of speech and freedom of the press came together to produce an effective political approach. The emergence of a Republican opposition also coincided with the passage of the Postal Act of 1792. This law established cheap postal rates for mailing newspapers, making them particularly effective vehicles for spreading partisan ideas to a growing and geographically dispersed electorate.[50]

From 1792 onward, Jefferson dedicated himself to establishing Republican newspapers, even in heavily Federalist areas, and encouraging a cadre of surrogates to frequently and vigilantly publish articles in newspapers and elsewhere attacking Federalists policies and offering other options. One of Jefferson's first efforts was *The National Gazette* of Philadelphia, published by Philip Freneau, which served as the leading attack dog against Hamilton's financial policies and his possible misdeeds.[51] Jefferson also supported numerous Republican newspapers through subscriptions, some more successfully than others.[52] In 1799, Jefferson wrote to Tench Coxe concerning a proposal "for the publication of a new gazette" entitled *The Constitutional Gazette; and Republican Courier,* adding "I shall still hope that it will not be abandoned."⁵³ By 1798, Republican newspapers could even be found in Federalist territory. Jefferson reported to James Madison with great enthusiasm that "a revolution of opinion in Massachusetts and Connecticut is working," with the establishment of two Republican presses in both states.⁵⁴ While a small step, these papers laid the groundwork for a Republican coalition in New England by providing both a critique of and an alternative to the dominant Federalist policies.

Beyond offering financial support and encouragement to the establishment of Republican newspapers, Jefferson regularly urged his political allies to publish anti-Federalist pieces in newspapers as well as in pamphlets, broadsides, and letters. From his Monticello home, Jefferson supervised an editorial operation among his supporters that rivaled those of a modern news service. During the debate over the pro-British Jay's Treaty, an exasperated Jefferson urged Madison, "For god's sake take up your pen, and give a fundamental reply" to Hamilton and the other leading Federalists.⁵⁵ Jefferson praised Edmund Pendleton for an article he had written concerning the XYZ Affair: "I observe however that it is running through all the republican papers, and with very great effect." Jefferson expressed regret that Pendleton's letter had not arrived in "Philadelphia a few days sooner that we might have sent it out in handbills by the members."⁵⁶ In other words, give the article to Republican members of Congress so they can then disseminate Pendleton's arguments to their constituents.⁵⁷

Many of the writers Jefferson cultivated had begun their careers supporting the Federalists. But as the 1790s progressed, they had grown so disenchanted with Federalist policies that they were eager to offer published rebukes of them.⁵⁸ Charles Pinckney of South Carolina fit this mold, but his conversion proved to be a particular coup for the Republican cause because of his family's political prominence. His cousins, Thomas Pinckney and Charles Cotesworth Pinckney, remained avid Federalists, while Charles Pinckney's opposition to Jay's Treaty precipitated his break with this party and resulted in a series of articles written by "A South Carolina Planter." Jefferson praised Pinckney's efforts, writing: "I have no doubt the piece you enclosed will run through all the republican papers, and carry the question home to every man's mind."⁵⁹ Pinckney's political conversion proved to have greater significance than merely a family embarrassment or a personal preference. During the highly contested 1800 presidential election, the Republican Pinckney played a pivotal role in persuading the South Carolina legislature to support the Jefferson-Burr ticket over the Adams-Pinckney ticket, which contained his kinsman, Charles Cotesworth Pinckney.[60] Despite Jefferson's frequent claims that he did not use newspapers to promote his political views, in fact, this was exactly what Jefferson did, although anonymously and through surrogates.[61]

The Republican rhetorical campaign also included several tracts penned by Jefferson himself, although his attempts to remain anonymous met with mixed success, requiring him to make some tactical adjustments in his war of words. In April 1796, Jefferson wrote a letter to his Italian friend, Philip Mazzei, a one-time Virginia neighbor who had been active in the American and French revolutions.[62] Jefferson offered Mazzei a candid assessment of the state of American politics: "In place of that noble love of liberty and republican government which carried us triumphantly through the war, an Anglican, monarchical and aristocratical party has sprung up, whose avowed object is to draw over us the substance as they have already done the forms of the British government."[63] Jefferson also wrote of the perpetrators of the pro-British approach: "men who were Samsons in the field and Solomons in the council, but who have had their heads shorn by the harlot of England," a reference most people interpreted to be an attack on George Washington's integrity and judgment.[64] While these observations were compatible with the ideological opposition that Jefferson had been formulating since 1792, the publication of this letter in the pro-Federalist *Minerva* in May 1797 caused an enormous uproar among his political opponents.[65] By the time of its American appearance, Jefferson had been elected as Adams's oppositional vice president, and his critics pummeled him for his partisan efforts, despite his repeated denial of such activities. They also accused him of traitorous activities for criticizing the United States government to a foreigner, as well as maligning Washington's character, a political tactic Jefferson was just beginning to employ. By modern standards, such a letter does not seem unusual, but because it emanated from a disinterested "retired" farmer living three hundred miles from the capital of Philadelphia, Jefferson's comments and his ambitions exposed qualities deemed unseemly by republican standards. Although Jefferson made several attempts to defend himself, the damage had been done and merely added to the heightened partisan tensions that characterized the presidency of John Adams during the late 1790s.[66]

Despite the criticism Jefferson endured during the Mazzei controversy, he refused to alter what had become a highly effective practice of promoting his ideas through letters and writings aimed at his political supporters. What Jefferson did change was the way he distributed his correspondence rather than modifying the substance of what he wrote, particularly as the presidential election of 1800 grew nearer. First, Jefferson limited sensitive information to his most trusted political associates like James Madison and James Monroe, and he repeatedly urged them to use discretion in sharing the contents of his letters. Second, Jefferson avoided sending correspondence through the U.S. Postal Service because he feared that Federalist-appointed patronage employees might intercept his letters and circulate them to pro-administration newspapers and politicians.[67] In 1799, a year before the election, Jefferson expressed his distrust of the U.S. mails to Madison: "I shall trust the post offices with nothing confidential, persuaded that during the ensuing twelvemonth they will lend their inquisitorial aid to furnish matter for new slanders."[68] Jefferson urged his correspondents to rely on private messengers or trusted friends to deliver messages. Typical of these pleas was one he shared with Revolutionary War hero Tadeusz Kosciuszko: "On politics I must write sparingly, lest it should fall into hands of persons who do not love either you or me."[69] In the period between the contentious presidential elections of 1796 and 1800, both Jefferson and his Federalist opponents had mastered the art of the rhetorical campaign, and both sides were willing to employ whatever tactics were necessary to promote their political point of view.

Jefferson experienced more success remaining anonymous with the second major political tract he penned and distributed in the 1790s, his monumental Kentucky Resolutions of 1798. Introduced in the Kentucky state legislature, along with Madison's companion resolutions in Virginia, these documents offered a broad defense of individual and states' rights in opposition to the Federalist-supported Alien and Sedition Acts of 1798.[70] A combination of French xenophobia and partisan chauvinism produced these four laws during the summer of 1798.[71] The first three acts dealt with the perceived threat foreigners posed to the United States by limiting the number who could emigrate, by restricting their rights once they got here, and by identifying them as potential enemies during war and peace.[72] The fourth law, the Sedition Act, targeted domestic threats, particularly those appearing in Republican newspapers, by making it a crime to publish "any false, scandalous and malicious writing or writings against the government of the United States, or either House of the Congress, . . . or the President . . . with intent to defame . . . or to bring them . . . into contempt." While

Republican editors were targeted (and prosecuted) under this law, its enactment offered a measure of the effectiveness of Jefferson's rhetorical campaign against the Federalists.

In countering the Alien and Sedition Acts, Jefferson (and Madison) employed a political strategy that had proved successful in the past: formulate a philosophical argument; designate a surrogate to advocate it; and disseminate the proposals as widely as possible. During the fall of 1798, Jefferson and Madison drafted resolutions that were introduced in the Kentucky and Virginia legislatures by John C. Breckinridge and John Taylor, respectively.[73] In his Kentucky Resolutions, Jefferson offered a nine-point rebuttal to Federalist policies that addressed the 1798 laws, but also affirmed a philosophical platform he had been developing since 1792. Jefferson urged the repeal of the Alien and Sedition Acts because they needlessly encroached on state and individual rights and because they violated the First Amendment rights of freedom of speech and freedom of the press. He also reaffirmed his support for a strict interpretation of the Constitution that respected the power reserved to states under the Tenth Amendment, and finally, he introduced the possibility of states' withdrawing from the Constitution in the face of excessive federal encroachment.[74]

Jefferson and Madison's selection of the state legislatures as the venue for their opposition to the Alien and Sedition Acts was not accidental. In fact, this choice possessed both philosophical and political significance. In encouraging state legislatures to adopt these resolutions, Jefferson and Madison were advocating the exercise of state authority to oppose federal laws that encroached on their rights and powers. With the Sedition Act criminalizing any sort of newspaper opposition to the Federalist government, Jefferson and Madison wisely chose the states, rather than the press, as the best arena to promote their ideas. Although only the legislatures of Kentucky and Virginia passed these resolutions, these ideas received consideration in ten additional states, while the four remaining states did not address them at all.[75]

Passed at a time of Federalist strength and popularity, the Alien and Sedition Acts proved to be a political disaster for the party because their policies neatly matched the critique Jefferson had formulated against them: they were monarchists who favored a powerful British-inspired government and this administration did not respect First Amendment rights.[76] Rather than silencing the opposition press, these intrusive laws produced a backlash that encouraged more newspapers and more supporters to join the Republican cause.[77] Chastened by the Mazzei controversy, Jefferson managed to conceal his authorship of the Kentucky Resolutions so that the focus remained on the Federalist policies, not on Jefferson, who was serving as vice president in the very administration whose policies he was attacking.[78]

The final piece of Jefferson's rhetorical campaign against the Federalists was his coining and dissemination of political epithets that succinctly and pointedly summarized the differences between the Republicans and their Federalist opponents. His letters from the early 1790s attacked the Federalists as "Monarchists" or "Monocrats" for their antirepublican fondness for monarchical trappings. To contrast the Republicans' pro-French policies with the strong British sympathies of Hamilton and Adams (and to reinforce the link to monarchy), Jefferson also called them "Anglomen." As the decade proceeded, he offered further distinction, conflating these terms and dividing his opponents into "Pure Monocrats" and "Anglo-Monocrats," the latter being the lesser of two evils. Another early nickname was "Papermen," a reference to Hamilton's financial and banking schemes. During the late 1790s, during the quasi-war with France, Jefferson added "war party" to the other epithets already in circulation. In a letter to John Wise in 1798, Jefferson described the political landscape: "It is now well understood that two political sects have arisen within the United States," one emphasizing the executive branch, the other the legislative. Jefferson added, "The former of these are called Federalists, sometimes Aristocrats or monocrats and sometimes tories . . . the latter are stiled Republicans, Whigs, Jacobins, Anarchists, Disorganizers. . . . Both parties claim to be Federalists and Republicans."[79] With these terms in widespread circulation, Jefferson successfully and succinctly described his opponents and provided an easy way for voters and supporters to explain the philosophical differences between the two.

Although Jefferson's rhetorical campaign occupied most of his partisan efforts as vice president, he increasingly concerned himself with the organizational side of politics, tracking election results and even encouraging candidates to run for office on the Republican ticket. Two letters written to James Madison in the aftermath of the 1796 presidential election neatly captured Jefferson's growing interest in practical politics. On December 17, 1796, Jefferson surmised: "it begins to appear possible that there may be an equal division where I had supposed the republican vote would have been considerably minor," and on January 22, 1797, he added: "the [Republican] vote comes much nearer an equality than I had expected."[80] As the 1800 presidential election grew closer, Jefferson's attention to electoral detail increased as well. By 1799, Jefferson had mastered the state-by-state rules for choosing presidential electors as well as the growth of the Republican cause in each state. Jefferson reported to James Thomson Callender, an almost notorious Republican newspaper editor: "Georgia, North Carolina, Tennessee, Kentucky, Virginia, Maryland, and Pennsylvania chose their electors by the people directly. In Massachusetts the choice is first by the people," although the legislature could intervene. In the remaining eight states, the legislatures named the electors."[81] Jefferson paid close attention to the voting in pivotal states like Pennsylvania, which possessed strong Republican and Federalist elements, concluding: "By the time you receive this, you will know the event of the Pennsylvania elections. These are all-important to the union at large, as the state nearly holds the balance between North and South."[82] Jefferson's interest in political developments at the state level extended to his opponents' political strategy in 1800. Writing to his son-in-law, Thomas Mann Randolph, on the Federalists' choice of Adams's running mate: "They held a caucus on Saturday night and have determined on some hocus-pocus maneuvers by running General Charles C. Pinckney with Mr. Adams to draw off South Carolina, and to make impression on North Carolina."[83] The final aspect of Jefferson's foray into electoral politics as a party leader was encouraging candidates to run for political office to help secure a Republican majority in the House of Representatives. Writing to John Page of Virginia, Jefferson argued: "I am told that if you will exert yourself you may be elected to the next Congress. Pray my dear Sir, leave nothing undone to effect it. We gain on the whole by the new elections, and if those of Virginia are uniform, we shall have a majority."[84] While serving as vice president, Jefferson's partisan portfolio expanded to include electoral concerns, alongside philosophical arguments, to ensure a Republican majority in at least the House of Representatives, and the presidency by 1800.

Jefferson's extensive rhetorical campaign and his growing electoral involvement would seem to have been enough to produce the Republican victory he was seeking in 1800, but he intended to leave nothing to chance. The final piece of his assault on the Federalists was an attack on this party's greatest asset: George Washington. By targeting the nation's quintessential republican, who continued to give enormous legitimacy to the Federalist cause, Jefferson sought to burst the cult of personality surrounding Washington in order to place the upstart Republicans on an equal footing with the more nationally established Federalist Party. While politically necessary, Jefferson's efforts served as a humiliating blow to the reputation of a man who had sought to remain above the political fray and had even tried to broker a partisan middle ground between his squabbling cabinet members, Jefferson and Hamilton, in 1792.[85]

Although Jefferson had taken indirect aim at Washington by criticizing the policies and practices he supported such as the national bank or his use of monarchical rituals, these attacks left Washington's reputation largely intact. By contrast, his whispering campaign of the mid-1790s represented a direct assault against the president's most prized assets: his character and his judgment. Jefferson's controversial letter to Philip Mazzei of April 24, 1796, marked the opening act of his assault. Upon its American publication in March 1797, all communication between Washington and Jefferson ceased, freeing Jefferson to escalate his attacks with impunity.[86] Writing to James Monroe in 1796, Jefferson explained the strategic need to go after Washington in order to defeat the Federalists: "they see that nothing can support them but the colossus of the president's merits with the people, and the moment he retires, that his successor, if a monocrat, will be overborne by the republican sense of his constituents."[87] In the aftermath of the 1796 presidential election, Jefferson portrayed the departing Washington as vain, shallow, and accustomed to unquestioning public adulation, a reference to public ceremony and presidential tours. Jefferson concluded in a letter to Archibald Stuart: "His mind had been so long used to unlimited applause that it could not brook contradiction, or even advice offered unasked."[88] Several days later, Jefferson underscored Washington's vanity while challenging his exalted integrity and judgment, when he wrote to James Madison that "he will have his usual good fortune of reaping credit from the good acts of others, and leaving to them that of his errors."[89] In the midst of the 1800 presidential election, Jefferson offered a succinct criticism of Washington, couched in philosophical musings about republican government. Writing to his Virginia neighbor, Dr. William Bache, Jefferson provided a list of the lessons he drew from the French Revolution for the benefit of American citizens, including "to beware of too much confidence in any man," suggesting that both Washington and the Federalist Party could and should be replaced.[90]

Jefferson's efforts as party leader culminated in the dissemination of detailed letters that announced his national candidacy and offered the philosophical ideas he called "the true spirit of the Constitution," which he believed would elevate him to the presidency in 1800.[91] Jefferson's platform contained an opposition to specific Federalist policies as well as an alternative approach that emerged from a long career spent contemplating monarchy, revolution, natural rights, sovereignty, and citizenship.[92] Seeking a wide national audience, Jefferson chose to share his philosophical and political intentions with two New Englanders: one a potential ally, the other a loyal supporter. On January 26, 1799, Jefferson wrote an extensive letter to Elbridge Gerry, a future Massachusetts governor and American vice president, laying out his philosophical platform in anticipation of the 1800 presidential election.[93] Jefferson declared his opinions to Gerry (and anyone else who was listening) in a series of succinct policy positions: "I do then with sincere zeal wish an inviolable preservation of our present federal constitution. . . . I am opposed to the monarchising its features by the forms of its administration. . . . I am for preserving to the states the powers not yielded by them to the Union. . . . I am for a government rigorously frugal and simple. . . . I am for relying, for internal defence, on our militia solely till actual invasion. . . . I am for free commerce with nations, political connections with none. . . . I am for freedom of religion . . . for freedom of press. . . . [T]hese my friend are my principles; they are unquestionably the principles of the great body of our fellow citizens."[94] Closer to the election, Jefferson offered an equally emphatic, although less detailed, juxtaposition of the philosophical platforms of the two parties to a loyal supporter, Gideon Granger of Connecticut. Jefferson wrote that he believed the Republican Party "shall obtain a majority in the legislature of the U.S. attached to the preservation of the Federal constitution according to its obvious principles," including "freedom of religion, freedom of the press, trial by jury and to economical government," in contrast to the Federalist Party which seeks "to sink the state governments, consolidate them into one, and to monarchize that."[95]

Jefferson's rhetorical and organizational efforts to unseat the incumbent party in national politics after twelve years of their rule almost went off smoothly. Although Jefferson won more electoral votes than his Federalist opponent, John Adams, a tied Electoral College vote between Jefferson and his running mate, Aaron Burr, forced the election into the House of Representatives to be resolved, producing, in essence, two presidential elections.[96] On the thirty-sixth ballot, occurring on February 17, 1801, Jefferson finally received enough votes in the House of Representatives to be officially elected president of the United States.[97] In 1800, the United States witnessed its first successful regime change, as one partisan ideology gave way to another, and the Republican Party gained the presidency, along with a sizeable majority in the House of Representatives and a slim one in the U.S. Senate, for the first time in the upper body.[98] Long after leaving the presidency, Jefferson dubbed the triumph as no less than the "Revolution of 1800."[99] As the mastermind of the political strategy and philosophical ideas that produced this outcome, Jefferson had earned the right to imbue the event with his own historical spin. Despite the contentiousness and animosities that had characterized this election, including the thirty-six ballots that occurred in the House of Representatives, Jefferson could still proudly claim to his son-in-law, John Wayles Eppes, "our campaign will be as hot as that of Europe. But happily we deal in ink only; they in blood," an affirmation of Jefferson's rhetorical efforts and the American citizenry's respect for the Constitution and the political process.[100]

The resolution of the electoral vote on February 17, 1801, gave Jefferson a mere two weeks to prepare for his legally mandated inauguration on March 4, 1801.[101] Prior to 1801, Jefferson's preference had been to emphasize the rhetorical and to avoid Federalist-produced ceremonial events. When he prepared for his vice presidential inauguration in 1797, he wrote to his son-in-law, Thomas Mann Randolph: "I mean to get into Philadelphia under shadow of the stage and unperceived to avoid any formal reception."[102] He expressed a similar sentiment to James Madison: "I hope I shall be made a part of no ceremony whatever. I shall escape into the city as covertly as possible."[103] Despite his best intentions, Jefferson's time during his vice presidential inauguration was swallowed up by what he described as "a thousand visits of ceremony, and some of sincerity."[104] In 1801, Jefferson could not rely upon words alone to fulfill the ceremonial expectations that accompanied his new job as America's head of state. So instead, he adopted an intentionally unadorned public style that announced a sharp ceremonial and philosophical departure from his Federalist predecessors.

Thomas Jefferson's performance as the unadorned republican at his inauguration (and subsequent political events) announced the arrival of a new political style and a more decentralized interpretation of the Constitution. Jefferson planned his own limited inauguration, writing to John Marshall on March 2 of his intention "to take the oath or oaths of office as President of the United States on Wednesday the 4th inst. at 12 o'clock in the Senate chamber," adding, "May I hope the favor of your attendance to administer the oath?"[105] Marshall responded, "I shall with much pleasure attend to administer the oath of office on the 4th and shall make a point of being punctual."[106] On the morning of March 4, Jefferson walked a short distance to the U.S. Capitol, after breakfasting with other residents at his Capital Hill boarding house. The Alexandria militia, marshals of the District of Columbia, and members of Congress, who had gathered on their own accord, escorted him.[107] Upon entering the Senate chamber at noon, where Vice President Burr, Chief Justice Marshall, and members of the House and Senate were already gathered, Jefferson delivered his inaugural address and was then sworn in by Marshall.[108]

Jefferson's carefully crafted statement expressed the vision of republicanism that he sought to promote through his unadorned style. He stressed that popular sovereignty promised the freest and the strongest government of any throughout the world, despite the doubts or concerns of some. Jefferson also emphasized that the republic's strength and wisdom came from the people themselves, rather than from some seemingly benign or omniscient figure. Jefferson stated: "Sometimes it is said that man cannot be trusted with the government of himself. Can he then be trusted with the government of others? Or have we found angels, in the form of kings, to govern him? Let history answer this question."[109] In this administration, republicanism would be cherished for its simplicity, and the gilt of monarchy would not cheapen or corrupt it. Jefferson also offered a list of governing priorities such as "the supremacy of the civil over the military authority," "economy in the public expence," "freedom of religion," and "freedom of the press" that echoed the campaign platform he had shared with Elbridge Gerry and others in 1800.[110] After his thirty-minute address, Jefferson signaled a new way to exercise popular sovereignty as he returned to Conrad and McMunn's to wait with the other boarders for dinner, while others in Washington continued to celebrate his inauguration.[111]

During his two-term presidency, Jefferson deliberately employed an informal style to present himself as a truly republican leader in both word and deed. He maintained a level of accessibility and a disregard for social standing that were unheard of in the carefully managed social interactions of the Washington and Adams administrations. Jefferson left the door open in his office to allow visitors, casual or scheduled, to have contact with him. He took daily horseback rides throughout the capital, an activity that brought him into conversation with mechanics, gardeners, and sailors, among others. And by 1804, Jefferson no longer issued invitations from "The President of the United States," but instead invited people as "Thomas Jefferson."[112]

Jefferson's rejection of social formality did not mean that he was a recluse or a social hermit. While he saw threats to republican simplicity in official birthdays and levees, he did entertain regularly in the President's House, primarily as the host of dinners for a regular rotation of congressmen and senators of both parties. Extreme informality characterized these meals, with Jefferson sometimes answering the door himself in slippers and shabby clothing. One frequent visitor, Senator William Plumer, a Federalist from New Hampshire, noted the president's inattention to sartorial matters: "Though his coat was old and threadbare, his scarlet vest, his corduroy small cloths, and his white cotton hose, were new and clean—but his linen was much soiled, and his slippers old."[113] Attendees remembered these meals for the quality of the food, the wine, and especially the conversation. Avoiding the subject of politics altogether, Jefferson charmed his political friends and enemies alike with his engaging discussion of diverse topics. Benjamin Latrobe, architect of the U.S. Capitol, raved that these meals were "an elegant mental treat" in which "literature, wit, a little business, with a great deal of miscellaneous remarks on agriculture and building, filled every minute."[114]

Jefferson also hosted annual gatherings at his home to commemorate New Year's Day and Independence Day, presidential traditions that Jefferson modified to accommodate his republican ideas. His Fourth of July parties lasted several hours and consisted of as many as one hundred invited guests enjoying cakes, wine, and punch. Samuel Harrison Smith, owner of the *National Intelligencer,* described the scene: "We found about twenty persons present in a room where sat Mr. Jefferson surrounded by the five Cherokee chiefs." During the party, Smith went on to say, Jefferson "mingled promiscuously [meaning freely or without hint of distinction] with the citizens, and far from designating any particular friends for consultation, conversed for a short time with every one that came in his way."[115] These more casual social interactions were a sharp departure from the imposingly formal levees and dinners that had characterized Washington's presidency.

In addition to his philosophical opposition to elaborate festivities, Jefferson's status as a widower freed him from offering the continual round of parties, balls, and receptions that residents of the nation's capital had come to expect from the president's wife.[116] The informal dinners he hosted were for men only and were exempt from the more formal rules governing social occasions where women were present. Etiquette demanded that a hostess be present at events that women would be attending.[117] On such occasions Jefferson bowed to social propriety and had his close friend, Dolley Madison, serve as his official hostess. Jefferson nonetheless exhibited the same ease and charm with his female guests that characterized his other social interactions. Margaret Bayard Smith, wife of Samuel Harrison Smith and a frequent guest at Jefferson's table, described a typical dinner: "He has company every day, but his table is seldom laid for more than 12. This prevents all forms and makes the conversation general and unreserved. I happened to sit next to Mr. Jefferson and was confirmed in my prepossessions in his favour, by his easy, candid and gentle manners."[118] Despite his popularity as a host, Jefferson's informal practices sometimes puzzled and frustrated those guests who did not appreciate that, in his administration, republican simplicity always trumped decorum.

Jefferson's inattention to diplomatic protocol created a minor stir in 1803 with the arrival in Washington of the new British minister and his wife. When Minister Anthony Merry arrived at the President's House to present his credentials, it took some time for Merry and Secretary of State James Madison to locate the president, who had been expecting them. They found Jefferson working in his study instead of in the reception hall. Jefferson's indifference to appearance and diplomacy appalled Merry. "I, in my official costume," Merry wrote, "found myself at the hour of reception he had himself appointed, introduced to a man as president of the United States, not merely in undress, but actually standing in slippers down at the heels, and both pantaloons, coat and underclothes indicative of utter slovenliness and indifference to appearances."[119] Merry interpreted Jefferson's behavior as an intentional slight from a president who long favored France over Britain, not realizing that Jefferson greeted everyone in an equally informal manner.

Relations between the Merrys and Jefferson sunk even lower when Jefferson's adherence to republican simplicity unleashed a comedy of errors at a formal dinner held in their honor. Even the socially adept Dolley Madison could not save the scene. When the dinner began, Jefferson escorted the nearest lady present, in this case Dolley Madison, rather than the British minister's wife, as was the custom at official diplomatic functions. Although Dolley Madison murmured, "Take Mrs. Merry," Jefferson ignored her protestations and led Mrs. Madison to the seat intended for Mrs. Merry, leaving Mrs. Merry to fend for

Dolley Madison, circa 1805. She sometimes acted as hostess for the widowed Jefferson. Upon her husband's election in 1809, she excelled at the ceremonial duties that accompanied her role as the president's wife. Source: Library of Congress.

herself. Because Jefferson squired his own hostess (who should have been escorted by the British minister), the embarrassment continued as a startled Minister Merry competed with the other guests to find a decent seat.[120] One guest remarked that this incident "will be cause of war," a fear that was not entirely unfounded.[121] Despite the shock and disapproval of official Washington, particularly the diplomatic community, Jefferson's charming disregard for rank, station, and formality demonstrated his deep commitment to his understanding of republican principles.

Jefferson's informality horrified his Federalist opponents. A critique in the Federalist magazine, *The Port Folio,* summarized the dangers of Jeffersonian republicanism: "There is reason more and more to apprehend that the moral principle of society is relaxed and tainted to the core; and that it is in the growing corruption of our national character that democracy, laboring still to increase that corruption, now feels her strength and hopes to preserve it."[122] Where the Republicans believed the monarchical elements of Federalist celebrations corrupted republican simplicity, Federalists saw the democratic elements in Republican accessibility as the real problem because these ideas championed individualism over community and virtue.

Jefferson did not believe that it took ceremonies to renew the government's ties to the people, but he ardently supported the idea that republican government drew its authority from its citizens. Instead of tours and festivities, he used accessibility and informality to link himself to the common men who embodied what he considered to be the essence of republican government. Jefferson formulated a way to celebrate the nation that dispensed with the monarchical relics that he saw as a threat to America's independence. A future generation of political leaders would emulate his example and develop a more democratic ceremonial culture. To the dismay of his detractors and the delight of his supporters, Jefferson introduced a new generation of voters to a new way of honoring republicanism that moved them from the sidelines of the festivities to the heart of the nation's government.

Jefferson's close friend and fellow Republican, James Madison, succeeded him as fourth president of the United States. Although they shared much in common philosophically, Madison did not reject social formality as Jefferson had. Ceremonial matters, primarily entertaining, had become the responsibility of the president's wife. Because of Dolley Madison's experience, she was uniquely poised to revive decorum in the American government. She skillfully balanced feminine propriety and political skills into an effective public role that had eluded her female predecessors and her more reserved husband. Having apprenticed as Jefferson's hostess for eight years, Dolley Madison was fully prepared to assume these responsibilities on a full-time basis in 1809. Madison's inauguration witnessed the partial return of the large, public celebration: troops of cavalry and militia escorted the Madisons to the capitol building, while ten thousand spectators lined the streets to greet them.[123] Signaling a ceremonial shift away from Washingtonian pomp and Jeffersonian austerity, Dolley Madison (and her husband) hosted a postinaugural open house at their home and then held the first inaugural ball at Long's Hotel that evening.[124] Although James Madison never cultivated a politically effective ceremonial style, his wife successfully wielded influence through the feminine realm of entertaining.[125]

During her husband's two presidential terms, Dolley Madison launched an active social schedule of weekly levees and dinners. Attending one of her receptions in 1811, Washington Irving described the contrasting styles of the two Madisons. According to Irving, Dolley Madison was "a fine, portly buxom dame who has a smile and a pleasant word for everybody . . . but as to Jemmy Madison, ah poor Jemmy—he is but a withered little applejohn."[126] While Madison preferred the sidelines, his wife made effective political use of these functions while maintaining the appearance of her prescribed feminine role. She effected this delicate balance by being gracious and hospitable to everyone, including her husband's enemies, and by putting the most uncomfortable guest at ease. She also used invitations to the White House to rally support for her husband from wayward congressmen and senators.[127] Dolley Madison dominated Washington's social scene for twelve triumphant years until the War of 1812 shut down the city. Through a unique combination of gregariousness, dignity, accessibility, and political acumen, Dolley Madison created a public role for herself as first lady effectively using the feminine realm of entertaining and ceremony to strengthen her husband's presidency.

While the informal presidential style of Thomas Jefferson has been well documented, its casualness belies the extensive efforts that underwrote his understanding of republican government. Jefferson interpreted the Constitution in a fundamentally different way than his Federalist opponents, and his dislike of monarchical rituals was just one area of disagreement. Washington favored a strong executive and a top-down approach to government that received reaffirmation through monarchical rituals; Jefferson supported a more limited national government and encouraged wide participation through partisan activities and newspapers. For eight years, Jefferson developed his approach to republican government by formulating and disseminating his ideas in writing and encouraging his followers to undertake similar activities. He also promoted political candidates and organizations to shepherd these ideas. Working as an opponent and as a behind-the-scenes writer, Jefferson encouraged his supporters to exercise their understanding of the Constitution, not through ceremony, but through political participation. While the Jeffersonian rhetorical reaction fostered a new understanding of republican government and permitted the exercise of popular sovereignty, it was not the final word on the best way to launch the Constitution. His protégé and Virginia neighbor, James Monroe, would offer his own understanding of republican government that would merge the ceremonial styles of Washington and Jefferson for the further approval or disapproval of the nation's sovereign citizens.

4

Desperately Seeking "Good Feelings"

Monroe's Northern Tour of 1817

Almost thirty years elapsed before another president adopted the ceremonial practices that Washington had introduced during his first term. The emulation came from an unlikely source, James Monroe, a Democratic-Republican partisan and a protégé of Thomas Jefferson. Monroe entered the presidency after the divisive War of 1812, a conflict that exposed deep regional, partisan, and ideological disagreements within the nation. Hoping to ease the lingering tensions, Monroe decided to tour New England and the southern states to promote a nonpartisan message of national healing. By following in Washington's literal and figurative footsteps, Monroe saw an opportunity to renew the sovereign bonds between the national government and its citizens, while embracing a more Federalist style of presidential leadership to atone for his own partisan sins. Monroe's tours lasted longer and covered more distance than Washington's, in part due to the country's intense territorial expansion. Monroe also made himself more accessible than Washington, lingering in each city and town he visited. In addition to healing partisan wounds in New England, Monroe's tours coincided with a generational shift in national politics as a younger generation of politicians vied with one another to assume the presidency. Traveling the nation as an exemplar of republican virtue, Monroe and his tours helped the nation and republican government make a smooth transition from a period of postwar uneasiness into a new political era beyond the founding generation.

While Washington's and Jefferson's public rituals had emphasized their competing interpretations of the Constitution, Monroe's tours targeted the three decades of partisan rancor that had emerged from these debates. As president, Monroe wanted to unite Americans around an understanding of republicanism based in partisan-free government. In his inaugural address, Monroe made his intentions clear, stating, "Discord does not belong to our system," and he pledged that promoting "this harmony in accord with the principles of our republican Government . . . will be the object of my zealous exertions."[1] During his northern and southern tours he promoted this vision to enthusiastic tour participants, critical newspaper editors, hopeful Federalists, and skeptical Republicans. After thirty years of experience with republican government, many participants and observers freely offered their opinions of Monroe's tours, a practice that reaffirmed the bonds of government and citizens.

Monroe's message of nonpartisan healing struck a popular chord with many Americans who agreed that disunity and selfishness had produced the lion's share of the nation's recent woes. The tour's supporters expanded Monroe's nonpartisan message to include a celebration of the nation's revolutionary glories and its republican principles. During the four-month northern journey, the tour's participants offered parades, welcoming speeches, and local boosterism to honor Monroe as a living symbol of the nation's founding ideas.[2] The organizers hoped that their participation in these rituals of citizenship would purify the government of its excesses and return the nation to its republican moorings.

Newspaper editors played a significant role in presenting Monroe and his republican vision to the nation during the two tours. While they avidly covered his progress and the public outpourings that greeted him, many openly criticized the tours' adherence to republican principles, while others served as cheerleaders for the Federalist cause. Reflecting the influence of newspaper editors in promoting and analyzing the tour's meanings, the most familiar legacy of the 1817 journey was the misleading but widely reprinted phrase "Good Feelings," coined by a Federalist editor eager to promote the political resurrection of his party.[3] The animated debate that ensued among editors across regional and political lines demonstrated the fierce ideological disagreements on the best way to fulfill the Constitution's republican mandate.

Route traveled by Monroe, summer 1817

Map of the route of James Monroe's northern tour, 1817. Source: *The Papers of James Monroe: A Documentary History of the Presidential Tours of James Monroe, 1817, 1818, and 1819*, Daniel Preston, editor. Copyright © 2003 by Daniel Preston. Reproduced with permission of Greenwood Publishing Group, Inc., Westport, Conn.

The greatest challenge to Monroe's nonpartisan vision of government came from the tour's most ardent supporters, the Federalists, whose political needs undermined Monroe's efforts to eliminate parties. While Monroe envisioned the elimination of all parties, including his own, the Federalists wanted to maintain their party identity and form a governing coalition within his administration. The refusal of the Republicans in Congress and in Monroe's cabinet to share power with their Federalist opponents exposed the flaws in this makeshift alliance.

Rather than eliminating parties, Monroe's tour reaffirmed their position in American political life because of their ability to represent and negotiate political differences. The northern tour proved to be a great disappointment for the Federalists and exacerbated their national decline, but their failure to find a new political home in Monroe's administration did not lead to the disappearance of parties. Instead, Monroe's northern tour signaled the beginnings of a major transformation in American politics as the founding generation abandoned hopes of partisan-free government, and disappointed Federalists sought a new political home elsewhere. During Monroe's northern and southern tours of 1817 and 1819, the seeds of the second American party system were planted as a new generation of leaders like Daniel Webster, Henry Clay, and Andrew Jackson shared the stage with the last founding father and began to form more vigorous political organizations to promote their policies and ambitions. While Monroe's northern tour did not yield a consensus on presidential ceremony or the beginnings of nonpartisan government, the ensuing discussion among participants, newspaper editors, Federalists, and Republicans succeeded in renewing the citizenry's sovereign bond after the turbulent War of 1812.

The War of 1812 provided the backdrop for Monroe's two-term presidency, as both the Federalist and Republican parties confronted philosophical and political challenges in the conflict's aftermath. Americans fought the War of 1812, sometimes referred to as the "Second War of American Independence," to liberate themselves from Britain once and for all. Despite considerable diplomatic efforts to establish America's autonomy, Britain had been unwilling to acknowledge American sovereignty, particularly in the area of trans-Atlantic trade. Impressment epitomized America's lack of independence. In this practice,

British ships gained access to American ships in order to seize American sailors, who they claimed were British deserters. Although this violation of citizenship outraged many Americans, particularly southerners and westerners, many coastal New Englanders enjoyed a cozy and profitable trading relationship with Britain and tolerated this behavior.[4] The war against Britain was the final straw for a party and a region that felt increasingly alienated from a national government that they saw as pro-French, anti-British, and headed by a never-ending succession of Virginia Republicans.[5] The New England Federalists gathered at the Hartford Convention in late 1814 to translate their unhappiness into a cohesive political platform that would revive their national fortunes.[6]

Unfortunately for the Federalists, their poorly timed convention had just concluded its work as the war took a victorious turn, with Andrew Jackson and his troops decisively defeating the British at the Battle of New Orleans in January 1815, and news of the Treaty of Ghent reaching America in February 1815.[7] While a relieved nation celebrated its renewed independence, victory cast a sinister light on the activities of the Federalist opposition. Their concern with regional advantage and political status during a war that assumed national significance made them seem disloyal, if not treasonous, during wartime.[8] Although the Hartford Convention was intended to revive a struggling national party, it hastened the Federalists' decline instead. Amidst the almost universal rejoicing, the War of 1812 produced one significant casualty: the Federalists, who retained pockets of regional strength, but began a swift retreat from the national political stage after 1815.[9]

Despite the considerable weaknesses plaguing the American war effort, the nation's successes at least equaled its failures, permitting America to claim victory. (Britain's preoccupation with the Napoleonic Wars did not hurt either.) Officially, the Treaty of Ghent restored the prewar status quo, since neither country ceded rights or territory to the other. However, America obtained a degree of autonomy that had not existed prior to the war, particularly in trading matters. What had been initially dismissed as "Mr. Madison's War" had assumed a national significance as a string of military victories enabled America to finally achieve its independence from Britain.[10]

The war's successful resolution permitted James Monroe to enter the presidency at a time of unusual calm as Americans and their leaders made sense of a dramatically altered landscape. Monroe's elevation to the presidency in 1816 was largely a foregone conclusion due to the Federalists' attenuated national standing. As secretary of state, as well as secretary of war during a portion of the War of 1812, Monroe knew firsthand the weaknesses that had undermined the nation's effectiveness in defeating the British. Monroe dedicated his presidency to the elimination of political parties, which had caused so much strife during the war. Monroe also tackled the military and transportation problems that had become so acute during the war. In his inaugural address, Monroe recommended a group of programs more traditionally associated with the Federalists, including fortifying coastal and inland frontiers, strengthening the Army, the Navy, and the militias, discharging the national debt, fostering domestic manufacturers, and improving roads and canals.[11] To his ambitious list, Monroe added the standard Republican caveat: "proceeding always with a constitutional sanction."[12]

Ironically, the nation's deficiencies during the War of 1812 affirmed the wisdom of many Federalist programs, but the party's diminished postwar status prevented its members from championing their beloved agenda. The Republican Party's abandonment of its more decentralized, state-based approach in favor of the Federalists' economic program further hastened their opponents' national decline. This program of internal improvements, a national bank, and tariffs, eventually packaged together as Henry Clay's American System, would dominate the national political debate for the next forty years.[13]

Monroe's desire to eliminate political parties had roots that went back to the beginnings of American republican government.[14] Dressed in old-fashioned knee breeches, Monroe's presidency evoked memories of an earlier era. A protégé of Washington and Jefferson as well as a war hero, Monroe served as a tangible link to the nation's revolutionary and republican pasts.[15] As the last of the founding presidents, Monroe, presided during his two terms over the gradual transfer of power from a generation who had participated in the revolutionary struggle to a new generation who had inherited its legacy.[16] Given Monroe's strong Republican credentials and his long political association with Jefferson, he seemed an unlikely person to adopt the Federalists' ceremonial mantle. In a bipartisan gesture, Monroe returned to the example of his first mentor when he embraced Federalist policies and emulated Washington's tours of the United States, while also atoning for his own partisan sins.[17]

In proposing an end to political parties, Monroe was revisiting a fundamental philosophical objective of the founding fathers: the best way to manage factions that threatened the government's stability and survival.[18] Despite qualms over the role of parties, these entities emerged during the 1790s because of competing interpretations among the nation's leaders and citizens regarding the meaning of republicanism. The early partisan organizations of Federalists and Democratic-Republicans eventually matured into the national political parties of Whigs and Democrats because they enabled sovereign citizens to communicate their opinions to their official representatives, a process that ironically strengthened republican government. Although Monroe saw the nation's future in the reclamation of this republican ideal, his predecessors, Jefferson and Madison, had come to recognize the importance of parties to representative government. Nonetheless, Monroe remained steadfast in his belief that political parties had been the source of much of the nation's recent discord, and he dedicated his presidency to their elimination.

In his efforts to eliminate factions, Monroe may have also hoped to make a lasting contribution to republican government, having long been in the shadow of Jefferson and Madison.[19] The most enduring portrait of Monroe came from his fellow Virginian and future attorney general, William Wirt, who described Monroe as a dedicated, if somewhat unimaginative, public servant. Disguising himself as the "British spy" in a series of newspaper essays published in 1803, Wirt wrote: "Nature has given him a mind neither rapid nor rich. . . . But to compensate him for this, he is endued with a spirit of generous and restless emulation, a judgment solid, strong and clear, and a habit of application, which no difficulties can shake."[20] Through this pattern of hard work, service, and emulation, Monroe would, Wirt presciently concluded, eventually become president.

Even before becoming president, James Monroe had begun to contemplate partisan-free government, as well as a trip to visit New England Federalists. While serving as secretary of state, Monroe dispatched Christopher Hughes to Boston with "instructions" to meet with Federalist leaders.[21] Writing to Monroe on April 13, 1816, to report on the visit, Hughes described his warm reception in Boston, despite expectations to the contrary. Hughes wrote, "I have received very distinguished attentions from all the first people here; this is my first visit, and I find everything in point of society, private and public establishment and political feeling and principle very much better than expected."[22]

While in Boston, Hughes met extensively with Hartford Convention leader, Harrison Gray Otis, who seemed particularly eager to redeem himself and his party in the convention's aftermath. Otis, recognizing Hughes's close association with Monroe, used the visit as an opportunity to explain the true motives behind the Hartford Convention.[23] In his comments to Hughes, Otis stressed that disunion was never the goal of the Hartford Convention. Hughes wrote to Monroe that, according to Otis, "the principle of the permanence of the Union of the States, was the very soul of the Hartford Convention."[24] Hughes then relayed Otis's suggestion that the next president should travel to New England, where he would receive a warm reception from the region's residents that would demonstrate their support for the union. Hughes added that Otis believed that such a visit would be beneficial for all concerned. It is unclear whether Monroe, via Hughes, proposed a presidential tour to Otis to seek his support, or Otis originated the idea of a tour. In either case, Otis and Monroe entertained an alliance of convenience that Otis believed would redeem himself and his Federalist colleagues.[25]

Despite the positive exchanges occurring between Otis and Monroe in 1816, the lingering taint of the Hartford Convention, along with Monroe's assumption of the presidency and his opponents' agenda, produced grim political prospects for the Federalist Party nationwide. Early in 1817, Jeremiah Mason, a U.S. senator from New Hampshire, assessed the political impotence of the Federalists in Congress. Writing to former senator Christopher Gore, Mason lamented, "On no occasion has anything like a Federal opposition appeared during this session, in either House," and he concluded, "It will never again be seen."[26] By June, Mason considered the situation so hopeless that he resigned his Senate seat, two years before his term expired. Daniel Webster, a congressman from New Hampshire, joined the ranks of exiting Federalists who no longer saw a political future for themselves or their party.[27] Writing to Mason, Webster cogently described the party's congressional decline: "Who remains, fit to prescribe any course to us?"[28] Between 1815 and 1817, the number of Federalists decreased from seventy-five in the fourteenth Congress to fifty in the fifteenth Congress.[29] With his own congressional term over in 1817, Webster relocated to Boston to practice law and to contemplate other options.[30]

Soon after his inauguration, Monroe alerted his friends and associates of his intention to tour the nation. The earliest mention of his plans came from Brigadier General Joseph Gardner Swift, chief engineer of the Army and superintendent of the U.S. Military Academy at West Point. In Swift's March 25 diary entry, he described an outing

Desperately Seeking "Good Feelings" 99

Christopher Gore and Jeremiah Mason, two Federalist senators from New England, who weighed their party's political prospects before, during, and after Monroe's visit to Boston. Source: Courtesy of Harvard Art Museum and Special Collections Department, Harvard Law School Library with the president along the Potomac River: "This excursion was made on horseback, and on the way back to the city the President informed me that he proposed making a tour of inspection of the fortifications and navy yards in the Union, and that he should require my services to aid him in that excursion." By April 4, Monroe and Swift had agreed to meet in Baltimore in early June "to proceed there and elsewhere on his contemplated tour."[31] With the preliminary itinerary of his tour established, word quickly spread in the capital and along the proposed route.

Although most of Monroe's correspondence sought to keep his friends informed of his plans and his whereabouts, his letter to Thomas Jefferson assumed a different tone as he sought to elevate the tour's mission. Monroe stressed the tour's importance in fulfilling his presidential responsibilities. He wrote: "Soon after my election to the present office, I determined to make a tour along our coast, and to the westward to enable me to execute with the greatest advantage the duties assigned me, relative to public defense, as to fortifications, dockyards."[32] Despite Jefferson's strong opposition to ceremonial forms, Monroe sought his mentor's approval. In late July, Monroe wrote to him again to share his detailed observations of the trip.[33]

As word spread concerning Monroe's plans, the Federalists exchanged letters canvassing opinion on how best to take advantage of a presidential visit. Former Federalist Nicholas Biddle, a close associate of Monroe who had served as his aide in London in 1806, responded to Monroe with his model of a strong national government headed by a powerful executive who promoted a comprehensive program to strengthen the economy.[34] Lamenting the loss of presidential influence, Biddle declared: "Ever since the time of General Washington, the President has unfortunately appeared to the nation too much like the Chief Clerk of Congress—a cabinet man, stationary at his desk relying exclusively on secretaries, and invisible except to those who seek him."[35] Federalists had always favored an energetic government headed by a strong executive. Biddle praised Monroe's proposed tour because it would reinvigorate the executive branch by reminding the nation of the president's influence in the national government. With the Republicans forced to abandon the Jeffersonian vision of a limited federal government, the Federalists remained hopeful that their governmental ideal would be restored under Monroe.

Biddle also believed that Monroe needed to conduct himself as a proper republican in order to enhance the dignity and the influence of the presidency. Biddle advised Monroe to abstain "from all exhibitions of mere ostentation or festivity" and to decline all personal invitations as a reminder to the nation that he was conducting public business. Adopting this approach, he went on to say, would insulate Monroe from criticism because "everyone will perceive the propriety of that course and no one could possibly object to it."[36] Curiously, Biddle's own admonishment did not prevent him from inviting Monroe to stay at his home when the president visited Philadelphia. As a friend and political supporter, Biddle must have considered himself insulated from the criticisms that might accompany invitations from others.

Biddle also used his letter to promote two sites for visits that he believed were compatible with Monroe's nationalist goals of internal improvements and national defense. First, he suggested that Monroe inspect the proposed canal to connect the Chesapeake and Delaware, a project he considered to be "a great national work which must be among the very first objects of the government of the U.S. whenever any system of internal improvements is adopted."[37] He also suggested that the president inspect Fort Mifflin, a revolutionary-era fort near Philadelphia, which had fallen into disrepair. During the War of 1812, Biddle had grown disenchanted with the regional approach of the Federalists, embracing Monroe's federal agenda of internal improvements and economic initiatives as the more prudent course for the future.

News of the impending tour reached a wider audience when newspapers along the eastern seaboard began announcing the president's plans to their readers. Thanks to the Postal Service Act of 1792, newspapers were charged a nominal postal rate, making it cheap for editors to exchange news among geographically distant cities and towns.[38] As soon as a Baltimore or Philadelphia paper reported the president's plans, the mail would carry these papers to Boston, Massachusetts, or Concord, New Hampshire, where the identical article would be reprinted several days later. Some newspapers even dedicated a separate column entitled "By the Mail" for the inclusion of articles from other towns.[39] The sharing of news played a critical role in the planning, promotion, and execution, as well as the analysis of the northern tour's meaning.

Newspaper reports of the upcoming tour provided Harrison Gray Otis, a recently appointed U.S. senator, with a fresh opportunity to communicate with Monroe about his impending visit to Boston. In his April 22 letter, Otis stated, "an intimation has appeared in a newspaper of this town, of an intention in you to make it a visit." Otis then extended an extraordinary invitation in an extremely humble fashion. He wrote, "I know not on what

Harrison Gray Otis, a younger Federalist, who sought political redemption during Monroe's northern tour by playing a leading role in inviting and welcoming the president to Boston. Source: *Harrison Gray Otis,* by Gilbert Stuart, 1809. Photograph by David Bohl. Courtesy of Historic New England.

foundation the report is heard, but in the hope of its reality I beg honor with Mrs. Otis to request that you and your lady and suite will do us the honor to take up your residence with us while you remain in town." Otis acknowledged that "on the score of personal acquaintance, we have no pretension that will justify the freedom we take in making this proposal," but he believed that his position as a federal official made this offer an appropriate one.[40] During Monroe's tour to heal party divisions, Otis intended to offer every possible courtesy to the Republican president in the hope that these gestures of friendship would be reciprocated with political appointments for the Federalists.

Monroe interpreted Otis's invitation as a continuing sign that the New England Federalists intended to dispense with previously held animosities and embrace his party-free vision. In recognition of this gesture, Monroe responded promptly and cordially to Otis on April 28, 1817, thanking the Massachusetts senator for his "very polite and obliging invitation." Monroe, heeding Biddle's advice to avoid personal invitations, continued, "Having already declined the invitation of some friends, in other cities, on the principle, that I deemed it improper, to burden them with such an intrusion, I am restrained, by respect and delicacy to them, from departing from the rule."[41] This remarkable interchange continued the process of reconciliation that Monroe and his former opponent had begun in 1816.

With the news of the tour widely known, towns along the proposed route turned their attention to establishing committees to welcome Monroe. Once again, newspapers provided the venue for a town to announce its plans to its local readership as well as the nation as a whole. On May 30, Philadelphia held "a large and respectable meeting of the civil officers of the General and State Governments . . . to make such arrangements as they may deem necessary for paying suitable respect to the President of the United States on his visit to this city."[42] Reflecting the uncertainty in Monroe's itinerary, many of the more northern cities waited until the tour was under way before they organized their committees. On June 14, the citizens of Portsmouth, New Hampshire, held a town meeting to make arrangements for the "respectful reception" of the president. In each of these meetings, the participants selected a committee of arrangements from an array of federal, state, and local officials, as well as distinguished citizens, to lead their community in receiving the president.

Many newspapers, particularly those in New England, described the political comity that characterized these civic meetings. Gideon

Beck and Daniel C. Foster of the *New-Hampshire Gazette* reported that "the most perfect harmony prevailed in the meeting—no trace of party spirit could be discerned, and all were equally zealous to pay that respect to the Chief Magistrate of the American Republic, to which his official character and his eminent services richly entitle him."[43] It remained to be seen whether this assessment was wishful thinking or whether a significant change was really occurring in the nation's political discourse. Monroe's tour would put that question to the test.

Travel in the United States in 1817 posed significant challenges due to poor roads and limited modes of conveyance. Inefficiency and danger were the leading characteristics of an American transportation system that depended almost exclusively upon horses, either ridden or leading stage coaches. In the early nineteenth century, the U.S. Postal Service unexpectedly led the way in building roads and providing reliable transportation between towns. During most of the northern tour, mail stages provided ground transportation for Monroe as he traveled between coastal cities and then west to Sackett's Harbor, New York. To avoid the appearance of impropriety, Monroe reimbursed the Postal Service $1,912 from his personal funds.[44] When Monroe reached the outskirts of a town, he mounted a horse and rode in with his entourage, emulating Washington's earlier example of the accessible and heroic republican president.[45] Monroe also took advantage of the newly available steamboats, traveling in them from Baltimore to Philadelphia, from northern New Jersey to New York City, and across Lake Erie from western New York state to Detroit, Michigan.

Upon Congress's adjournment for the summer, Monroe departed Washington and began his trip. The northern tour began on June 1, 1817, when the 59-year-old president and his entourage traveled fifty miles north from Washington to Baltimore. Accompanying Monroe were John Mason, Jr., a grandson of revolutionary patriot George Mason, who served as Monroe's personal secretary during the entire northern tour, and Brigadier General Joseph Gardner Swift, the Army's chief engineer, who provided Monroe with technical expertise concerning the nation's coastal defenses.[46]

While Monroe envisioned his 1817 tour as an opportunity to foster partisan healing and to inspect coastal defenses, visits to cities and towns along the route expanded the tour's length and its meaning into a celebration of their civic achievements and the wisdom of republican government. The city of Baltimore revived the rituals that had been a standard feature of Washington's tours and now would be reinstituted during Monroe's northern and southern tours: an escorted procession, a welcoming speech, a dinner or ball in Monroe's honor, and, if time permitted, a tour of the locale's highlights. The widespread circulation of newspapers permitted communities along the route to monitor Monroe's expected arrival date while also keeping abreast of the welcoming rituals offered by other communities. A vigorous rivalry emerged as cities and towns strove to match, if not exceed, the hospitality extended by others.

In June 1817 the city of Baltimore teemed with civic pride as it continued to bask in the glow of the Battle of Baltimore, an event that provided the nation with a much-needed military victory during the War of 1812. In the celebrated British assault on Fort McHenry in September 1814, the Americans rebuffed their opponents, paving the way for a peace treaty that no longer required American territorial concessions. With trading resumed with Britain in the postwar years, Baltimore experienced an economic boom and emerged as a major Atlantic port. Reflecting its growing pride and prosperity, the city's population had nearly doubled between 1810 and 1820, beginning the decade at 35,583 and ending it at 62,738.[47] Although Monroe's northern tour began in Baltimore because of its geographic proximity to the nation's capital, Baltimore's mayor, George Stiles, interpreted this honor differently. Evincing considerable local pride, Stiles declared, "That a city which bore so conspicuous a part in the national defence, should first be honored with the presence of the magistrate, is flattering as it is natural."[48] As Monroe attempted to unify the nation, he also confronted regional pride and rivalries that threatened this vision.

The welcoming address of Mayor Stiles provided the first opportunity to define the republicanism that the tour intended to celebrate. Stiles declared the nation's republican government as "superior to any that has hitherto existed," and praised Monroe for undertaking a tour that highlighted the strengths of this system. By traveling among the nation's citizens as their equal, Monroe also promoted republican accessibility and renewed the bond between the government and the governed. Stiles remarked that citizens could "see the chief magistrate of this great and powerful nation, making an official tour through their country in the style of a private citizen, guarded only by the respect paid to the high station he occupies, and the affections of a virtuous people." In his response, Monroe emphasized the central theme of his tour: national unity. He declared, "From the increased harmony of public opinion, founded on this successful career of a government, which has never been equaled . . . I unite with you, in all the anticipations which you have so justly suggested."[49] After the exchange of remarks and a sightseeing tour of the city, the president declined the mayor and city council's invitation to a public dinner, citing his desire to avoid social invitations during the tour, and instead he returned to his lodgings at Mr. Barney's Hotel.[50]

While Mayor Stiles's remarks emphasized Monroe's accessibility and the superiority of republican institutions, the Baltimore newspapers highlighted additional ways that republicanism was being celebrated during the northern tour. Isaac Munroe, the editor of the *Baltimore Patriot,* remarked that the city's citizens transcended party distinctions when they honored their republican president. He observed, "It was the particular wish of the president to avoid all parade on his present tour, but this disposition the people generally, we can say without distinction of party, do not feel disposed to gratify." Munroe also described the specific ways Monroe embodied republican values: "In his deportment, the president is plain, dignified, and truly republican; presenting an example of that general demeanor which is peculiarly the delight of our citizens."[51] Hezekiah Niles in his influential *Niles' Weekly Register* contrasted Monroe's modest appearance with the crowns and robes associated with monarchs. Niles praised the president's republican style and demeanor: "His dress and manners have more the appearance of those supposed to belong to a plain and substantial, but well-informed farmer, than such as, from our perverted notions, are attached by many to a personage so distinguished."[52] Amidst this praise for his appearance, one newspaper believed that Monroe had failed to present a truly republican demeanor because "he did not make his appearance in a suit of American Manufacturers."[53] While popular opinion began to coalesce around Monroe's republican vision, his tour also triggered dissenting voices.

Monroe's Baltimore visit, which was widely reported in the nation's newspapers, stirred up additional excitement for the tour and resulted in more elaborate welcoming ceremonies and longer visits as he headed up the coast. Although Monroe had considered visiting the entire nation in a single trip, after his enthusiastic reception in Baltimore, he recognized the need to scale back his plans. He wrote to Andrew Jackson on June 2, "I am so far on my tour, to the northward and westward, in which, it would give me great pleasure, if in concluding it, I could, so far, extend it, to pass by, your residence." He continued, "I fear, it will be impossible for me, to accomplish this object."[54] This letter gave shape to the southern tour that would take place in 1819.

On June 3, Monroe departed Baltimore by steamboat and proceeded to Philadelphia. Following Nicholas Biddle's recommendation, Monroe inspected Fort Mifflin along the way. In Biddle's estimation, this fort possessed historical and strategic significance due to its location on the Delaware River, and he hoped to see it returned to its former glory.[55] Slightly northwest of the fort was the mouth of Schuylkill River, which Monroe entered in order to reach Philadelphia. Entering the city from west, Monroe crossed the Gray's Ferry Bridge, retracing the route Washington had taken during his triumphant preinaugural tour of 1789.[56]

Philadelphians repeated the welcoming rituals established in Baltimore by providing Monroe with a military and civilian escort into town, a welcoming address, and a tour of Philadelphia's leading attractions. Although Philadelphia was no longer the nation's capital nor the largest city in America, having been eclipsed by New York during the previous decade, the city continued to lead the nation in cultural and educational endeavors. Between 1805 and 1814, the Pennsylvania Academy of Fine Arts, the Academy of Natural Sciences, and the Athenaeum of Philadelphia opened for business.[57] During his weeklong stay in Philadelphia, Monroe visited these institutions as well as the "the Prison, the Hospital, the Museum of Charles Willson Peale, and the Navy Yard."[58] Eschewing Biddle's offer of hospitality, Monroe stayed in a fashionable hotel known as the Mansion House, where he hosted a seemingly never-ending succession of well-wishers. During Washington's tenure in Philadelphia, the Mansion House had functioned as the unofficial social and political center of his presidency when it was part of the elaborate estate of Federalist senator William Bingham and his wife Anne Willing Bingham.[59] By staying at this former bastion of Federalist politics, Monroe paid homage not only to President Washington, but also to the Federalists of Philadelphia.

During his visits to Philadelphia as well as Trenton, New Jersey, the tour's organizers strengthened the journey's republican vision by tangibly linking the nation's revolutionary heritage, particularly Monroe's own heroic service, with contemporary politics. The Society of Cincinnati in Philadelphia, a fraternal organization of Revolutionary War officers, saluted him as their former comrade-in-arms and their current president.[60] Connecting the nation's past to the present, the society "renewed their personal intercourse" with Monroe and expressed their support "for the firm and impartial administration of the government, . . . which . . . will promote the best interests of the United States." In his response, Monroe confirmed the power of the past to inform the present and the future. He declared, "In attending to the naval and military defence of the United States, nothing can be more gratifying to me than to meet the surviving members of my associates in arms." Promoting his administration's goal of party unity, Monroe added "tranquility at home, and respect abroad by a firm and impartial administration, are among the highest duties of the chief magistrate."[61] A day later, the welcoming reception in Trenton, New Jersey, praised Monroe's revolutionary service, but in more personal terms. The mayor congratulated Monroe on his arrival and offered a "most cordial welcome to this city, the scene, sir, of some of the services you have rendered our country."[62] The mayor, of course, was referring to the serious wounds Monroe had sustained during the Battle of Trenton in 1777.[63] The messages delivered in Philadelphia and Trenton were crystal clear: America's revolutionary heritage, embodied by Monroe's own heroism, would elevate the political discourse and sustain the nation into the future.

The American Revolution was not the only war being celebrated during the northern tour. In addition to the militia companies who participated in the tour's welcoming parades, many current military officers and naval heroes from the War of 1812, such as Commanders Oliver Perry and Isaac Hull, traveled with Monroe and made appearances with him during his visits. Monroe was the first president with military experience since Washington, and the leaders of the nation's inchoate Army and Navy remained hopeful that he would prove to be a more effective commander-in-chief than his predecessors. General Swift, Monroe's tour escort, summarized Madison's deficiencies as a wartime leader: "Mr. Madison's mind and disposition are averse to military pursuits. During the war he had conceived no plan for its military conduct, evinced little talent in selecting commanders, and was far too exclusive in a party sense in those selections."[64] As the first graduate of West Point as well as its current superintendent, General Swift epitomized the professionally trained career officer that the military considered vital to its success. With the election of "Colonel" Monroe to the presidency, Swift and many other Army officers believed they had found a leader willing to correct the mistakes that had plagued the military during the War of 1812.[65] Appearing with the president throughout his northern tour, these officers were eager to support Monroe's efforts to examine as well as strengthen the nation's defenses.

After Monroe departed from New Jersey by steamboat, he arrived at Staten Island on June 9, where he stayed at the home of his vice president, Daniel D. Tompkins. Fatigue forced Monroe to recuperate at the vice president's for several days before receiving his official welcome into New York City. As the city awaited the president's arrival, the *New-York Gazette*, the state's oldest newspaper, linked Monroe's efforts with the republican past, particularly the visit to New York by his illustrious predecessor, George Washington.[66] Its editor, John Lang, declared: "Tomorrow being the day on which his Excellency will reach this city, this occasion will bring back to the recollection of many of our aged readers, that interesting epoch when our immortal and beloved Washington arrived in this city, to take the presidential oath."[67] With the link to the first American president formally established, the tour's republican vision was complete. Its salient features included a reverence for revolutionary heroism, a pride in republican institutions and their leaders, a desire to eliminate parties, and an expression of respect to Monroe as the symbolic embodiment of these qualities. With the content of his tour established, the serious business of celebrating republicanism could now begin.

On the morning of June 11, Monroe's floating entourage docked at the Battery, the most southern point of Manhattan, where a committee from the corporation, led by the mayor and the city council, received him. In his welcoming address, New York Mayor Jacob Radcliff affirmed the city's concurrence with the republican vision expressed in earlier cities.[68] He remarked on the high regard citizens had for Monroe's "past conduct" in service to the nation as well as "their confidence in the able and faithful discharge of the important duties assigned to your present station." He also praised the superiority of republican government, which had blessed the nation with untold benefits. Radcliff concurred with the prevailing consensus that developed during the northern tour: Monroe's republican leadership, combined with America's superior political institutions, would result in peace and prosperity for the nation.[69]

After the welcoming reception, Monroe was "escorted up Broadway to the City Hall, where the troops passed in review."[70] Monroe continued his policy of refusing personal invitations. In order to meet with well-wishers, he borrowed rooms in the City Hall and hosted "respectable citizens" on the afternoon of his arrival from 1:00 to 3:00. The festivities continued into the evening when "the City Hall and Theatre were brilliantly illuminated, and decorated with appropriate transparencies, exhibiting, perhaps, one of the most beautiful spectacles that can be well imagined." While in New York City, Monroe lodged at Merchant's Hall, located nearby the City Hall on Wall Street.[71]

In the past decade, New York City had become the nation's largest city, sporting a population of close to 123,000 in 1817.[72] As the nation's busiest and most accessible port, the city experienced an economic boom in the early nineteenth century that increased its population and its wealth. As Monroe traveled up Broadway, he would have seen thousands of recently constructed classically inspired Federal-style townhouses that reflected the city's commitment to republican simplicity as well as its growing prosperity. These residences housed the city's middle class, which consisted of master craftsmen, small merchants, and the new professionals who were beneficiaries of the city's expanding economic base. Not to be outdone by Philadelphia or Boston, the city spent the early decades of the nineteenth century building cultural institutions worthy of its newfound status as America's largest city. During the northern tour, the city proudly introduced Monroe and the rest of the nation to these institutions.[73] While Monroe, consistent with his interest in defense, inspected Fort Bellows and the Navy Yard, he also visited the recently established New York Academy of Fine Arts and became a member of the New-York Historical Society, the Lyceum of Natural History, and the Literary and Philosophical Society.[74]

From New York City, Monroe traveled up the Hudson River where he spent several days visiting the U.S. Military Academy at West Point. Demonstrating his interest in the academy's training and its curriculum, "he reviewed the pupils at that Academy, in all the various branches of their education; and examined those of the higher classes individually."[75] Monroe's attention to this institution must have heartened his military supporters, who were eager to correct the deficiencies that had marred the American military during the recent war.[76]

After spending eleven days in New York City, Monroe departed on June 20 and traveled to New Haven on the steamboat *Connecticut*. Samuel Green of the *Connecticut Gazette*, a scion of the venerable Green family of colonial printers, wrote that "the shore was thronged on his arrival— and the roaring of cannon, the streaming of flags, and the ringing of the bells, testified the joy our citizens felt in welcoming the Chief of the American Republic, in their city."[77] During his three-day visit, Monroe reviewed the uniform companies of artillery and cavalry, received an address from the committee of arrangements, and visited Eli Whitney's gun factory as well as Yale University.[78]

Upon leaving New Haven, Monroe temporarily departed from his coastal route in order to visit the Springfield Armory. Located inland along the Connecticut River, the Armory owed its prominence to its military and technological capabilities, as well as its leading role during Shays' Rebellion in 1786. As Monroe traveled through Connecticut over a two-day period, the towns of Durham, Middletown, Wethersfield, and Hartford treated him to a familiar round of military and civilian escorts, welcoming speeches, and parades. In Middletown, "he viewed the pistol, sword, and rifle manufactories," and en route to Hartford, he crossed a bridge, "which was elegantly ornamented with three lofty arches thrown over it, composed of evergreen and laurel—from the central one was suspended a label—March 4, 1817," the date of Monroe's inauguration.[79] In the tradition of Washington, Monroe was honored as a national hero.

The excitement and novelty of a presidential visit attracted a diverse audience whose reactions ran the gamut from unbridled enthusiasm to guarded optimism. As young men, two future reformers embraced their sovereign status as citizens when they eagerly welcomed Monroe into their communities. In Providence, Rhode Island, a Brown University college student named Horace Mann described the president's visit in a letter home to his family. Mann, who became famous as a champion of public education, wrote that Monroe "arrived in town on Monday evening amidst the firing of cannon and the shouts of the citizens, and was conducted to his lodgings accompanied by a numerous crowd." Mann joined his fellow Brown University students in welcoming the president, reporting that "the streets through which he passed were partially illuminated, the students from the affection they bore him, illuminated the college which made a most splendid and brilliant appearance."[80] At the age of twelve, the radical abolitionist William Lloyd Garrison participated in political street theater when he joined other schoolboys in throwing flowers along the president's path as he passed through Newburyport, Massachusetts.[81] For young men like Mann and Garrison, Monroe's tour introduced them to the rituals of citizenship as they greeted a sitting president.

More guarded reactions came from other observers who seemed surprise by the widespread impact Monroe's tour was having. John Pintard, the founder of the New-York Historical Society, reported the excitement the president's visit generated: "We have been all in a flutter with the arrival of President Monroe." He noted the president's accessibility: "He is followed whenever he appears in the streets by all classes and has expressed himself I understand highly gratified with his reception."[82] A frustrated David Cobb, trapped in Boston while he awaited the arrival of a schooner from Maine, described the paralysis gripping the city as it awaited the president's arrival. He wrote: "All business is suspended in this part of the state, that their respect may be paid to the Commander in Chief of the Union." Criticizing Boston's incompetence in coping with the impending visit, he added disparagingly: "For every appearance to me, these Bostonians only know how to get information."[83] Sarah Connell Ayer offered a more optimistic assessment of the president's tour. She wrote in her diary, "There appeared to be an entire oblivion of party spirit, and all hearts seemed to harmonize in the honors paid to the President."[84] With its ability to attract Americans of diverse backgrounds, perhaps Monroe's tour could succeed in uniting Americans through an embrace of their shared heritage.

A month into the president's trip, highly partisan newspaper editors freely offered a wide range of reactions to the tour. John Lang of the *New-York Gazette* declared, "A more noble and dignified spectacle has never been exhibited in a free and civilized nation, than the reception and conduct of the President of the United States and his Constituents."[85] In the *New-Hampshire Gazette*, New England's oldest newspaper, Gideon Beck and Daniel C. Foster praised the republican values that the tour promoted: "Our citizens, in republican simplicity, meet and converse with their president, face-to-face, hand-in-hand." They added, "No royal diadems, no court sycophants, no military guards, as in nearly all other countries, to keep the people at a useless, gazing distance."[86] For many Americans, Monroe's tour produced an appealing celebration of America's revolutionary and republican values. What remained to be seen was whether this vision could transcend the nation's recent difficulties and truly unite it.

Amidst the enormous public outpouring and excitement associated with the president's visits, a more critical assessment began to appear in some newspapers. As the tour proceeded, many editors struggled with the best way to report on a newsworthy event without appearing sycophantic and unrepublican. John Lang of the New-York Gazette described the balance he hoped to achieve when he wrote, "we have endeavored to avoid fulsome adulation, and to give an unvarnished idea of the interesting intercourse which has taken place between the first Magistrate of our beloved country, and the citizens who have elevated him."[87] The pro-Republican National Intelligencer also labored to avoid "too great a profusion of the outward testimonials of respect for his character and office and too much of the pomp of military and civil parade." The newspaper conceded that the rarity of a presidential tour combined with Monroe's popularity had triggered this unexpected outpouring of sentiment. Its editors, Joseph Gales and William Seaton, concluded that the president's reception was appropriate to his position and his personal qualities, "though it has certainly been more pointedly flattering than we had anticipated."[88]

In a preview of the bumpy road ahead, some comments assumed a more contentious tone as southern newspapers criticized the actions of northerners, northern cities chided one another, and newspapers of both regions blamed Monroe for the tour's excesses. Timothy Green, editor of the Fredericksburg-based *Virginia Herald*, assumed a more critical stance toward the tour than his brother, Samuel Green, editor of the *Connecticut Gazette*, did.[89] Reflecting his personal familiarity with the president as well as political and regional disagreements between North and South, Green took Monroe to task for the public's unrepublican behavior. He wrote: "Knowing something of the character of Mr. Monroe . . . we had hoped that he would shrink from the glittering 'pomp and circumstance' of courtly parade, and courtier-like attention, which the good people of the North lavish upon him." Green scolded Monroe that "instead of lending himself to be made a show by those men, he would have dared to put down such degrading adulation."[90]

The *New York Evening Post*, a leading Federalist paper, mocked George Stiles for declaring that the president visited Baltimore first because of its recent glories rather than its geographic proximity to Washington. Lamenting the absence of common sense in this interchange, its editor, William Coleman, scolded Monroe for not intervening. Coleman then offered Monroe and Baltimore an instructive anecdote about King Henry IV's visit to a French town. According to the newspaper, when the king entered the town, the mayor apologized for not discharging a cannon and began to give ten reasons why this had not happened. When the king heard the first reason, which was that the town did not have a cannon, he interrupted the mayor and said that he did not need to hear the other nine.[91] In a sly critique of Monroe and his tour, the *Evening Post* believed that America's republican president should have demonstrated as much regard for common sense as a French monarch.

Other newspapers stressed that the public's adulation, however well intentioned, was inconsistent with republican values. Because of its comprehensive national coverage, *Niles' Weekly Register* had emerged as required reading for politicians of both parties, as well as readers at home and abroad. During the tour, Hezekiah Niles strove to provide comprehensive but restrained coverage of the president's progress. He declared: "We shall not follow the president step-by-step, and retail all the chit chat stuff that appears in the papers about him—as irksome to the republican mind and manners of Mr. Monroe as to the people at large."[92] But despite Niles's best efforts, the novelty and excitement of the tour overwhelmed any attempts at restraint. In the same passage as his critique, he conceded, "But as it belongs to this work to keep a sort of journal of his official proceedings . . . we shall keep copies of them, and occasionally insert some of them in regular succession."[93] Although many editorials took issue with the manner in which the president was being honored, their comments did not oppose the bond that the celebrations forged between the government and its citizens. The real threat to Monroe's vision came from the New England Federalists, whose political needs tested whether his version of republicanism could transcend party differences. Monroe's visit to Boston inserted politics in an explicit way that had been absent earlier in the tour.

The mood among Federalists lifted some as Monroe made good on his promise to journey into New England. The discussion temporarily shifted away from the party's demise toward an evaluation of the practical ramifications of Monroe's plans to reach out to the Federalists. Jeremiah Mason wrote to Rufus King to describe the elaborate preparations under way for the president's reception in Boston. At a minimum, Mason reported, these festivities are intended "to work out the stain of the Hartford Convention and their other rebellions."[94] During Monroe's visit in New York City, King had met with the president, and he described their exchange as friendly but vague. Responding to Mason, King summarized his impressions of the president's intentions: "I think the chief must, and will, be mainly influenced in his course by the perpetual changes in the political horoscope."[95] Mason echoed King's assessment when he wrote to Christopher Gore, "No one can foretell what this will produce; but I do not believe the Federalists, or quasi-Federalists, have anything to expect from Colonel Monroe."[96] Despite their pessimistic assessments, Mason, Gore, and other Federalists nonetheless took an active role in welcoming the president.

While his Federalist colleagues handicapped their political futures, Harrison Gray Otis continued his campaign to curry favor with the Republican president. Although Monroe had declined Otis's previous offer of accommodations, the Massachusetts senator did not allow this minor setback to interfere with his broader plans. Instead, Otis dedicated his energies to playing a prominent role on Boston's Committee of Arrangements. As chairman of Boston's Board of Selectmen (similar to a city council), Charles Bulfinch, the leading architect of the period, was the obvious person to head the committee and deliver Boston's welcoming address.[97] For his part, Otis led the delegation that greeted and escorted Monroe into Boston. This position afforded Otis considerable access to the president as he traveled with him, conducted him to his lodgings in Boston, and attended to his needs.[98] During a two-day horseback ride to Boston, a Federalist senator and a Republican president finally met face-to-face to address their shared goal of political reconciliation.

There was one Boston Federalist who seemed less anxious than his younger colleagues about Monroe's upcoming visit, and this was former president John Adams. Writing to Dr. Benjamin Waterhouse, Adams jested: "Have you adjusted your Bib and Tucker to visit the president," a reference to the intense planning and formality under way in Boston. Adams then concluded his letter on a more charitable note, declaring, "His plain manner will please in general. Tranquility and prosperity to his Administration. Amen."[99] As the Boston visit drew closer, Adams wrote a letter to Monroe that captured the regional and partisan healing that the tour was intended to promote: "In the good old English Language of your Virginian and my New England Ancestors, I am right glad to see you in the oldest Plantation, in Old Massachusetts . . . where you will be received with more splendor and I hope equal cordiality."[100] There are two obvious explanations for Adams's almost giddy tone. At the age of 82, Adams had long since retired from national politics, and his future did not hinge on the success or failure of the Republican president's visit. Also, John and Abigail Adams were delighted that Monroe had invited their son, John Quincy Adams, to serve as his secretary of state. A culmination of the young Adams's impressive diplomatic career, this position also established him as Monroe's presidential heir apparent.[101] The Boston visit would provide an opportunity for two former partisan combatants to affirm their friendship, while also allowing the Adamses to thank Monroe in person for their son's appointment.

Despite the superficial appearance of harmony between the Federalists and Monroe, their contrasting needs placed them on a collision course that eventually doomed the aspirations of both. The first sign of trouble came even before Monroe entered Massachusetts. As was the custom throughout the tour, Boston dispatched a representative from its committee of arrangements to escort the president into the city. However, Boston produced rival welcoming committees with competing political affiliations. On June 30, a Federalist committee led by Senator Otis met Monroe in Providence, Rhode Island, to escort him into Boston. A day later, in Pawtucket, Rhode Island, Monroe's entourage encountered a Republican committee, headed by General Henry A. S. Dearborn and Justice Joseph Story, who also intended to accompany Monroe into Boston.[102] Brigadier General Joseph Gardner Swift directed the second contingent to "fall in and form a part of the cortege," and the two committees then escorted Monroe to Dedham, Massachusetts. This delicate compromise could not last because, as Swift explained, both groups wanted "to take charge of the president," and neither party was willing to share power with the other. Engaging in "ceremonial consultations" with the two committees, Swift selected the Federalist committee as the legitimate escort because Boston's Committee of Arrangements had appointed them.[103] Adding insult to injury, the Republican committee was invited to present a written address to their party's president, once they reached Boston.

Unlike other cities along the tour route, in Boston party animosities remained high because of the current political needs of the Massachusetts Federalists as well as their long-standing philosophical beliefs. Committed to the principles of stability, hierarchy, dependence, and the common good, the Boston Federalists saw themselves as the true philosophical heirs of the nation's republican tradition, while they viewed the Republicans' belief in opportunity, mobility, and self-reliance as a threat to these ideals. Since the late 1790s, the Federalists had formulated their most strident, but coherent, opposition to the Republican Party from a city where they controlled the civic and commercial institutions as merchants, bankers, and manufacturers.[104] During Monroe's visit to this Federalist stronghold, this party sought a rebirth that would return them to what they considered to be their rightful place at the head of the federal government. The Boston Republicans, who lacked their opponents' political and economic clout, nonetheless dedicated themselves to blocking any sort of alliance between Monroe and their partisan enemies. Unlike earlier cities where partisan tensions remained largely confined to newspaper editorials, in Boston, the rival welcoming committees had publicly and explicitly uncorked the genie of party. Once unleashed, it would prove extremely difficult to bottle up these tensions again.

The intensity of the partisan rivalry came as no surprise to Christopher Gore, who observed to Jeremiah Mason that the two parties were engaged in a contest to appear more devoted to the president. Hedging his bets, Gore added that the Federalists seemed "to have got the start in the race."[105] However, the Federalist press in Boston was so eager to promote an image of loyalty and unity to the rest of the nation that, in their otherwise overheated coverage, they failed to mention the city's competing welcoming committees.

With Boston's considerable commercial and civic resources at their disposal, the Federalists offered Monroe a welcoming ceremony and a non-stop swirl of receptions, dinners, concerts, sightseeing trips, and honors unmatched by that in any other city during the northern tour. To escort Monroe into Boston, the town fathers convened a mile-long procession consisting of cavalry squadrons, military officers, militia units, the committee of arrangements, the civil officials of the United States government, a cavalcade of citizens on foot and on horseback, and lines of carriages.[106] In the middle section of this grand procession, Monroe rode into Boston as a heroic figure on his customary white horse.[107] This parade snaked through the streets of Boston along a two and a half–mile route, where a crowd of forty to fifty thousand assembled to greet the president.[108] The *Columbian Centinel* reported that "the sideways, avenues, windows, roofs, and even chimney tops were thronged with a smiling population," while streamers hung from windows and balconies and bands played patriotic music.[109] Just in case Monroe forgot why the Boston Federalists had prepared such a lavish reception, the Republican president received a vivid reminder when he entered the Boston Common. There, Monroe witnessed four thousand children "of both sexes, about two-thirds boys; who were principally dressed in blue coatees, with white underclothes, and the girls in white" carrying bouquets of red and white roses.[110] As the ardently pro-Federalist *Columbian Centinel* pointed out in its coverage, these roses stood as "an emblem of the union of parties," the principal theme of Monroe's visit to Boston.[111]

After the parade ended, Monroe took up residence at the Exchange-Coffee House, consistent with his desire to stay in public establishments. From the first floor of this six-story tavern and inn located in the heart of Boston's government center, Charles Bulfinch delivered the city's welcoming address to Monroe and the assembled crowd.[112] The Federalist committee of arrangements eagerly embraced the tour's republican vision in order to expunge the sins of the Hartford Convention. Bulfinch, articulating this enthusiasm, expounded upon the themes of political unity, the nation's glorious origins, and Monroe as the living embodiment of these values.[113] He linked Federalist to Republican by invoking memories of Washington's visit to Boston, which brought to mind recollections of Monroe's "illustrious predecessor, the father of his country," and of course, the first Federalist president. He continued by commending Monroe's revolutionary and political service to the nation: "Called to the service of your country at an early period of life . . . you are now raised to the highest dignity which can be conferred by a free people." Bulfinch added a veiled reference to the "solicitude" of Boston's residents in the hope that Monroe would exercise his constitutional powers "with a sincere regard for the welfare of the people."[114] With their loyalty to Monroe and to the nation dramatically illustrated in their welcoming reception and opening remarks, the Boston Federalists now waited to see if this visit would produce more tangible results such as political appointments.

During Monroe's weeklong visit, Boston's leaders eagerly sought to present a picture of a growing and vibrant city and state, even if this was not necessarily true. The Federalists' political decline coincided with the state's diminished population as its residents increasingly moved south and west to seek cheaper land and less restrictive communities. By 1820, due to the loss of Maine as well as continued emigration, Massachusetts fell from second to fifth place in population, ranking behind New York, Pennsylvania, Virginia, and Ohio.[115] To counter the impression of decline, Boston offered the president a whirlwind of official visits and social calls. In return, Monroe embraced the Federalists' hospitality as proof that his former foes were relinquishing their partisan armor. Monroe visited the Navy Yard, the Arsenal, as well as Forts Independence and Warren along with ships of war.[116] His hosts also introduced him to the city's leading attractions such as Bunker Hill and Harvard University, where he received the penultimate Federalist honor, an honorary Doctor of Law degree.

The Boston visit provided Monroe with an opportunity to join the pantheon of distinguished presidential images when he sat for a portrait with Gilbert Stuart.[117] Monroe's fashion-conscious wife, Elizabeth, who did not accompany her husband on the northern tour, encouraged her husband to take advantage of Stuart's residence in Boston to initiate his presidential painting.[118] Over the course of three sittings, Stuart produced a bust-size image of the fifth president as the epitome of republican simplicity and dignity. Dressed in a black coat and a white shirt and cravat, the gray-haired, blue-eyed president maintains a direct and serious gaze. The notoriously slow Stuart sent the completed portrait to Monroe in Washington, D.C. in December 1819, permitting the president and the nation to have a tangible souvenir of his historic visit to Boston, as they had done with Washington in 1789.[119]

The president's stay in Boston coincided with the celebration of Independence Day, America's most sacred and also its most contested civic holiday. The holiday owed its most important association to the writings of Thomas Jefferson, a foe of Federalists, and since the government's inception, the festivities had become partisan rallies as each side declared themselves the true heirs of the nation's revolutionary tradition. By celebrating Independence Day together, Monroe and his hosts achieved a symbolic reconciliation as they labored to expunge the long-standing partisan hostilities from the day's festivities.[120] In addition, the holiday provided the Federalists with an important occasion to express their national loyalty directly to the president. Serving as a reminder of the limits of this newfound political comity were the Boston Republicans, who did not participate in the president's gathering with the Federalists, but met with him separately on July 4 to deliver their long overdue welcoming address.

Led by Henry A. S. Dearborn, the federal collector of customs, the Republican delegation praised Monroe's message of unity, but advised him to remain faithful to constitutional principles.[121] Hinting at the recent missteps of the Federalists, the Republicans declared that while they understood Monroe's desire to eliminate "the asperity of party dissentions," they remained hopeful that he would show equal respect to constitutional principles. Reluctant to draw attention to Boston's competing parties, Monroe offered a brief response, which was not reprinted, and then offered them a full reply later that day. In his written response, Monroe reiterated that the "union of the whole community, in support of republican government" was his top priority.[122] To the disappointment of his fellow Republicans, Monroe intended to pursue any policy that would unify the country, including the elimination of

A tactile souvenir of the northern tour. The portrait of Monroe painted by Gilbert Stuart during the president's Boston visit in July 1817. Source: *The Papers of James Monroe: A Documentary History of the Presidential Tours of James Monroe, 1817, 1818, and 1819,* Daniel Preston, editor, vol. I. Copyright © 2003 by Daniel Preston. Reproduced with permission of Greenwood Publishing Group, Inc., Westport, Conn.

parties. Overshadowed by its Federalist opponents, Monroe's own party was relegated to the sidelines during his historic visit to Boston.

In an effort to advance a political reconciliation with the Federalists, halfway through his Boston visit Monroe broke with his policy of declining personal invitations and began to attend dinners and parties at private homes. John Adams had participated in several welcoming dinners for Monroe in Boston, and Monroe then visited John and Abigail Adams at their Quincy home, where they hosted a dinner for forty people in his honor.[123] Adams fostered both partisan healing and a personal friendship with Monroe when he declared: "Sir, I am happy to welcome you and your friends, and to acknowledge my high appreciation of the distinction which you propose to confer on my son as Secretary of State."[124] As a former Federalist president and the father of a possible future president, the political situation, at least for the Adams family, looked relatively sanguine.

Monroe continued his outreach to other Federalists outside of Boston. After visiting the Adamses, he extended his stay in Quincy to socialize with Josiah Quincy, a former Federalist mayor of Boston, at his family's farm. A relaxed Monroe wandered around the farm and "mounted on the fence to look at the carrot field and regretted he had not time to go down to the salt works," and then visited with the Quincy family for an hour before departing.[125] Monroe also traveled to Medford to pay a personal call to former senator Christopher Gore.

Not to be forgotten amidst this nonpartisan socializing was Harrison Gray Otis, who, along with his wife Sally, scored the major social coup of the northern tour by hosting a lavish ball at their home in the president's honor. Described in the newspapers as a "brilliant party; enlivened by a band of music placed in the garden and a display of fireworks," the ball represented the fruits of Otis's considerable efforts to ingratiate himself with the Republican president.[126] Eliza Quincy, daughter of Josiah Quincy, relayed the excitement of the evening: "The crowd was great both within and without the mansion." She added, "I passed a most amusing evening, walking about the rooms, talking to the beaux and belles and listening to Mr. Monroe's conversation, with my father and mother."[127] A day after the triumphant ball, Monroe departed from Boston on July 8, confident that he had achieved his goal of eliminating parties, while the Federalists believed that they had taken a major step forward in preserving theirs.

The highpoint of the Federalist Party's newly acquired influence occurred right after Monroe's Boston visit, and the Federalists took advantage of this window of opportunity to promote one of their own for a position in Monroe's cabinet. Two days after Monroe left Boston, Congressman George Sullivan of New Hampshire proposed Daniel Webster as the next attorney general. In his letter, Sullivan supported Monroe's quest to eliminate traditional party structures, and he added that Federalists would rally to Monroe's side if he gave them "some pledge that they will be received into your counsels." Sullivan believed that appointing Webster would provide the commitment that the Federalists desired. In recommending his friend as the bridge between the two parties, Sullivan summarized Webster's assets: "You would find him a rock, on which your administration might rest secure against the violence of almost any parties. His admission to your counsels would be a sufficient pledge to the mass of federalists and their leaders could ask no more. His popularity with the republicans every where would exclude all jealousy of federal influence."[128] Webster represented the best hope for the Federalists' return to national politics because he embodied the party's values while avoiding the political baggage of an earlier generation. For his part, Webster remained conspicuously absent during the tour, having privately encouraged Monroe to travel to New England.[129] Although an idealistic Monroe might welcome Webster's appointment as an important step in his campaign to reconcile the two parties, the Republicans and many Federalists refused to share power with their opponents.

The Federalist outpouring in Boston horrified not only the Republicans, but many Federalists as well, who believed their colleagues had relinquished the party's last shreds of political dignity in an embarrassing attempt to gain favor with Monroe. Joseph Hopkinson, a Federalist congressman from Philadelphia, scolded Daniel Webster for the excessive and transparent reception the members of their party extended to Monroe during his visit to Boston. Hopkinson wrote, "I think Boston federalism is in a fine way—you erect triumphal arches—and glittering thrones, and sing songs of triumph to Mr. Monroe, whose path is strewed with flowers by virgins (or those who pass for such) . . . and all this for harmony and brotherly love." While Hopkinson recognized the need to offer Monroe "every mark of a dignified and proper respect," he believed that the New England Federalists had "pushed the thing to the very borders of the ridiculous."[130] Although Hopkinson's criticism captured the excesses of the Federalists, their declining political fortunes explained their desperate behavior. Hopkinson's own career illustrated the problems of being a Federalist. Without a viable

Daniel Webster, another younger Federalist who sought political redemption during Monroe's New England visit. He worked behind the scenes to secure appointment as Monroe's attorney general. Source: *Daniel Webster, Member of Congress from Massachusetts,* by Charles Bird King, 1817. Courtesy of Redwood Library and Athenaeum, Newport, R.I.

political home, Hopkinson left politics in 1819 to pursue a career as a lawyer, participating in landmark Supreme Court cases such as *Dartmouth College v. Woodward* (alongside Webster) and *McCullough v. Maryland*.[131]

Other New Englanders criticized the Federalists' outpouring of sentiment for Monroe. William Abbot wrote to Leverett Saltonstall that he was pleased that the president had visited New England and that he was equally happy that Monroe was received warmly.[132] However, Abbot added: "I should have been as well pleased with a little more simplicity and godly sincerity." Abbot expressed hope that the visit would benefit the region, although he feared the tour's excesses might outlive its contributions. Paraphrasing Thomas Ritchie, the Republican editor of the *Richmond Enquirer*, Abbot wrote that Monroe's reception in New England "out-herods Herod," an allusion to the grandiosity, ostentation, and lavish wealth associated with the Judean king's reign.[133] In the wake of the president's triumphant visit to Boston, the Federalists remained on shaky ground as they waited expectantly for hopeful news from Monroe, while enduring criticism from their constituents and leaders elsewhere.

Despite the superficial comity that the Federalists and Monroe achieved, the Boston visit revealed the deep-seated partisan tensions that would ultimately doom Monroe's republican vision. Nothing illustrated the gap between Monroe's ideas and the political realities better than the *Columbian Centinel*'s exaggerated coverage of the tour. Owned by Benjamin Russell, a member of Boston's Committee of Arrangements, the *Centinel* unabashedly promoted the resurrection of the Federalist Party during Monroe's visit. Throughout his newspaper career, Russell had been an ardent Federalist, actively defending the Sedition Act of the Adams administration in his newspaper. When Jefferson was elected in March 1801, Russell presented an epitaph for his party, declaring: "Yesterday expired, deeply regretted by millions of grateful Americans, and by all good men, the Federal Administration of the Government of the United States."[134] Along with his Federalist colleagues, Russell hoped to see the return of his beloved party to national politics.

A few days after the president left Boston, the *Centinel* achieved the pinnacle of its overwrought coverage when it announced the Federalist redemption to the rest of the nation, declaring: "During the late Presidential Jubilee many persons have met at festive boards, in pleasant conversation, whom party politics have long severed. We recur with pleasure to all the circumstances which attended the demonstrations of good feelings."[135] Exaggerating the degree of political unity in Boston and elsewhere, Russell's declaration of "good feelings" suggested that the controversial Hartford Convention was a distant memory and that the Federalists were no longer pariahs. In the *Centinel*'s rosy assessment, it was only a matter of time before the Federalists resumed their proper role at the head of the national government. It remained to be seen whether the Federalist rebirth would survive beyond Boston.

Despite compelling evidence to the contrary, particularly in Boston, the *Centinel*'s optimistic declaration was widely reprinted in the nation's newspapers, leading many to describe Monroe's first term as the "Era of Good Feelings." This phrase endured because it embodied the hopes of many Americans that Monroe's tour had succeeded in eliminating the destructive forces of parties and had returned the nation to its republican roots. Rather than promoting good feeling, the *Centinel*'s announcement increased partisan tensions, as the Federalists shifted their efforts from achieving redemption to gaining political appointments, and the Republicans worked vigorously to block them. The *Centinel*'s coverage also unleashed rivalries with newspapers not in New England, which challenged its jingoistic coverage of Monroe's tour. Although Monroe and his supporters continued to celebrate his republican vision during the remaining two months of the tour, Monroe's message began to lose its impact as he headed west, due in part to the partisan and regional tensions stirred up during and after his Boston visit.

The regular exchange of newspapers through the mails permitted Republican editors to launch a vigorous rebuttal to Benjamin Russell's dramatic claims. Joseph Gales and William Seaton of the *National Intelligencer* described the *Centinel*'s coverage as "fatiguing," while the *Centinel* responded that there was a "Clay-cold fastidiousness in several newspapers," a reference to Henry Clay's opposition to the tour and his association with Gales and Seaton.[136] Reflecting regional disagreements as well as partisan ones, Thomas Ritchie, the Jeffersonian editor of the *Richmond Enquirer*, offered a broader criticism of the unrepublican nature of "coteries" and "corteges" found during the president's tour, a critique Russell published and entitled "Sour Grapes."[137] In a second exchange, entitled "More Sour Grapes," Ritchie aimed his criticism directly at Russell, declaring: "Who is a patriot! The printer who can best dog the heels of a President, and tell how many times he partook of refreshments, where he dined, and with whom he supped, what pageantry accompanied the procession which led him to his lodging."[138] While Monroe continued to celebrate republicanism as he toured the nation, his message of national unity was unraveling in the nation's newspapers.

Forced to confront the challenges of other newspapers, the *Centinel* assumed an increasingly defensive tone that demonstrated the fragility of the political revival it was trying to promote. Under siege from its political enemies, the *Centinel* abandoned its declaration of "good feelings" and presented a party and a nation plagued by discontent and disagreement. On September 13, its front page declared that "at no period since the adoption of *their Constitution*, in 1788, have the Federalists, as a party, been more the objects of violent but senseless abuse and recrimination." The *Centinel* followed with extracts from a Pennsylvania newspaper's editorial that defended the honor and historical legacy of the Federalist Party. While this editorial counted among Federalist achievements the Constitution, the presidency of George Washington, and the prudent financial program of Alexander Hamilton, their partisan interpretation of early American history seems to have revived the political disagreements that Monroe's tour was supposed to have resolved.[139]

Responding to its regional critics as well, Russell also decided to undermine whatever national harmony Monroe's tour might have engendered. Declaring Ohio too backward to erect triumphal arches to welcome Monroe, the *Centinel* acknowledged that Ohio nonetheless "condescended" to imitate New England's welcoming rituals, even though the Ohio papers had criticized them as "anti-republican."[140] With the paper's overly optimistic assessment of the Federalist revival challenged by its opponents, the *Centinel* responded by lashing out at its critics and renewing those disagreements that Russell and his political associates had claimed were extinguished. The short shelf life of "good feelings" demonstrated that this ephemeral sentiment had never existed in the first place and had been the creation of a group of Federalists eager to announce their political revival to the rest of the nation.

On September 17, 1817, an exhausted Monroe returned to Washington, having completed a two-thousand-mile journey over four months up the Atlantic coast to its most northern point in the Maine territory, and into the western reaches of the United States in Michigan and Ohio.[141] Despite the political controversies stirred up in New England and elsewhere, Monroe remained committed to his goal of party unity. Monroe, who was seeking to revive his own reputation, avoided making public comments about the tour for fear of undermining the republican persona he had carefully crafted. Instead he shared his assessment of the tour's accomplishments with few close friends such as Jefferson and Madison, and even limited what he said to them. His most candid comments were reserved for his son-in-law and political confidant, George Hay.

In his letter to Jefferson, Monroe described the growing evidence of political unity and national harmony the tour engendered. Despite the physical and mental strain of the trip, Monroe expressed satisfaction with its unifying results, especially in the cities that had opposed the war. He concluded, "I have seen enough, to satisfy me, that the great mass of our fellow-citizens, in the Eastern States are as firmly attached to the union and to republican government as I have always believed or could desire them to be."[142] Although Monroe admitted that he had encountered some roadblocks in his efforts to eliminate partisan distinctions, he reported to Jefferson that "In all the towns through which I passed, there was a union between the parties," conceding that Boston remained the notable exception.[143] Given the lingering animosities between the two parties, Monroe reiterated the need to proceed cautiously in order "to guard against any injury arising from the step taken to the republican cause, to the republican party," in accommodating the Federalist desire to amalgamate.[144] In embarking upon the tour, Monroe sought to reconcile the worlds of Washington and Jefferson. His observations made it clear that he believed he had begun to accomplish this goal.

Although Monroe eagerly sought his mentor's approval, Jefferson, an opponent of ceremony in republican government, never expressed in writing his opinion or reaction to the tour. During his own presidency, he had steadfastly rejected the ceremonial forms embraced by his Federalist predecessors because they contained elements more compatible with monarchical pomp than republican simplicity. Although Monroe offered a symbolic olive branch to the Federalists by emulating Washington's tours, Jefferson recognized that ceremonial rituals dramatized deep philosophical differences that were not so easily surmounted. Writing to Albert Gallatin during the early days of the tour, Jefferson remarked upon the weakness of the Federalist Party in the 1812 and 1816 presidential elections, noting that their decline in power would not result in an elimination of the philosophical differences that separated the two parties, because "nature has made some men monarchists and tories by their constitution, and some, of course, there always will be."[145] Opposing both the form and the goals of his protégé's efforts, Jefferson preferred to remain silent as he awaited the return of politics as usual.

Along with his carefully crafted descriptions of the tour's achievements, Monroe's efforts to rehabilitate his reputation also made an appearance in these letters. Writing to Jefferson, he declared his intention to tour the nation as a true republican president in an "inferior station and even as a private citizen."[146] However, later in his presidency, Monroe demonstrated the limits of his republican generosity when he complained to Congressman Charles J. Ingersoll that he was forced to reimburse the postal service for the use of their mail stages, even though he had undertaken the tour for the public good.[147] In a revealing letter to George Hay, Monroe complained that William Wirt's less than flattering assessment of his intellect had resurfaced during the tour.[148] Many newspapers, eager to provide their readership with biographical information about the traveling president, reprinted Wirt's description of Monroe as a dull and dutiful public servant. Monroe wrote, "In the course of this tour I have been compelled to answer four or five addresses in a day as I have passed forward, not one of which, I had seen, or heard, till read, and in some instances, have had cause to presume, that I had been peculiarly successful." Alluding to Wirt's attack on his intellectual abilities, Monroe rhetorically asked: "How does this fact, if true, correspond with the dullness, and slowful operation of faculties, imputed to me by Mr. Wirt." Monroe concluded his spirited defense on a resigned note, "I have been much mortified to see, that portrait, circulated about, by those who quoted it, in my favor, apparently, at least."[149] Despite Monroe's tremendous efforts to establish a reputation as a wise and responsible public servant, voices from the past conspired against his personal rehabilitation.

Although less sanguine than Monroe in assessing the tour's accomplishments, many newspapers offered their own evaluation of the tour's success in eliminating political parties. Several acknowledged that parties were an integral part of the American political system, and Monroe's tour, rather than ending parties, occurred during a transition between parties. Isaac Bates of the *Hampshire Gazette*, based in Northampton, Massachusetts, wrote, "We may expect that a new party will spring up, either sectional or political, and the tranquility we now enjoy, will be but as a calm betwixt the storm that is spent, and the storm that is gathering."[150] Henry A. Ranlet, editor of the *Exeter Watchman*, also recognized the endurance of parties, despite the present decline of the Federalists. He wrote, "One day we are all united in the enthusiasm of fraternal affection, doing homage to our political father, and the next day our enthusiasm has turned to suspicion and our affection to hostility."[151] While Monroe's tour offered a temporary respite from party strife in many locations, these newspapers recognized that it was only a matter of time before newly configured parties reasserted their position in the political arena.

Months after their triumphant celebration for Monroe, the New England Federalists, who had gambled their entire fortunes on the tour, pondered what tangible signs of reconciliation they could expect to see. Shortly after the president passed through Portsmouth, New Hampshire, an excited Jeremiah Mason shared his observations with Rufus King: "[Monroe] was fully determined to do every thing in his power to exterminate it, and to produce an union of talents for national objects."[152] The devil was in the details, though. Despite his optimism, Mason conceded that the president "did not, in any degree, designate the means by which he intended to accomplish this important object." While Mason trusted Monroe's motives, writing, "I think it probable that he is inclined to conciliate the federalists, and gain their support if he can without offending his old adherents," he reluctantly concluded that "I doubt whether he is prepared, at present, to risk much in this experiment."[153]

While the Federalists awaited positive news from the president, members of Monroe's Republican Party privately expressed deep reservations about sharing power with their opponents. Secretary of the Treasury William H. Crawford wrote to his predecessor, Albert Gallatin, and grimly concluded, "Seriously, I think the President has lost as much as he has gained by this tour."[154] Crawford believed that the inroads Monroe had made with the Federalists had undermined his ability to lead his own party. Henry Clay, the Republican speaker of the house, offered a caustic critique of the Federalists' motives, writing, "The pomp and ostentatious parade with which the President has been received in New England has an object too obvious, I should think, to deceive any one." Clay dissected the Federalists' aspirations in reaching out to Monroe: "Disappointed in getting power by disloyalty and gasconade, the Leaders are now anxious to bury the past, and what they could not gain by force, to obtain by sycophancy." Exposing what he saw as the Federalists' disingenuousness and Monroe's naïveté, Clay concluded, "If indeed they are real converts to the true faith, and their conversion is attributable to the tour of Mr. Monroe, he merits the honors of a political saint."[155] Still angry that Monroe had not appointed him as secretary of state, Clay emerged as Monroe's most ardent critic, a position that allowed him to express views that other party members could not.[156] While many Republicans publicly supported the tour, they shared Clay's deep reservations regarding the Federalists' motives and Monroe's efforts to reach out to them.

In the end, partisan realities trumped ephemeral good feelings when it came time for Monroe to consider political appointments for the Federalists. Despite a vigorous lobbying effort, Monroe did not make a bold gesture and appoint Daniel Webster as attorney general, selecting a fellow Virginian and Republican (and his biographer) William Wirt instead.[157] Rufus King summarized his party's disappointment: "Our Boston folk have not been honored by an admission to the Cabinet; I allude to the office of Attorney General."[158] While John Quincy Adams's appointment as secretary of state might be interpreted as a significant Federalist achievement, the younger Adams possessed only superficial connections to his father's party. Serving as a U.S. senator from Massachusetts between 1803 and 1808, Adams tended to vote with the Republican Party more often than with his own.[159] Also, Adams had been living abroad as a diplomat since 1809 and was not steeped in Federalist politics like his contemporaries Harrison Gray Otis and Daniel Webster. In fact, Monroe found Adams appealing because of his lack of overt partisan credentials. Monroe believed that Adams's long absences from the United States meant he lacked the political following to be a competitive presidential candidate, and he would be less divisive figure as secretary of state than William H. Crawford, who actively sought the appointment and possessed a strong political following.[160]

The few Federalists Monroe did appoint to office were cautious and uncontroversial choices, such as Charles Bulfinch, whose selection as the new architect of the U.S. Capitol was a direct result of the president's stay in Boston. Bulfinch had served as Monroe's official host and escort while in Boston, and Monroe was impressed by both Bulfinch's political tact and skill during the visit, as well as the numerous examples of Federal-style architecture that Bulfinch had designed in Boston.[161] In December 1817, Monroe asked Bulfinch to replace the troublesome Benjamin Latrobe in order to complete construction of the Capitol.[162] Monroe's other noteworthy Federalist appointment was his selection of Nicholas Biddle to head the Second Bank of the United States. Although this choice would eventually become fraught with significance during Andrew Jackson's presidency, Biddle was a close associate of the president who had already worked for Monroe in England.¹⁶³ Biddle's pet project, Fort Mifflin, also received attention when Monroe named his brother, Brevet Major Thomas Biddle, Jr., to command the fort and begin its rehabilitation.¹⁶⁴

Ultimately, the New England Federalists succeeded in reaffirming their national citizenship during the northern tour, but a return to national politics remained more elusive because of pressure from Monroe's own party. While the Federalists achieved what Abigail Adams referred to as an "expiation" of their political sins during Monroe's Boston visit, their national revival stopped well short of the political resurrection they had also sought. ¹⁶⁵ The greatest opposition to Monroe's idealized vision of governing came from the party system he had hoped to dismantle, because neither the Republicans nor the Federalists were willing to relinquish their philosophical and organizational differences. Monroe envisioned the elimination of all parties, including his own, whereas the Federalists wanted to maintain their party identity and form a governing coalition within his administration. The refusal of the Republicans in Congress and in Monroe's cabinet to share power with their Federalist opponents exposed the flaws in this makeshift alliance. While Otis and the Federalists orchestrated a campaign to achieve redemption and political power, Clay prevailed because he recognized that the Federalists sought power at the expense of his party. Unlike many of the founding fathers, who had initially opposed parties, younger politicians like Clay and Crawford entered politics at a time when parties were an integral part of republican government because of their ability to represent ideological differences and dictate patronage. By 1817, the two-party system was almost three decades old and had become a fact of life in American politics.¹⁶⁶ Having worked their way up the party structure, Clay and Crawford were unwilling to cede power to their political opponents.

Despite opposition from within his party and his limited success in appointing Federalists to patronage positions, Monroe remained committed throughout his two-term presidency to the elimination of parties from national politics. In 1822, Monroe proudly announced to James Madison that this goal had been achieved. He declared, "we have undoubtedly reached a new epoch in our political career, which has been formed by the destruction of the federal party."¹⁶⁷ Monroe predicted that the end of parties would result in a brief period of turbulence, which would quickly subside once America adjusted to the change. He concluded, "Surely our government may get on and prosper without the existence of parties," adding, "I have always considered their existence as the curse of the country, of which we had sufficient proof, more especially in the late war."[168] Although Monroe expected Madison and Jefferson to congratulate him on his accomplishment, he received a different reaction from his Virginia neighbors. Despite initially advocating a similar course, both Madison and Jefferson had come to recognize the valuable role parties played in a republican government.

In his response to Monroe's letter of May 1822, Madison gently refuted his friend, writing: "I am afraid you are too sanguine in your inferences from the absence here of causes which have most engendered and embittered the spirit of party in former times and in other Countries."[169] Offering his friend a philosophical overview, Madison wrote, "There seems to be a propensity in free Governments which will always find or make subjects, on which human opinions and passions may be thrown into conflict."[170] Believing that the elimination of political disagreements was unrealistic and even undesirable, Madison offered an alternative scenario in which conflict might be minimized. He wrote: "The most, perhaps that can be counted on, and that will be sufficient, is, that the occasions for party contests in such a Country and Government as ours, will be either so slight or so transient, as not to threaten any permanent or dangerous consequences to the character and prosperity of the Republic."[171] Even Madison, the author of the famous *Federalist #10* essay that had warned against the destabilizing effects of factions, recognized the inevitability and importance of political disagreements (and even parties) because they provided a forum for the free exchange of ideas.

Jefferson offered an even blunter refutation concerning the disappearance of parties. In a letter to Albert Gallatin, written in October 1822, Jefferson argued that ideological differences still existed even if the party structures did not: "You are told, indeed, that there are no longer parties among us; that they are all now amalgamated; the lion and the lamb lie down together in peace. Do not believe a word of it. The same parties exist now as ever did. No longer, indeed, under the name of Republican and Federalists."[172] Although Jefferson avoided commenting directly on Monroe's claims that parties had been eliminated, his writings before and after the tour leave little doubt regarding his opinion of his protégé's accomplishments. For Jefferson, the nomenclature may have changed but the philosophical differences still remained. Ironically, the most eloquent rebuttals to Monroe's dream came not from his political enemies, but from his two closest friends.

During the summer of 1817, President James Monroe toured the northern portion of the United States to promote national unity and partisan healing among the nation's citizens.[173] His visits generated enormous public reaction as spectators embraced Monroe's unifying message and transformed his tour into a celebration of the nation's revolutionary past and its republican ideas. Members of the Federalist Party also participated in his northern tour with the hope of achieving a political revival. And finally, newspapers across the nation offered detailed coverage and pointed commentary of the presidential spectacle they were witnessing.

Despite Monroe's best efforts and the hopefulness associated with the phrase "good feelings," his northern tour did not succeed in eliminating political parties. Instead, his 1817 journey affirmed their necessity in republican government. Monroe's unwillingness to be the partisan leader of his own Republican Party and his inability to make substantive Federalist appointments hastened the decline of both major political parties.[174] The dream of partisan-free government quickly yielded to political reality in the aftermath of the inconclusive presidential election of 1824, in which a younger generation of regional candidates—John Quincy Adams, Andrew Jackson, Henry Clay, and William Crawford—lacked the national following or political organization to win the presidency decisively. With the Federalist Party no longer a national force and the Republican Party languishing under too many competing political ideologies, younger politicians like Jackson and Clay realized they would need to establish a new set of vigorous political institutions to launch their ideas and ambitions. Jackson's supporters immediately began organizing what became the Democratic Party to support his presidential candidacy in 1828, while the National Republicans, led by Clay and Adams, eventually reorganized themselves into the Whig Party in the early 1830s, in part to oppose Jackson and his policies.[175] Amidst the collapse of the Federalist and Republican parties of the founding period, the second American party system was born to represent and negotiate a new era of politics.

The failure to secure political appointments in Monroe's administration forced Federalist well-wishers from the northern tour to seek a new political home elsewhere. Many younger Federalists found an ideological resonance in the Whigs' national message of social and economic progress.[176] Nicholas Biddle, who had encouraged Monroe to embrace his former opponents in 1817, emerged as Jackson's chief nemesis during the Bank War. Daniel Webster, who had pushed for the tour and had hoped to be named Monroe's attorney general, joined the Whigs as a U.S. senator from Massachusetts, while Nathaniel Silsbee, a member of Salem's Committee of Arrangements, led the Massachusetts Whig convention in 1832 and later served as a U.S. senator from this state and party.[177] Monroe's namesake and nephew, Lieutenant James Monroe, also became a member of the Whig Party and served as a congressman from New York City from 1833 to 1835.[178] And finally, Harrison Gray Otis, who perhaps best epitomized the efforts of younger Federalists to revive their party during Monroe's Boston visit, became active in Whig politics during the 1830s as a supporter of Henry Clay.[179]

Beyond the affirmation of political parties, Monroe's northern tour made another enduring contribution to republican government. A revolutionary hero and the last founding father to serve as president, his tour provided a badly divided nation with the opportunity to reflect on the meaning of republican government and reaffirm their commitment to it. Although the tour generated many competing understandings of the best way to fulfill the Constitution's mandate, including Monroe's own nonpartisan vision, what was important was not the attainment of a consensus but the vigorous discussion that emerged. In this lively debate about the meaning and form republican government should take, Americans renewed the essential sovereign bond that linked them to their government at a pivotal moment in the nation's political development.

5

"The Success and Stability of Our Republican Institutions"

Monroe's Southern Tour of 1819

After returning from his northern tour, Monroe remained committed to visiting the southern portion of the country, just as George Washington had done in 1791. In May 1818, Monroe ventured to Annapolis, Maryland, and Norfolk, Virginia, until pressing matters forced him to cut his trip short and return to Washington. Finally, in 1819, Monroe was able to depart the nation's capital and fulfill his goal of touring the southern coasts of Virginia, the Carolinas, and Georgia, and the western frontier of Kentucky and Tennessee. By symbolically bringing the nation together during his tours, Monroe hoped to achieve the national unity and political healing that he regarded as the greatest contribution of his presidency.

Despite Monroe's best intentions, the political realities of 1819 intruded upon his idealistic vision. In two years the partisan intrigues and regional disagreements that had undermined the achievements of his northern tour had become even more pronounced. As Monroe journeyed south, the nation faced a severe economic downturn while a contentious debate over slavery's future began to consume congressional attention.[1] These troubles were symptomatic of the cultural, political, and societal differences that distinguished the North, the South, and the

Map of the route of James Monroe's southern tour, 1819. Source: *The Papers of James Monroe: A Documentary History of the Presidential Tours of James Monroe, 1817, 1818, and 1819*, Daniel Preston, editor, vol. I. Copyright © 2003 by Daniel Preston. Reproduced with permission of Greenwood Publishing Group, Inc., Westport, Conn.

West from one another. The greatest barrier to Monroe's plans for unity and political healing was the growing regionalism that began to redefine the nation's politics in the 1810s.

These regional stirrings found expression during Monroe's 1819 tour, as younger members of the Republican Party traveled with him through the South and West to promote themselves as future presidential candidates. Secretary of War John C. Calhoun of South Carolina accompanied Monroe along the Atlantic coast, while Andrew Jackson of Tennessee, the commanding general of the southern region, traveled with the president through the western frontier. William H. Crawford of Georgia, the treasury secretary, made several unsuccessful attempts to join the tour but nonetheless supported Monroe's efforts. Speaker of the House Henry Clay of Kentucky, who remained angry that Monroe had not chosen him as secretary of state, concurrently staged his own celebratory trip, traveling to New Orleans and to his home state.

Monroe's southern tour signaled a substantive change in politics as a new generation of leaders achieved national prominence, not as heroes of the revolutionary and republican struggles, but as standard bearers of their region's concern. Among the southern contenders, an intense competitiveness developed in 1819 as these four closely connected candidates from the same party sought to distinguish themselves from one another. While Jackson gained fame (and notoriety) as a military leader, the biographies of Calhoun, Clay, and Crawford were almost indistinguishable as they rose to the pinnacle of southern leadership through successful law practices and socially advantageous marriages.[2] Their paths continued to cross as each played a prominent role during Monroe's presidency. From the cabinet, Calhoun and Crawford had addressed Jackson's behavior during the recent Seminole War in which he acquired Florida using extreme measures and possibly disobeying orders, while Clay led the campaign for his censure in the House of Representatives. Thanks to the Seminole controversy, animosities and alliances ran deep among these four men.

The southern tour lasted longer and covered greater distances than its northern counterpart, in part because Monroe's greater familiarity with the region led him to extend his stay in cities such as Charleston and Savannah. The more arduous nature of travel in the South and the greater distances between cities also produced a longer southern tour and even resulted in Monroe's "disappearance" for two weeks as he journeyed through the remote wilderness of western Georgia into Alabama.[3] As Monroe traveled through the South, newspaper editors throughout the nation offered their readers regular coverage of the president's progress. And as they had during the northern tour, these editors freely expressed their partisan preferences and exposed their regional rivalries as they debated the best ways to welcome a republican president.

Despite overwhelming evidence of regional tensions and political disagreements, Monroe remained committed to promoting his inaugural goals of national unity and political harmony during the 1819 tour. The tour became a celebration of a distinctive southern way of life that increasingly had little in common with northern ideas and values. Rather than bringing the nation together, the coastal portion of the tour reaffirmed the political and economic dominance of a planter class led by men like Calhoun and Crawford. The western portion of the tour witnessed the aggressive promotion of the region's economic needs through the competing political visions of Clay's federal program of internal improvements and economic tariffs and Jackson's military efforts to open additional lands for settlement.

While the northern tour served as a journey into the nation's heritage in which Monroe and the Federalists sought to correct their past mistakes, the 1819 tour represented a journey into the nation's political future as regional differences in the South and West became solidified and a new generation of leaders shared the stage with the last founding father.[4] Washington's tours had introduced the nation to its new Constitution, and Monroe's southern tour (and its northern counterpart) served to remind Americans of their shared republican heritage, as they experienced the first major political transformation since the government's establishment in 1789.[5]

Monroe made his first attempt to launch his southern tour in the spring of 1818, but pressing business in Washington forced him to cut his plans short. Emphasizing the national themes of defense and a shared revolutionary heritage, Monroe began his companion trip by visiting the strategically important cities located on the Chesapeake Bay. On May 28, 1818, after Congress adjourned for the summer, Monroe departed from Washington and proceeded to Annapolis, Maryland.[6] Accompanying him were his secretaries of war and navy, John C. Calhoun and Benjamin Crowninshield, and his nephew, Lieutenant James Monroe, who served as his private secretary.

This truncated tour, beginning with the reception in Annapolis, highlighted the cultural differences that separated North and South. While the city emulated its northern counterparts by offering the president a military escort, a public dinner, and a welcoming address, the Annapolis visit also included such southern practices as toasts and volunteers at the public dinner, rituals which became a standard feature during the 1818 and 1819 tours. Adding a personal and parochial touch to these festivities, Mayor John Randall reminded the president of his previous stay in Annapolis as a member of the Confederation Congress.

In his response, Monroe stressed national themes, reminiscing about the year 1783 as a turning point not only for his entry into national service, but also for the entire country, because the ratification of the Treaty of Paris that year had secured the nation's independence.[7]

After spending several days in Annapolis, Monroe traveled south down the Chesapeake Bay to Norfolk, Virginia. Because Monroe often traversed geographically isolated regions, the *American Beacon* of Norfolk anticipated a frequent theme of the 1819 tour by relying upon word of mouth to track the president's progress. In its June 6 edition, the newspaper reported on the president's approach: "We learn from a friend . . . that the President of the United States . . . left Annapolis on Tuesday in the U.S. Schooner *Nonsuch*."[8] Monroe arrived in Norfolk on June 8, where he was honored with a military salute from Craney Island, Forts Norfolk and Nelson, and the Navy Yard, and enjoyed a rousing reception.

Despite its significance as a port and a site of defense, Norfolk had been weakened on both fronts by the War of 1812. During Monroe's visit, its residents were eager to gain presidential assistance in strengthening the local economy and the city's defenses. Monroe briefly left Norfolk to visit Elizabeth City, North Carolina, and along the way, he stopped at the Dismal Swamp Canal. Intended to rival the Erie Canal as an inland transportation system, this project was designed to link Norfolk's rivers in order to lift this port city out of an economic depression caused by the Embargo of 1807 and the War of 1812. While Monroe inspected the site with great interest, he was reluctant to direct federal dollars to it because of a lack of explicit constitutional authority for such projects, so the canal continued to languish.[9]

Monroe was more receptive to the city's proposals to strengthen its fortifications, because he considered the improvement of the nation's defenses to be a fundamental presidential responsibility. While Mayor John E. Holt praised the nation's superior form of government and Monroe's service to it in his welcoming remarks, he also addressed the city's military needs. Holt complimented Monroe for his "personal attention . . . by the General Government, for the defense of our inland frontier, and sea coast, and the establishment of naval arsenals." In his response, Monroe declared that improving the nation's defenses in Norfolk and elsewhere was the government's highest priority: "No object is more interesting to the United States, than the adoption of a judicious system of defense, and the establishment and construction of such fortifications as may be found necessary for the security of our maritime and inland frontiers."[10] After America's uneven performance during the War of 1812, Monroe intended to fortify coastal and inland military resources as part of his campaign to unify the nation and heal its lingering wounds.

Monroe's coastal tour of 1818 never made it beyond Elizabeth City, North Carolina, because on June 11, he abruptly reversed course to deal with the controversy surrounding General Andrew Jackson's conduct during the recent Seminole War. Although his abortive southern tour lasted only two weeks, his brief visit still managed to generate an outpouring of enthusiasm, curiosity, and homage to republicanism similar to the one that had characterized the northern tour. Reporting that Norfolk had never "witnessed such an indiscriminate assemblage on any occasion," William C. Shields of the *American Beacon* proudly concluded: "It might indeed be said, that the reception was in a style of genuine republican simplicity."[11] It remained to be seen whether the republicanism of the South had anything in common with its northern counterpart.

The issue confronting Monroe and his cabinet on his return to Washington was the American acquisition of Florida and the methods employed by General Jackson to achieve this valuable prize. At the age of 51, Jackson, a veteran of the American Revolution and the War of 1812, as well as a hero of the American frontier, generated feelings of admiration or outrage, and rarely anything in between. His nickname "Old Hickory" attested to his strength and determination as well as his stubbornness and pettiness.[12] A man of action, Jackson could not be bothered with details or nuance. It should not be surprising, then, that Monroe's vague instructions allowing Jackson to enter Spanish-controlled Florida with a contingent of one thousand armed men resulted in the quintessential Jacksonian mixture of stunning achievement and embarrassing excess.

Although Jackson acquired Florida during his six-month assault, he also authorized the execution of two British officials, led a vicious campaign against several Indian groups, and, most importantly, conducted a war against Spain without formally notifying them. Afterwards, Monroe and his cabinet, and later Congress, grimly assessed these events to determine whether Jackson had disobeyed orders and, if so, whether he should be punished for his actions. At the heart of this controversy were the actual directions issued by President Monroe that Jackson should bring troops into Spanish-controlled Florida, and the implied order that by entering Florida on January 22, 1818, Jackson was expected to wage war against the Seminole Indians and seize this territory for the United States.[13]

During the summer of 1818, two positions emerged in the cabinet: defend Jackson and retain Florida, or censure Jackson and return Florida.[14] The patrician John Quincy Adams, eager to negotiate a treaty with the recalcitrant Spanish minister, emerged as Jackson's unlikely (and sole) defender in the cabinet. Secretary of State Adams argued that the unfolding events in Florida justified the general's actions. War secretary Calhoun, angry at Jackson's insubordination, led the campaign for censure, while treasury secretary Crawford, aware of the general's power as a possible rival, backed Calhoun. Monroe, always trying to stay above the fray, eventually supported the Calhoun-Crawford approach. He then sent a letter to the Spanish minister, Luis de Onis, which formally returned Florida to Spanish control.[15] While this letter was traveling through official diplomatic channels, Adams worked behind the scenes to negotiate a treaty with Spain to acquire Florida legally.

In the meantime, in early 1819, Congress began to debate whether Jackson should be censured. Henry Clay, balancing principles and politics, led the charge against Jackson in a powerful indictment on the House floor. Seeing an opportunity to embarrass Monroe for his failure to control Jackson, while also gaining political advantage over his western presidential rival, Clay delivered a two-hour denunciation of the general. The eloquent Kentuckian interpreted the general's behavior in Florida as an intolerable act of insubordination that violated the nation's republican and constitutional principles. Clay argued that if the Congress accepted Jackson's behavior, they were giving "fatal sanction, in this infant period of our republic, scarcely two score years old, to military insubordination."[16] In his stirring conclusion, Clay declared that the Congress must censure Jackson for his actions, because its silent approval of his behavior would serve as a "triumph of the principle of insubordination—a triumph of the military over the civil authority—a triumph over the constitution" and most profoundly, "a triumph over the liberties of the people."[17] When Clay finished his remarks, the House chamber erupted in cheers and applause.

The embattled general, residing in Washington while he awaited his fate, wrote to his wife Rachel a letter assessing the damage after Clay's powerful speech. Declaring his opponent's remarks to be "very lengthy and inflammatory," Jackson maintained that he would not be punished because he had the backing of former presidents Jefferson and Madison, as well as the support of a majority in Congress. Despite his declared optimism, Jackson sounded a more cautious note when he added that he planned to maintain a low profile in Washington, declining "all invitations of dining out or visiting until the question before the House is decided."[18]

Clay's high-profile speech forced Congress to contemplate the philosophical and political ramifications of the general's behavior. Despite the constitutional concerns raised by Clay, Jackson's enormous popularity and his achievements allowed him to escape congressional censure. As he had predicted to his wife, a majority of House members voted on February 8, 1819, to reject the committee report disapproving of his actions by a vote of 107 to 63.[19] With General Jackson's behavior no longer at issue, Secretary of State Adams could finally achieve diplomatically what had been accomplished through force. On February 22, 1819, Spain formally relinquished Florida through the Adams-Onis Treaty, allowing Monroe and his administration to move beyond this internal triumph and international embarrassment.[20]

Due to the intense reactions and personal animosities that this crisis generated, the rivalries that had already begun to develop among the nation's rising political stars solidified, producing complex battle lines that were not easily forgotten or forgiven. Jackson and Clay became lifelong enemies, and Jackson erroneously identified Crawford as his prosecutor in the cabinet, leading to a one-sided antagonism toward the Georgian that should have been directed at Jackson's future vice president, John Calhoun.[21] Despite its diplomatic resolution in 1819, the Seminole controversy would continue to influence national politics well into the next decade.

Although the fate of Florida had been resolved, the consequences of the economic downturn and the controversy surrounding Missouri's petition for statehood roiled the political waters.[22] Nonetheless, Monroe remained committed to completing his southern tour, and in late March 1819, after Congress adjourned, he began his journey along the Atlantic coast and into the southwestern interior. While the two regions were distinct in many ways, they shared a common heritage in the southern slave culture that informed the celebrations and the politics that Monroe encountered during his tour.

Many of the settlers who relocated to the western states of Kentucky and Tennessee came from the slave South, particularly because these territories had been under the control of Virginia and North Carolina, respectively, during the colonial era.[23] In their pursuit of economic success through cheaper and more plentiful land, these farmers also transported the slave system to the west. The fundamental feature of the slave culture was the ability of a small group of white property holders to dominate the lives and labor of a majority population of African men and women deemed chattel by state law. The southern planters justified their unmitigated power because it permitted them to attain a political and economic independence that resulted in the disinterested virtue that classical republicanism required and also led them to believe that national leadership was their birthright. Because planters could act and think freely, they thought themselves best equipped to act as checks on the excesses of the federal government. The fact that their independence was premised upon the dependence and deference of others was irrelevant. Instead, the planters saw themselves as the leaders of an agrarian civilization that was the true fulfillment of the nation's republican tradition.[24] In contrast to the North's two-party politics, its vibrant mercantile economy, and its social fluidity, the institution of slavery produced an oligarchic society in the South in which a small number of wealthy landowners dominated the region's agrarian economy as well as its political offices.

No group more vigorously claimed the prerogatives of the planter class than the favorite sons who, having reached the pinnacle of southern leadership, sought to succeed Monroe as president. All four men were born into the slave South: Clay and Crawford in Virginia, Jackson in North Carolina, and Calhoun in South Carolina, with the first three relocating to Kentucky, Georgia, and Tennessee, respectively, to begin their legal and political careers. In short order, Clay, Crawford, and Calhoun fulfilled the prerequisites for membership in the planter class by establishing successful law practices, allying themselves with locally prominent families through marriage, and purchasing plantations and slaves. Clay and Calhoun gained national notice when they served in Congress as "War Hawks," leading a youthful group of congressmen from the South and West who pushed for war with Britain to resolve trading and territorial issues. Elected to the United States Senate in 1807, Crawford caught the attention of the Republican Party and President Madison when he pushed for the renewal of the First Bank of the United States. While Andrew Jackson's career followed a similar path as he pursued a legal career, acquired a plantation and slaves, and served in the United States Senate, Jackson achieved national prominence as a military hero. While the Federalists were committing political suicide in Hartford, Jackson was busy immortalizing his reputation as he defeated the British during the final battle of the War of 1812. Later, as an Indian fighter against the Creeks and Natchez, he became a frontier legend because he opened up additional lands for white settlement.

As members of the planter elite, the South's rising political stars also participated in rituals that enabled them to establish authority over their plantations while also distinguishing them from those they dominated.[25] A benign ritual involved drinking toasts at ceremonial occasions, a practice that forged a common bond among planters as they saluted those issues and individuals they considered important.[26] Some of these practices, such as duels and whippings, were intended to illustrate a planter's willingness to use violence to defend his reputation or to control his plantation.[27] During their careers, each of these men had engaged in duels that confirmed their worthiness to be a leader of the slave South. As William H. Crawford worked to establish himself in Georgia politics, he fought a duel in 1802 that resulted in his opponent's death, and he engaged in another one in 1806 that ended in a draw.[28] In 1813, Calhoun almost faced off against Thomas P. Grosvenor, a Federalist congressman from New York, while Henry Clay participated in several skirmishes throughout his political career.[29] The master of the duel was Andrew Jackson, who complemented his battlefield reputation with at least three contests between 1788 and 1812.[30] Although Monroe avoided this ritual, he was a member of the planter elite and the owner of seventy slaves.[31] As governor of Virginia during the slave revolt of 1800 known as Gabriel's Rebellion, Monroe had immediately called up the Virginia militia in order to employ force to quell this uprising and restore the social order.[32]

Although Clay and Jackson came to be associated with frontier politics, like other transplants to the West they brought elements of the old slave South with them. Crawford and Calhoun, who never left the South, embodied its values from their positions of economic and political prominence. The celebrations in the South and the Southwest incorporated the rituals and hierarchy of the slave culture, which in the coastal states produced a reaffirmation of southern society and in the interior states provided a public forum for westerners to express their political and economic concerns directly to the president.

As soon as Monroe left Washington on March 30, the tour provided a forum for the celebration of an idealized image of the planter class,

John Calhoun, Monroe's secretary of war and one of the younger politicians who shared the stage with the president during his southern tour. Calhoun traveled with Monroe through Virginia, North Carolina, and his home state of South Carolina. Source: John C. Calhoun, Secretary of War, Charles Bird King, 1818. Courtesy of Redwood Library and Athenaeum, Newport, R.I.

while also allowing communities to raise local concerns. Accompanying Monroe during the coastal leg of the trip was John Calhoun, the first would-be successor as well as his secretary of war. From this position, Calhoun promoted the strategic benefits of constructing roads and canals. Unlike Monroe, Calhoun supported using federal money for these improvements, even in the absence of constitutional authority. In his *Report on Roads and Canals,* issued in January 1819, Calhoun had removed references to public financing out of deference to Monroe, but the South Carolinian nonetheless used the 1819 tour to inspect potential projects while also enhancing his political stature.[33]

In his travels down the coast, Monroe took advantage of the recent invention of steamboats, which began to appear on the nation's waterways during the War of 1812. Although these early conveyances could be hot and smoky due to the inefficiency of their wood-burning engines, their relative speed compared with horse-drawn carriages more than compensated for these inconveniences.[34] Unlike the means of travel used in the hectic northern tour, steamboats allowed Monroe's coastal journey to assume a more relaxed pace, one sufficiently measured to permit Calhoun to bring his wife, Floride, and their two small children along.

As Monroe headed west from Georgia, his mode of conveyance and his entourage changed significantly. Primitive roads through dense forests forced him to downshift from steam power to horseback. After visiting Georgia, the Calhouns returned to their plantation in South Carolina, and Monroe acquired a new traveling companion accustomed to the rugged backwoods when the recently exonerated General Andrew Jackson greeted him in Tennessee. Serving as Monroe's personal aide and personal secretary during the entire journey were his two nephews, Lieutenant James Monroe and Samuel Gouverneur, respectively. Reflecting the greater distances between southern towns and cities, Monroe traveled 2,600 miles over six months compared with 2,000 miles during his four-month northern tour.[35]

After paying a second visit to Norfolk, Monroe and his entourage navigated the jagged North Carolina coast and disembarked in the state's maritime cities, where the celebration of the planter class began in earnest. Every aspect of the southern tour served as a reminder of this group's dominance. The welcoming committees were smaller in size than their northern counterparts and reflected the small world of plantation owners and politicians—many of whom were related—who dictated the rules governing the larger population of African slaves and poorer white farmers. In Washington, North Carolina, the eight-person welcoming committee included former congressman William Kennedy, as well as two brothers, Thomas H. Blount and William A. Blount, whose father, William Blount, was the first territorial governor of North Carolina.[36] In Charleston, South Carolina, the committee of arrangements included Colonel William Drayton, a War of 1812 veteran and current city recorder, as well as Thomas Lee, a jurist and presidential elector.[37]

The cities and towns in 1819 honored Monroe with a military salute, a welcoming reception, and a public dinner. Unlike their northern counterparts who addressed the nation's broader revolutionary heritage, the southern speeches celebrated Monroe as one of their own whose career and service epitomized the planter class's understanding of republicanism. In New Bern, North Carolina, the appointed committee praised Monroe as representing the stellar qualities present in American society, declaring, "We cannot express to you our devotion to liberty and the honor and interests of our country, without associating a love and veneration for you."[38] In his response, Monroe deflected praise away from his leadership and modestly attributed the nation's success to larger forces: "to the favor of Providence" and "to the energies and virtues of a free and enlightened people."[39]

The public dinners held in Monroe's honor provided an additional opportunity for the planters to deliver toasts that reaffirmed their leadership position and their republican vision. In New Bern, the city's residents toasted the national government's leading components such as the Constitution, Congress, the Judiciary, the Army, and the Navy (excluding the presidency from this list). The celebrants also chose to salute the leading components of a civil society such as agriculture, commerce, manufactures, the arts, the press, the clergy and the polity, and literature. Bowing to parochial concerns, the New Bern celebrants saved their final toasts for the state of North Carolina and its governor.[40]

Despite the positive sentiments expressed in the speeches and toasts, the North Carolina cities were plagued with economic woes and strategic concerns, and the state's leaders used Monroe's visit to request federal assistance. Foremost on their minds was the lack of a suitable port in the state because of the shallow, unnavigable waterways that comprised their share of the Atlantic shore. This coast was so unforgiving that seventeenth-century pirates like Blackbeard would lure commercial ships into the harbor knowing full well that these vessels would become stuck in its numerous sandbars. With their prey trapped and helpless, the pirates would loot the marooned ships.[41] The *National Intelligencer* added to the sense of the state's remoteness when it reported: "The line of the president's progress along the maritime frontier of North Carolina is not as easily traced as that was which he made along the more populous part of the Atlantic border, two years ago."[42] North Carolina, having earned the dubious distinction of being the most backward of the coastal states, saw many of its residents relocate west and south to seek a more fruitful way of life elsewhere.[43]

During his visit along the North Carolina coast, Monroe visited a proposed canal site in the Albemarle Sound, near Edenton. This waterway was intended to solve the state's commercial and navigation problems by opening a direct passageway through the sound into the Atlantic Ocean. While Calhoun enthusiastically supported this project, Monroe remained interested, but noncommittal.[44] Although the citizens and politicians in the northern portion of the state saw their economic future in this project, leaders in the other parts of North Carolina opposed the construction of a waterway because they did not want to support a program that did not offer any benefit to them. Lacking support at the federal and state levels, the goals of this program were never realized.[45]

Residents of coastal North Carolina were also eager to share their defense concerns with the president. During the recent war, the North Carolina legislature had complained bitterly that the national government had left the state vulnerable to British invasion by neglecting to build forts or devote warships to the coast. They also resented the commitment of the North Carolina militia outside the state.[46] In his welcoming address, Hanson Kelly, the magistrate of Wilmington, reminded Monroe of the state's desire for the federal government's "fostering care, in peace and in war, should our shores again be visited." Reiterating his interest in strengthening the nation's coastal defenses, Monroe enthusiastically committed the "unwearied attention of the general government" in protecting this potentially vulnerable coastal site.[47] After thoroughly visiting the North Carolina coast, Monroe and his party proceeded along the Atlantic Ocean to South Carolina where a grand celebration of the southern way of life awaited him in Charleston.

The pinnacle of Monroe's southern tour occurred in Charleston, South Carolina. Despite the economic troubles sweeping the nation, the cotton boom of the past two decades had enriched almost everyone who planted cotton, and South Carolina as its leading producer benefited handsomely. The leading planters were particularly eager to celebrate their recent economic good fortune and to demonstrate their superiority over their northern neighbors. Unbeknownst to South Carolinians, 1818 represented the economic high point of its love affair with King Cotton as the price peaked at thirty cents a pound. In subsequent decades, this state's leadership in cotton production would drop precipitously as its black and white residents headed west and south to farm more fertile and less expensive land.[48]

Charleston represented the commercial and social hub of the slave South due to its fortuitous placement at the confluence of two rivers, as well as its access to slave labor to run its markets and its skilled trades. In 1820, the city had a slight black majority, while the outlying plantation areas were predominantly black. The state's white minority devoted a great deal of energy to the development and enforcement of laws to control the massive slave population and to prevent revolts, including a prohibition on black literacy and limits on the number of slaves who could travel together.[49] Charleston also served as the social center for plantation owners who spent the winter and spring in the city participating in a round of festive and civic events, and then retreated to their upcountry homes during the stifling summer months. Monroe wisely chose to visit Charleston in late April and early May, before the annual yellow fever outbreak closed down the city from July until the middle of November.[50]

The port city threw an elaborate welcoming celebration for Monroe intended to rival that held in Boston two years earlier. On April 26, an elegant barge, prepared by the City Corporation, transported Monroe, the Calhouns, and Monroe's traveling party into the city. A cavalry unit, joined by hundreds of citizens on horseback, escorted Monroe into town, where the governor of South Carolina received him on behalf of the entire state. After the welcoming reception, Monroe and his entourage, along with the governor and civic leaders, paraded through the streets of Charleston before an enthusiastic audience. The *Charleston Courier* proudly described the universal acclamation and approval that Monroe received from his fellow southerners during his visit, declaring, "The whole population appeared to be present, who pressed on the procession in a manner, which, if it did not contribute to the harmony and order of the scene, at least evinced their ardent attachment for the man, whom all were emulous to honor."[51]

In his welcoming address, the city intendant, Daniel Stevens, struck a mixture of national and regional themes as he praised the peace and tranquility that happily characterized the United States, while also highlighting local values and concerns. Saluting the city's distinguished leadership, Stevens reminded Charleston and the rest of the nation that a fellow planter, the venerable George Washington, had made a similar trip through the South in 1791. Stevens concluded his remarks with an explicit reference to southern concerns when he praised Monroe's acquisition of Florida because it will "give a safe frontier to the southern section of the union."

Monroe, although grateful for the city's support, used his remarks to remind his supporters that they were celebrating republican government, not him. He explained, "With a free people, enjoying every blessing of which society is susceptible, the presence of their Chief Magistrate, would excite but little interest, if it did not impress them with a high sense, of the excellence of the government, under which they live, the source from which all these blessings flow."[52] It is doubtful that Monroe's exaltation of the nation's republican values made much of an impression on a southern city eager to draw attention to those qualities and achievements that distinguished it from northern cities.

Lurking beneath the surface of this idealized presentation of southern life was a power struggle between the city council and the governor over the welcoming festivities. As Monroe made his way down the coast, he began to receive competing instructions from Governor John Geddes and Intendant Stevens concerning his arrival in South Carolina. The city council wanted to receive the president by water, in order to replicate Washington's 1791 visit, while state officials preferred receiving the president by land.[53] Letters traveled to Monroe from Geddes and Stevens explaining their respective intentions, forcing Monroe to dispatch his personal aide, Lieutenant James Monroe, to Charleston to resolve the dispute.[54] Demonstrating the power of the state over the city, the city council acquiesced to the governor's plans, although the compromise allowed the city to act as host as Monroe was transported into Charleston. The day before Monroe arrived in Charleston, Aaron S. Willington, the owner of the *Charleston Courier*, publicly apologized for the dispute, explaining that it would not interfere with "the cordial salutations of all our fellow citizens."[55] Governor Geddes defended the competition between the city and state because it demonstrated their high regard for the president.[56] Absent from this political one-upmanship were the exalted republican values of disinterestedness and virtue, which were supposed to prevail in southern life and politics.

During his weeklong visit, consistent with his original intentions, Monroe inspected forts in the Charleston harbor. The city organizers also arranged visits to cultural institutions such as the theater, the library, and the Museum of Natural and Artificial Curiosities of the Literary and Philosophical Society. Monroe was the guest of honor at a large public dinner that included Charleston's elite as well as invited guests. Despite this city's palpable rivalry with its northern neighbors, its city leaders drank toasts to national themes such as the United States of America; the American Constitution; Adams, Jefferson, and Madison; the Congress; the Army and Navy; the Judiciary; Agriculture and Commerce; and Science and Literature.[57]

Charleston concluded its elaborate festivities by commissioning Samuel F. B. Morse to do a full-length portrait of Monroe, reminiscent of the one John Trumbull painted of Washington after his 1791 visit there.[58] Not only would this painting commemorate the president's visit, it would provide the city with an opportunity to rival Boston's celebration two years earlier when Monroe sat for Gilbert Stuart. The Morse painting contrasted with Stuart's in two important ways. First, Morse's painting portrayed Monroe wearing a sword and holding a revolutionary hat in recognition of his military service to the nation. Second, this portrait did not assume the national significance associated with Gilbert's presidential gallery, which already included images of Washington, Adams, Jefferson, and Madison. Instead, Morse's painting was displayed in the Charleston City Hall as a reminder of the southern values of honor and physical bravery.[59]

Charleston's desire to rival Boston's reception underscored the growing separation between the North and South. Both were vibrant coastal cities that served as the spiritual and cultural centers of their regions' concerns and values. Boston was the home of the Federalists and the center of New England's mercantile economy, while Charleston embodied the economic promise, social reality, and political power of the slave South. As the nation began to split apart in the 1830s and beyond, these cities led their regions in offering competing visions of the union's futures: Boston supported and guided the movement to abolish slavery, while Charleston supported nullification and later secession in order to preserve this institution. Unbeknownst to these cities, the elaborate celebrations they staged during Monroe's visit in honor of their way of life served as a last hurrah rather than a rebirth, as each city entered a period of decline.[60]

Portrait of James Monroe by Samuel F. B. Morse, commissioned by the city of Charleston during Monroe's southern tour. Source: *The Papers of James Monroe: A Documentary History of the Presidential Tours of James Monroe, 1817, 1818, and 1819,* Daniel Preston, editor. Copyright © 2003 by Daniel Preston. Reproduced with permission of Greenwood Publishing Group, Inc., Westport, Conn.

Amidst the hoopla of South Carolina's official visit, Monroe's travels afforded him the opportunity to continue the political healing between the Federalists and Republicans that had begun during his northern tour. Despite the growing emphasis upon regional and personality politics, Monroe remained committed to freeing republican government from the stranglehold of factions, and he believed that meeting with former opponents like Thomas and Charles Cotesworth Pinckney would bring him closer to this goal. The Pinckney brothers were born to a prominent South Carolina planter family, and each had enjoyed a distinguished career as a revolutionary officer. Both men became Federalists during Washington's administration when they supported the policies of Alexander Hamilton. Thomas Pinckney served as Washington's minister to Great Britain and later ran for vice president alongside John Adams in 1796. Pinckney lost to Adams's Republican opponent, Thomas Jefferson, and served in the House of Representatives instead.[61] Charles Cotesworth Pinckney ran for vice president with John Adams in 1800 and served as the Federalist candidate for president in 1804 and 1808 against popular Republican incumbents, Jefferson and Madison. Although there had not been any personal disagreements between Monroe and the Pinckneys, the Republican Monroe entered Charleston alongside the Federalist Thomas Pinckney to symbolize his desire for partisan reconciliation.[62] In a letter to his advisor and son-in-law, George Hay, written after meeting with Thomas Pinckney and before he would visit Charles Cotesworth Pinckney, Monroe described his outreach to Federalists as "an illustration of the principles on which I act." Monroe encouraged Hay to publish an editorial that praised Thomas Pinckney, believing that this statement "would have conciliatory effect, in drawing the country together, [and] shaking the foundations of party animosities."[63] As a reformed partisan warrior, Monroe considered the elimination of parties to be the primary goal of his presidency. Rather than reducing tensions and disagreements, his refusal to lead the Republican Party or notice the disappearance of the southern Federalists increased the political jockeying and competition among his successors even during his tour of reconciliation.

Monroe completed his trip along the Atlantic coast in Georgia, whose economic successes and political rivalries illustrated the best and worst aspects of the planter elite's control of the slave South. In 1802, the state acquired 80 million acres when the federal government vitiated the Creek Indians' title to these lands. The availability of cheap and plentiful acreage triggered an economic boom when Georgians scrambled to acquire land and slaves to plant more rice and cotton. Georgia's major port city, Savannah, benefited from this agriculture upswing, as more ships arrived to handle the increased output of goods. Although this prosperity did not last forever, the land windfall carried the state's economy into the 1820s.[64]

Amidst this economic good fortune, the state's residents had to contend with a highly personal, factionalized politics that pitted William H. Crawford and his supporters against General John Clarke and his followers. This rivalry epitomized the destabilizing effects of single-party rule in the slave South. Crawford represented Georgians like himself who had relocated to the state from Virginia after the Revolutionary War, while Clarke led those residents who had settled in the state before the Revolution, either directly from Europe or from North Carolina.[65] Crawford's followers tended to be wealthy coastal planters, while Clarke attracted frontiersmen and small farmers in the western portion of the state. This rivalry permeated almost every aspect of Georgia's society with churches, militias, bars, and families divided into Crawford or Clarke camps. As Clarke and Crawford competed for control over Georgia's politics, they exercised the perquisites of power that distinguished white southerners from those they dominated. This code of honor provided the white elite with a prescribed set of rituals for resolving disputes and defending their reputations.[66] Supporters of Clarke and Crawford frequently engaged in duels, hair-pullings, gougings, and bitings in order to gain political advantage over one another.[67]

As Crawford's national profile became more prominent in the 1810s due to his service as secretary of treasury, the animosity between the two groups had begun to subside. Crawford was a particular favorite of the Virginia caucus, which almost nominated him for president over Monroe in 1816. Despite his rising popularity, Crawford left nothing to chance. As the president toured Georgia, Crawford made several efforts to appear with Monroe to shore up his political base. The recent failure of western banks forced the treasury secretary to stay in Washington. Expressing his disappointment to Monroe, Crawford wrote, "My failure to join you at Augusta is more mortifying to me than it will be inconvenient to you."[68] To ensure his political presence during the president's visit, Crawford arranged for his supporters to attend to Monroe's needs. An ambitious member of the planter class and a national leader among a new generation of Republican politicians, Crawford recognized the

"The Success and Stability of our Republican Institutions" 155

William H. Crawford, Monroe's secretary of the treasury, who made several unsuccessful attempts to join Monroe during his visit to Crawford's home state of Georgia. Source: Courtesy of the Pennsylvania Academy of Fine Arts, Philadelphia. Gift of Charles Roberts.

political value of appearing with a distinguished founding father who was also the current president.

With Crawford unable to leave Washington, the Calhouns continued to escort Monroe down the Georgia coast to Savannah and inland to Augusta and Washington. Calhoun and Crawford enjoyed a fragile alliance based in their shared criticism of Jackson's conduct during the Seminole War. Reflecting the economic well-being of the coastal planters, Savannah launched an enthusiastic round of military parades, welcoming receptions and speeches, and public dinners that complimented Monroe for his distinguished presidential leadership. Expanding on this burgeoning national pride were the toasts that praised the federal union, the country, and the Constitution. Local interests also slipped in as celebrants saluted the cession of Florida and the heroics of Andrew Jackson. In a sign of the growing awareness of regional tensions in the nation, attention was paid to the "concord between the north and the south, the east and the west" as an antidote intended to "falsify the timid fears of those who predict dissolution."[69] Several years after Monroe's visit, the *Daily Georgian* reported that Savannah's youthful mayor (and future Supreme Court justice), James M. Wayne, had spent the astronomical sum of $13,000 in an "ostentatious display" to welcome the president. Wayne's defenders explained that this amount was an exaggeration, and instead the city's funds had been dedicated to an antimalarial planting program.[70] In either case, this largesse reflected the economic prosperity that was sweeping through Savannah and the rest of Georgia.

Out of deference to his ally in the cabinet, Calhoun and his family completed their travels with Monroe on May 19 and did not accompany the president to Crawford's hometown of Lexington, returning home to South Carolina instead. Although the Georgian was not able to leave Washington in time to join the president, Lexington promoted its favorite son during Monroe's visit. In its toasts, the city saluted Crawford, declaring: "We, his neighbors, know his honesty. His country has awarded him the reputation of great talents." The city of Lexington also continued the pattern of praising the nation's attributes such as the Constitution and Congress, while extending equal attention to local concerns such as Georgia in particular and the integrity of the states in general.[71] In contrast to their northern neighbors, who considered a commitment to republican values as the way to maintain the union, Lexington's speakers expressed their belief that the key to preserving the union and its republican ideas resided in promoting the autonomy of the states. This shifting fealty from the national good to the power of the states was a harbinger of the regional concerns sweeping the slave South.

By May 22, the western portion of the tour had begun, as Monroe and his two nephews slowly made their way across Georgia by horseback. Attesting to the absence of people and towns in the Georgia wilderness, Monroe "disappeared" several times during his two-week journey to Tennessee. The *National Intelligencer,* based in Washington, reported that they had "lost the President" and added a very dramatic description of the western United States: "We shall probably hear nothing of him for some days to come, on his passage from the abode of civilized man, through the depths of our Southern forests, and alternate burning sands to the borders of Tennessee."[72] The term "civilized man" stood in contrasted with the "uncivilized" Cherokees who occupied land in western Georgia. As Monroe passed among them, it was later reported that he visited an Indian missionary school attended by about sixty students.[73] During Andrew Jackson's presidency, white demand for additional land made these Cherokees the subject of a landmark Supreme Court case, *Worcester v. Georgia* (1832), which defended their rights, but still resulted in their forcible removal to Oklahoma.[74]

Because the president's whereabouts were unknown to everyone but Monroe and his two nephews, no one knew when they should expect to see him again. Remarkably, none of the newspapers seemed particularly concerned for Monroe's safety. Instead they waited patiently for a report of his progress to surface. On June 1, the president of the United States startled the residents of Huntsville, Alabama when he unexpectedly showed up in their town. Describing the town's surprise, the *Western Monitor* of Lexington, Kentucky reported, "No intimation of his intention to visit our town had been received by any one in it," but the city managed to emulate the other cities along the tour route by hosting a welcoming reception and a public dinner in Monroe's honor for the next evening.[75] On June 5, the southern tour officially resumed, two weeks after Monroe's "disappearance," when he and his nephews arrived at the Hermitage, the Nashville area plantation of General Andrew Jackson. As the first president to visit the West, Monroe encountered familiar elements of the slave culture, along with this region's unique concerns as it attempted to play a vital role in the nation's economic and political life.

As the embodiment of the region's frontier spirit and its insatiable quest for land, Jackson was extremely popular, particularly in his home state of Tennessee. He had received a hero's welcome after the resolution of the Seminole controversy. Still, Old Hickory's actions in Florida and elsewhere reminded many people that the general was an intemperate and insubordinate military leader. In 1817, Jackson had engaged in a very public dispute with Brigadier General Winfield Scott, a commander during the War of 1812, when Jackson erroneously identified Scott as the author of a newspaper article that called him "mutinous." While Monroe traveled through the northern states to heal the nation's wounds, Jackson engaged in a full-throttle attack against Scott in the nation's newspapers, even going so far as to challenge him to a duel. Scott wisely ignored Jackson's accusations and the controversy finally subsided, leaving Jackson's reputation in tatters and confirming the worst fears of his critics.[76] A defiant but publicly chastened Jackson now waited among his supporters to receive the president.

Nashville's demographics helped to explain Jackson's enormous popularity among its residents. Although Tennessee had been a state since 1796, Nashville still retained the characteristics of a frontier town thanks to a transient population of 1,800 that consisted largely of white males and their slaves.[77] Jackson was the hero of these settlers because he had secured their economic future through the acquisition of Indian lands in Tennessee and beyond. As with the welcoming committees in the coastal slave states, the Nashville delegation consisted of the city's economic and political leaders, who were also ardent supporters of Jackson. The reception for Monroe was built around Jackson and the values he represented, and the organizing committee was stacked with Old Hickory's political cronies, who were interested in promoting his rehabilitation and his presidential ambitions. Among those chosen to welcome the president were Dr. Samuel Hogg, a military physician who had served with Jackson during the Creek War of 1814, and William B. Lewis, who had fought alongside Jackson in the Natchez and Creek campaigns of 1812 and 1813.[78] Other committee members included the Tennessean's personal physician, James C. Bronaugh, and Felix Grundy, an ardent supporter and future U.S. senator.[79] Delivering the welcoming address to Monroe was Senator John H. Eaton, an intimate of Jackson and his future secretary of war. In the 1830s, a scandal involving his wife, Peggy Eaton, would nearly topple Jackson's presidency.[80]

Although influenced by settlers from the South, as well as from the North, the West was more than a hybrid of southern agrarianism and northern mercantilism. Instead it had emerged as a distinctive region with unique political concerns. Blessed with prominent national leaders

Major General Andrew Jackson was another younger politician who shared the stage with Monroe during his southern tour, accompanying the president as he traveled through his home state of Tennessee. Source: *Major General Andrew Jackson*, by Ralph Earl.

like Henry Clay and Andrew Jackson, the states that composed the West were looking for ways to participate more fully in the nation's political decisions and its commercial successes. While southern states recognized the need for bridges and canals, some like Georgia were content to encourage private investors to provide these services. Lacking the capital found along the coast, many westerners, led by Clay, looked to the federal government to pay for roads and waterways. While the economic troubles of 1819 affected the entire nation, the West was particularly hard hit as a postwar drop in European demand reduced the need for locally produced goods, while a land boom became a speculative bubble as farmers and investors began risking borrowed money on shaky investments. When the recently rechartered Second Bank of the United States restricted credit, local banks foreclosed on bad loans, and many farmers lost their farms and their livelihoods. During Monroe's 1819 tour, people who turned out for his appearance in the West spoke openly about their economic troubles and urged Monroe to support an ameliorative tariff to make domestic manufactures more competitive.[81]

Like their southern counterparts, the westerners invoked the planter tradition of toasts, along with the standard tour features of welcoming speeches, parades, and public balls and dinners. In his address, Senator Eaton celebrated the western way of life that Jackson embodied: the acquisition of Indian lands as the path to economic prosperity and political power. Eaton then devoted the balance of his remarks to Jackson's heroism and his devotion to the nation. First, he saluted Jackson's military service during the War of 1812, referring to him as the "major general" who repelled "our haughty invaders" and gave "security to our country." Eaton also praised the men who served with Jackson, saying, "Before you, attired and armed as when they moved to battle, are many of those brave men who with him encountered the hardships and privations of that period." Reminding Monroe of the popularity of the Florida invasion, he added that Jackson's soldiers "are the same who traversed the wilds of Florida in pursuit of a foe who had murdered our peaceful citizens."[82] In his response, Monroe offered the Nashville celebrants the unequivocal praise for Jackson that they were seeking. Addressing the War of 1812, Monroe declared, "To meet any of the brave men who with the [major general] distinguished themselves in that great exploit, affords me peculiar satisfaction." He also honored their efforts during the Seminole War, citing "their good conduct on a more recent occasion."[83] With Monroe's remarks in support of the "major general" widely reprinted in the nation's newspapers, Jackson's public rehabilitation was largely complete.

A public dinner held in Monroe's honor provided the final venue for Jackson's supporters to salute the general during the president's visit. Out of deference to their distinguished guest, James Monroe earned the first toast of the evening as the embodiment of republican government. The celebrants declared, "More enviable than the mightiest monarch, is the republican ruler, who so justly possesses the confidence of a free and enlightened people." Following closely behind the president's was a more heartfelt toast in honor of Major General Andrew Jackson: "His reasons unconnected with his military functions were love for his country; hostility to her enemies."[84] Subsequent toasts addressing the Seminole campaign, Florida, and the Heroes of the Revolution provided additional opportunities for the residents of Nashville to salute Jackson.

Monroe's visit to Tennessee occurred at a fortuitous time because it allowed Jackson to appear alongside the president and present a less controversial image to the nation. Although Monroe was aware of Jackson's impulsiveness, the president's respect for his talents outweighed his reservations. Monroe's decision to visit Old Hickory at his home and then travel with him across Tennessee and Kentucky publicly symbolized the president's high regard for him and helped to rehabilitate his badly damaged reputation outside the western states. Thanks to Monroe's visit and his commitment to political reconciliation and healing, Jackson gained a new lease on his political life that allowed him to contemplate the presidency in 1820, 1824, and beyond. After spending over a week in Nashville, Jackson accompanied Monroe into Kentucky on June 15, and the two men traveled together and received accolades as they made their way through Kentucky before Jackson returned home upon reaching Lexington on July 1.[85]

The president's visit to Kentucky provided an opportunity for Henry Clay, the most antagonistic of Monroe's possible successors, to promote himself and his agenda. Unlike Jackson, Crawford, and Calhoun, who served at the pleasure of the president and tempered their personal opinions to reflect Monroe's policies, Clay, as speaker of the House of Representatives, enjoyed a political independence that he exercised with impunity. A member of the planter class, Clay was the most talented politician of his generation and the most complex. Despite his abilities and achievements, he was thin-skinned and held damaging grudges

Unlike Calhoun, Jackson, and Crawford, who eagerly sought to join Monroe, Henry Clay, speaker of the house, staged his own tour when Monroe visited Clay's home state of Kentucky. Source: *Henry Clay,* by Matthew Jouett, 1819. Courtesy of Ashland, The Henry Clay Estate, Lexington, Kentucky.

that sabotaged his substantive accomplishments. His most recent slight centered on Monroe's unwillingness to appoint him as secretary of state, an influential position that had become a steppingstone to the presidency.[86] Designating himself as Monroe's chief annoyance, Clay opposed the president whenever and wherever he could. In 1817, Clay had been an outspoken critic of the northern tour. When he attacked Jackson's behavior during the Seminole crisis in early 1819, he also intended to embarrass Monroe for allowing the general's excesses to occur during his watch. The president's visit south and west provided Clay with a new venue to challenge him.

Clay's active and public opposition to a president from his own party should have rendered him a political pariah. But because Monroe wanted to abolish parties, he refused to enforce loyalty and unity among his fellow Republicans, a policy that robbed him of valuable authority and made him vulnerable to attack. Despite Monroe's desire to stay above the political fray, his supporters in Kentucky warned him of the opposition he would encounter in Clay country. Before embarking on his southern tour, Monroe received a letter from Worden Pope of Louisville, which described the popularity the president enjoyed in this state. Pope wrote that the president's supporters regarded "Clay's opposition to your administration . . . as the effect of disappointed ambition and resentment." Pope believed that Monroe's visit would "defeat his plans" to oppose your presidency and would "be attended with much public good."[87] Pope, a descendant of the city's founder, later served on its welcoming committee, along with his brother William, in the hope of blunting the effect of Clay's supporters.[88]

As Monroe and Jackson headed north from central Tennessee into Kentucky on June 15, their choice of a land route into this state was unusual. Most people who visited Kentucky (or Ohio or Indiana) traveled by boat, beginning their journey in Pittsburgh and floating down the Ohio River into Louisville.[89] This water route enabled the state to ship its agricultural and manufactured goods such as hemp and rope directly to northern and eastern markets and gave this state its unique economic outlook.

Unlike the celebrants in Tennessee who saw their future in the availability of land, many residents of Kentucky, including Clay, believed that the federal government should encourage internal improvements and protective tariffs to enable this state to transport its goods to market while also being able to compete against European imports. While

Clay staged his own tour in order to antagonize Monroe, his followers stressed the state's economic problems as they greeted the president and highlighted these federal programs as the path to economic recovery. Although not as influential as Clay's supporters, his opponents tried to temper their influence and make the president feel welcome despite the palpable hostility. As in the coastal states, the tour through Kentucky included elements of the slave culture such as toasts and the involvement of the state's leading figures. The important difference was that the welcoming committees in these cities were divided between Clay's friends and his detractors.

The economic downturn of 1819 hit Kentucky particularly hard, and Clay's supporters stressed these difficulties to encourage Monroe to take action. In preparing for his visit, Amos Kendall, the editor of the *Argus of Western America* and the former tutor to Clay's children, urged Frankfort's citizens to share the city's economic distress with the president, rather than "sending a sycophantic messenger to make him an address full of flattery and falsehood."[90] In particular, Kendall recommended that a committee of citizens "show him our deserted houses and ruined manufactories" and explain to him "the absolute necessity of creating at home a market for our produce by encouraging our domestic manufacturers."[91] In other words, Clay's supporters would attempt to score political points by presenting a less rosy picture as the president visited their state.

When Monroe arrived in Louisville on June 24, the anti-Clay forces greeted him first, and they made every effort to emphasize their support for him and his administration. In a direct rebuttal of the views held by Monroe's opponents, the welcoming committee declared, "We believe, sir, that the Western people do approve of your administration, and repose an entire confidence in your intentions and exertions to do away with sectional prejudices—to destroy the bitterness of party spirit; and to unite the nation in a social, commercial and military connection."[92] In the toasts offered at the public dinner that evening, the celebrants did not mention regional concerns or economic difficulties. Instead they praised the country, the president, General Jackson (Clay's other nemesis), the Constitution, and the leading branches of the national government.[93] The rest of Kentucky would be less friendly to Monroe.

The welcoming speeches and toasts in the capital city of Frankfort provided Clay's supporters with the opportunity to promote their program of internal improvements and tariffs. After listing the American republic's many virtues in their welcoming speech, they lamented, "It pains us to turn from those prolific sources of national prosperity, to the miserable and almost ruined state of our Western Manufactures which now oppress the interior." Continuing their plea for an ameliorative tariff, they declared, "Our distance from markets renders the enhanced value given to our products."[94] In his response, Monroe slyly mentioned that Congress had devoted a great deal of attention to the plight of domestic manufactures, and he believed that they would continue to do so. The promotion of Clay's national agenda continued during the evening's toasts, with internal improvements being saluted before James Monroe.[95]

The last city of significance that Monroe visited during his 1819 tour was Lexington, Kentucky, Clay's hometown as well as the cultural center of the West. Challenging outside perceptions of the frontier as backward, Reverend Timothy Flint, a missionary from Massachusetts, declared Lexington "the Athens of the West" because the city's residents regularly discussed serious topics such as science, religion, and classical literature.[96] Monroe's visit to Lexington, coinciding with the Fourth of July, allowed this hub of western sophistication to throw a celebration that rivaled those held in the regional capitals of Boston and Charleston. Along with the standard array of welcoming parades and speeches, a public dinner, and toasts found during the northern and southern tours, the city proudly displayed its many institutions dedicated to culture and learning including the Lexington Athenaeum and Matthew Jouett's gallery of paintings. At the heart of the city's intellectual life was Transylvania University, which Monroe also toured. Not to be outdone by Harvard University's reception during the 1817 tour, a member of Transylvania's sophomore class delivered an address to the president in Latin.[97] Although local politics were never far from the surface during Monroe's stay in Lexington, the city's desire to emphasize its accomplishments outweighed parochial concerns as the West worked to secure its position alongside the North and South in the regional rivalries sweeping the nation.

As Monroe and Jackson made their way through Clay's home state, the Kentuckian staged a mini-tour of his own, where he received honors in New Orleans on May 19 and in Hopkinsville, Kentucky on July 3.[98] Although Clay's actions were hostile and insubordinate, he pursued several disingenuous strategies to hide his true motives. On July 19, Clay sent a letter to his friend and political supporter, Joseph Gales, Jr., the editor of the *National Intelligencer*, to explain why he was unable to join the president during his visit to Kentucky. Expecting the letter to be circulated, Clay expressed regret that he missed Monroe, writing, "I lamented my absence from this place when the Chief Magistrate did us the honor to visit it." Then, Clay placed the blame on Monroe and partially on himself for the missed opportunity, explaining, "It would not have happened if he had performed the whole of the tour that he had marked out, or if I had not encountered unusual delay in my returning voyage."[99] Then an even more remarkable event occurred. On July 10, Clay and Monroe briefly met each other in Harrodsburg, Kentucky, as the president was preparing to leave the state.[100] Although Clay intended to oppose and antagonize Monroe, he also made efforts to cover the trail of his political intrigues.

Exhausted by his six-month tour, Monroe dropped his plans to visit Cincinnati and began to make his way back to Washington.[101] William H. Crawford still hoped to travel with the president and contemplated joining the president at a halfway point between Kentucky and Washington. Crawford finally conceded that the "jolting of the stage a second time over the mountains" rendered such a trip physically impossible.[102] Although the Georgian was not able to travel with Monroe, the president's southern tour afforded three other presidential hopefuls with the opportunity to promote themselves and their candidacies during this trip. Monroe finally returned to Washington on August 8, having achieved his goal of touring the northern and southern states in the tradition of George Washington.[103]

Although Monroe believed his two tours united the nation and healed political disagreements, newspaper coverage of the 1819 tour provided further evidence that the nation was growing into three distinct regions. Southern newspaper coverage of the coastal portion of the tour was almost as avid as it had been during the northern tour. With the spotlight now trained on the South, the region's newspaper editors had to decide how to cover the president's visit, while avoiding the excesses they criticized in the northern tour coverage. William C. Shields of Norfolk's *American Beacon* chose to praise the city's cordial reception of the president as evidence of its adherence to republican values. He wrote, "The avidity with which all classes of our fellow citizens, seized upon the opportunity . . . to approach the Chief Magistrate of the Nation . . . was indeed, such a spectacle as is congenial with the most felicitous view of the tendencies of such a form of government."[104] In anticipating the president's arrival, John Kean of the *Augusta Chronicle* adopted a defensive tack, declaring,

"Although we may be out-done in the 'pomp and circumstance' of parade which has greeted the President in various places, yet, no doubt, we shall make as animated a display as any, in warmth and honesty of feeling."[105] His comments served as a warning to his fellow citizens to act with restraint in welcoming the president, as well as a criticism of other cities that had offered excessive receptions.

Having already covered Monroe's 1817 tour, many northern newspapers snubbed the southern tour, while their western counterparts castigated the southerners for their unrepublican conduct. Many northern editors decided that the president's progress was newsworthy, whereas the southern receptions were not, so they tracked the president's movements, but did not include the welcoming speeches or toasts. Even the Baltimore-based *Niles' Weekly Register*, which acted as the nation's newspaper of record, contained only perfunctory reports on the president's progress through the South. These papers committed a serious error in failing to notice the growing differences between the North and the South that were being expressed on a regular basis during the 1819 tour.

Recognizing the political power of the coastal states, the western newspapers, particularly those in Henry Clay's home state of Kentucky, critiqued the sycophantic conduct of leaders in the southern states. Joshua Norvell of the Lexington-based *Kentucky Gazette* chided the citizens of Savannah as they "commenced their plans of pomp and parade." Aiming his pen at the conduct of northern and southern states, Norvell added, "In his passage through this state, we feel confident he will have a plain and welcome reception—be we are equally confident that no civic wreaths will be presented—no triumphal arches will be erected—no flowers strewed in his walk."[106] Putnam Ewing, editor of the *Kentucky Republican,* also weighed in with his perspective on appropriate republican conduct, writing, "We regret to perceive, that the Southern people have disgraced themselves as much as the people of the East, by the disgusting aristocratic pomp with which they have received this officer of the government." Ewing added that American citizens should show the president respect and politeness, "but nothing more—no pomp, no parade and adulation—can become a republican people."[107] The meaning of republicanism emerged as a verbal battleground with three distinct regions competing to inherit its mantle.

Newspapers provided further evidence of the nation's growing regional and political differences as they openly speculated about potential presidential candidates in 1820. Although Monroe's predecessors and fellow Virginians, Jefferson and Madison, had been elected to second terms, Monroe's refusal to act as the head of his party created a political vacuum that left him vulnerable to challenges from within the Republican Party. During the early months of the 1819 tour, Joshua Norvell of the *Kentucky Gazette* commented that the *American Aurora* of Philadelphia had compiled a list of six favorite-son candidates, including Monroe and Crawford in the South; Clay in the West; DeWitt Clinton and Monroe's vice president, Daniel Tompkins, both of New York, in the center; and John Quincy Adams in the East.[108] In 1819, Monroe was regarded as just one of many possible presidential contenders in the next election.[109]

In 1820, Monroe ran unopposed for reelection thanks largely to his two presidential tours, which had served as proto-campaign swings that allowed him to appear presidential, republican, and most importantly, nonpartisan. During his tours, Monroe embodied the values of political healing and national unity that he hoped other politicians would emulate in order to keep the destructive forces of parties at bay. Paradoxically, Monroe's obliviousness to party, particularly his outreach to Federalists, yielded an electoral advantage that postponed rather than resolved the tensions among his Republican successors. Although political and regional disagreements characterized his first term, his decision to tour the nation as the last of the republican presidents produced a sense of national harmony and ensured his unopposed reelection in 1820. Despite the early exposure gained by Calhoun, Crawford, Clay, and Jackson during the southern tour, these favorite sons would have to wait another four years to find out who would succeed Monroe.

Monroe's unwillingness to lead his party, which yielded a short-term electoral victory, had disastrous consequences for the Republicans during the presidential election of 1824. That election was fraught with significance because it was the first presidential election in which none of the contenders was a founding father. With no clear front-runner, four candidates representing different regions and constituencies within the Republican Party faced one another: Adams, Clay, Crawford, and Jackson. As president, Monroe was the putative head of the Republican Party, but he refused to lead it and chose to remain neutral during the campaign. His unwillingness to exercise his considerable political authority ironically increased partisanship, even though it had been always been his goal to eliminate political infighting. Lacking a party leader or a structure with the authority to select a nominee, the election resulted in a stalemate and was thrown into the House of Representatives for resolution. Given the generational change in political leadership, the loss of a party structure, and the growing regionalism, it is not surprising that the 1824 election failed to produce a candidate with a majority of popular and electoral votes. One of the unexpected legacies of Monroe's idealistic mission to transcend political parties was the chaotic presidential election to succeed him. In subsequent years, Jackson, Clay, and their supporters would work to develop national party structures designed to counter the regionalism and infighting that doomed their chances in 1824.

By August 1819 Monroe had achieved his goal of touring the nation to heal its political wounds and to promote national unity, as Washington had done thirty years earlier. In his inaugural address, Monroe had dedicated his presidency to the elimination of political parties because he considered them incompatible with republican government. Despite Monroe's best intentions, the Federalist and Republican parties served a valuable function in republican government by negotiating differences among the nation's citizens. Even early critics like Jefferson and Madison had come to recognize their usefulness. While Monroe's presidency was committed to tackling lingering political issues from the 1790s, the 1819 tour uncovered a politics increasingly based in the regional differences of the South, North, and West and the growing prominence of a new generation of political leaders committed to these local concerns. During his 1819 tour, Monroe, the last of the founding fathers, promoted an older vision of a national government without parties, accompanied by favorite-son politicians who practiced a newer form of regional politics in the hopes of succeeding him as president. While Monroe did not succeed in solving partisanship, his two presidential journeys affirmed the "success and stability of our republican institutions" so that a younger generation of politicians could smoothly assume the reins of power.[110]

Conclusion
Celebrations, Parties, and Antebellum Politics

On March 4, 1829, large numbers of people descended on the nation's capital to witness the inauguration of Andrew Jackson as the seventh president of the United States. An estimated fifteen to twenty thousand people gathered at the Capitol to get a glimpse of Jackson. After he took the oath, crowds mobbed the new president to congratulate him, forcing Jackson to slip out the west side of the Capitol and return to the White House. As Jackson made his way down Pennsylvania Avenue on horseback, an unofficial procession consisting of "Country men, farmers, gentlemen, mounted and dismounted, boys, women, and children, black and white. Carriages, wagons and carts all pushing him to the President's House"[1] escorted him to his new home. The scene became even more chaotic once they reached the mansion. All the downstairs rooms were packed with people eager to greet the president and enjoy some refreshments. China and glassware were broken, and "men with boots heavy with mud stood on the damask-stained covered chairs in order to get a better look at their president."[2] In order to relieve the overcrowding, the mansion's staff lured the public on to the lawn with liquor and punch, while Jackson escaped to his temporary quarters at Gadsby's hotel. While the excitement continued at the official residence, Jackson dined with his vice president, John Calhoun, and went to bed early. The inaugural organizers hosted a subscription ball for the respectable citizens of Washington, but Jackson's recent status as a widower exempted him from attending.[3]

The chaos and mob mentality that characterized the "people's inauguration" of March 4, 1829, seemed to be a far cry from the atmosphere at the inaugurations of April 30, 1789, or even March 4, 1801. But perhaps not. The goal of presidential ceremony—putting sovereign citizens in contact with their government—was still a vibrant idea when Jackson became president. What had changed since 1789 was that a younger generation of political leaders were adopting a more accessible and democratic ceremonial culture that reflected the political changes occurring among a geographically and numerically expanding American electorate.

From 1789 to 1825, the first five presidents of the United States struggled to bring the abstract constitutional principles of popular sovereignty to life in order to successfully launch the new national government. While George Washington and James Monroe introduced ceremonial forms that borrowed from monarchy, particularly through tours of the United States, Thomas Jefferson chose to foster partisan organizations as the best way to secure republican government. Rather than achieving a consensus, these approaches promoted a lively conversation among the nation's citizens and the even more vocal newspapers' editors concerning the best way to exercise their sovereign responsibilities. Thirty years of presidential ceremonies and parties, and the accompanying discussion, made republican government a tangible presence in the lives of many Americans and led to the successful launching of the new Constitution. By ensuring the relevance of a new and unfamiliar type of national government, the early presidents made a tremendous contribution to the nation's founding. But even beyond the establishment of republican government for current and future generations, Washington, Jefferson, and Monroe also affirmed the use of ceremonial activities and political parties as appropriate ways to promote and maintain the bond between government and citizen. A younger generation of politicians embraced these lessons when they launched the second American party system, embarked on their own tours, and participated in festivities that celebrated the nation's heritage.[4]

By the end of Monroe's second term, the party organizations of the founding period had run out of steam. The Federalist Party was no longer a national force, although it remained strong in several states.

The dawn of a new age in American politics as the people take a vocal and visible role in Andrew Jackson's 1829 inauguration. Source: Library of Congress.

The Republican Party housed too many competing ideologies and personalities to be effective, ranging from the states' rights approach of William H. Crawford and the frontier bravado of Andrew Jackson to the nationalist vision of Henry Clay and John C. Calhoun. Another sign of a changing political environment were a younger group of favorite-son presidential candidates who lacked the national stature that had characterized the founding generation. The inconclusive outcome of the 1824 presidential election illustrated the decline of the Republicans as well as the need for effective political organizations. This election pitted four candidates against each other—John Quincy Adams, Clay, Crawford, and Jackson—all of whom had strong regional support but lacked a sufficient national following to win the election.[5] Although Jackson won a plurality of the popular vote, he did not gain enough electoral votes to secure the presidency. Adams finished second in both popular and electoral votes, with Crawford and Clay coming in third and fourth, respectively. The campaign to gain political support outside their strongholds moved into the House of Representatives as these four men and their supporters turned their attention to the congressional delegations of each state. Clay eventually released his thirty-seven electoral votes to Adams, giving Monroe's secretary of state enough votes to claim the presidency over Jackson.[6]

The chaotic presidential election of 1824 affirmed the need for vigorous political parties to support lesser-known candidates across a geographically expanding and growing electorate. Jefferson's efforts in launching the Democratic-Republican Party in the 1790s had affirmed the value of partisan organizations in strengthening republican government and demonstrated their importance in representing philosophical differences.

Clearly, the exhausted Federalist and Republican parties of the founding period were no longer capable of launching successful presidential bids. In their place a new two-party system eventually spread throughout the nation.[7]

The second American party system began to take shape immediately after Adams's accession to the presidency in 1825.[8] Believing that Jackson had been unfairly robbed of the presidency, his supporters began work on the establishment of a party structure that would result in his undisputed election in 1828. When Adams later appointed Clay to the coveted position of secretary of state, Jackson and his supporters cried foul, suspecting that Clay had cut a deal to make Adams president. While Clay wanted to become president, supporting Adams guaranteed that his western rival, Jackson, would not attain this office either, at least not in 1824.[9] With the Clay-Jackson rivalry renewed, Old Hickory's supporters redoubled their efforts to ensure the popular general's election.

Many of the organizers who participated in Monroe's tours continued their political involvement by working to establish the Democratic and Whig parties. The inner circle of Jackson's party consisted of his closest supporters in Tennessee, including John H. Eaton, Felix Grundy, and William B. Lewis.[10] These men had already gathered together to promote Jackson's political career as Nashville's Committee of Arrangements during Monroe's visit in 1819. Jackson also shored up his political base by heading a loose coalition formed to challenge the policies and the legitimacy of the Adams administration. This anti-Adams stance enabled Jackson to transcend regionalism and build a national party by attracting the southern supporters of Calhoun and Crawford.[11] Jackson expanded his national base by reaching out to the political leaders in the northern states who had already backed his candidacy and were eager to do so again. After 1824, Jackson built a personality-driven national coalition that became the Democratic Party and ensured his unequivocal election to the presidency in 1828 and 1832.

From 1824 to 1832, the Republican Party attempted a comeback as the political opposition to the Jacksonian Democrats. Jackson's departure from the Republicans and Crawford's retreat from politics due to poor health closed down the states' rights side of the Republican Party.[12] This change permitted the national wing to prevail, at least temporarily, under the leadership of Adams and Clay. After 1828, Jackson's electoral successes in gaining the presidency and both houses of Congress proved too much for this already weakened party, and Clay and his supporters began to contemplate other ways to oppose Old Hickory and his political juggernaut.[13] An opportunity presented itself when Jackson declared war on the Second Bank of the United States and its president, Nicholas Biddle. Jackson's opponents believed that the president had overstepped his authority when he vetoed the bank's rechartering in 1832 and then killed the bank by transferring its considerable assets to state banks. Jackson's opponents labeled him a tyrant, and they circulated politically effective cartoons that portrayed him as "King Andrew."[14] The Bank War encouraged this coalition to abandon the moribund Republican Party and to form a more effective political organization in its place. The name Whig allowed the party to identify themselves with the American colonists who confronted another monarch, King George III, during the American Revolution.[15] In addition to supporting the bank and opposing Jackson, this party attracted manufacturers and merchants who advocated social reform and Clay's American System of internal improvements and protective tariffs.

Some of the Federalists who welcomed Monroe during the northern tour found the political home they had been seeking in the Whigs' national message of social and economic progress. Nicholas Biddle, who had encouraged Monroe to embrace his former opponents in 1817, emerged as Jackson's chief nemesis during the Bank War. Daniel Webster, who had pushed for the tour and had hoped to be named Monroe's attorney general, joined the Whigs as a U.S. senator from Massachusetts, while Nathaniel Silsbee, a member of Salem's Committee of Arrangements, led the Massachusetts Whig convention in 1832 and later served as a U.S. senator from this state and party.[16] Although he participated in the 1818 and 1819 tours, Monroe's namesake and nephew, Lieutenant James Monroe, also became a member of the Whig Party and served as a congressman from New York City from 1833 to 1835.¹⁷ While many former Federalists became Democrats, those who participated in Monroe's northern tour allied themselves with the National Republicans in the 1820s and later the Whig Party in the early 1830s to contribute to the nation's political realignment.¹⁸

In addition to encouraging the formation of two new political parties, the presidential ceremonies of the founding period inspired a decade's worth of festivities that introduced a new generation of politicians to the nation. These celebrations of the republican past allowed a group of untested regional figures to link themselves and their careers to the distinguished founding fathers they hoped to succeed. Unlike Washington, Monroe, and their contemporaries, who had spent their entire careers in service to the nation, these younger politicians were largely unknown outside their home states or regions. Lacking an American Revolution or Constitutional Convention to make them household names, they emulated Washington and Monroe and engaged in their own occasions to honor the nation's history and government.

The ceremonial renaissance of the 1820s coincided with a change in the conduct of American politics. After 1824, the presidential election process became democratized due to two important changes. First, most states permitted the popular election of electoral slates, and the voting qualifications had been expanded to allow nearly universal white male suffrage.¹⁹ These changes combined to increase popular participation in the election of the president. In turn, presidential candidates now appealed directly to the voting public with open-air rallies and dramatic public events.²⁰ Inspired by Monroe's recent tours and Washington's earlier ones, a new generation of politicians celebrated the nation's past in order to succeed in the popular politics of the future.

One of the first successors to honor the nation's heritage was De Witt Clinton, the governor of New York. Clinton had unsuccessfully challenged James Madison for president in 1812. After this defeat, he staked his national ambitions on the success of the Erie Canal, a waterway that connected the farms in New York State with the trading and commercial opportunities in New York City. Born in 1769, Clinton was too young to have participated in the American Revolution or the nation's founding. Although he might link himself to these earlier events because of his uncle George Clinton, a governor of New York as well as Thomas Jefferson's second vice president, the younger Clinton needed a more tangible connection to the past if he were to emerge from the growing pack of presidential contenders. Clinton linked the nation's economic prospects and his political future with the nation's revolutionary glories by holding the canal's groundbreaking ceremony on the nation's most important secular holiday, July 4, 1817, and then opening the canal on July 4, 1825.[21] Despite the enormous success of this project, Clinton did not live long enough to reap its political benefits, dying in 1828 at the age of 58.[22]

Daniel Webster was another rising political star who enhanced his national profile by applying his oratorical skills to celebrations of the nation's past. On December 22, 1820, Webster participated in the two hundredth anniversary of the landing of the Pilgrims at Plymouth Rock by offering an address entitled "The First Settlement of New England."[23] Five years later, Webster enjoyed another opportunity to link his career and his aspirations with the achievements of an earlier generation when he offered an equally celebrated speech at the dedication of the Bunker Hill Monument on June 17, 1825, the fiftieth anniversary of this battle.[24]

While political leaders participated in celebrations of the founding period that prepared the way for their political accession, the American public symbolically embraced their political future as republicans when they honored the Marquis de Lafayette as he toured the United States in 1824 and 1825. Although a French citizen, Lafayette came to exemplify republican virtue because of his willingness to fight unselfishly for American independence. Lafayette served as a tangible link to the revolutionary era, as well as a surrogate for George Washington, who had regarded the young soldier as a son. At the age of 67, the Marquis visited every state in the Union as the official guest of Congress and President Monroe. Occurring during Monroe's second term, Lafayette's visit replicated the processions, welcoming speeches, and public dinners that had characterized the president's two tours. Americans thanked Lafayette for his service to the nation, while also expressing hope that they would continue to honor its revolutionary and republican ideas.[25] During Lafayette's fourteen-month visit, the nation's aspiring politicians appeared with him to bask in the republican glory his tour generated. Daniel Webster's triumphant speech at Bunker Hill occurred during Lafayette's visit to the monument, while Henry Clay welcomed the French hero to the House of Representatives.[26] Lafayette's visit to the White House afforded Monroe's cabinet secretaries, including John Calhoun, William Crawford, and John Quincy Adams, with an opportunity to appear with the revolutionary hero.[27]

Monroe's tours also inspired his successors to employ similar journeys to promote their political goals and presidential candidacies. Following in the footsteps of Washington and Monroe, these trips appeared apolitical when, in fact, they functioned as proto-campaign swings. At the beginning of his second term in 1833, a triumphant Andrew Jackson decided to tour New England, ostensibly to unite the nation. Traveling in a region where he was most unpopular, Jackson nonetheless demonstrated his political strength over his opponents in the aftermath of the Bank War and the nullification crisis.[28] Competing with Jackson's trip, Daniel Webster embarked on his own journey in the spring of 1833 in preparation for his presidential campaign in 1836. Webster traveled to northern New York and then through the Ohio Valley by stagecoach, visiting Buffalo, Columbus, and Cincinnati. His tour concluded at the Lexington, Kentucky home of Henry Clay, his political ally in the Whig Party.[29] An ailing Clay staged a tour of the east coast in 1847 to denounce the Mexican-American War and to test the political waters for another presidential run in 1848. Although he was enthusiastically welcomed in visits to Philadelphia, Wilmington, and Baltimore, his presidential prospects were over, due in large part to his defeat in the 1844 election.[30] By the 1840s, campaign swings by presidential hopefuls had become a normal part of the political process, inspired by the earlier tours of George Washington and James Monroe.

The ceremonial renaissance of the 1820s ended on a somber note as the nation marked the fiftieth anniversary of the Declaration of Independence on July 4, 1826. Although this holiday began with the traditional round of speeches, parades, and public rallies, the occasion assumed a more solemn cast when Americans learned that Thomas Jefferson and John Adams had died on this revered day.[31] (James Monroe died exactly five years later on July 4, 1831, although his passing lacked the commemorative coincidence of his colleagues' deaths.)[32] Their deaths marked the symbolic passing of the founding father era as well as the end of the Republican and Federalist parties they once headed. John Quincy Adams, Adams's son and the current president, represented the transition to a younger generation of political leaders, who did not participate in the Revolution or in the Constitutional Convention.[33] Through their ceremonial salute of the founding generation, younger men like Adams, Clay, Webster, and Jackson inherited the Revolution and demonstrated their worthiness to lead the nation.

George Washington, Thomas Jefferson, and James Monroe each entered the presidency with his own ideas on the best way to promote republican government through the use of cultural forms, whether ceremony, tours, parties, or rhetoric. Not only did these three men succeed in launching republican government during the nation's critical founding years, they also introduced and legitimized the use of celebrations and parties as the best way to preserve republican government for subsequent generations.

Notes

Introduction—"Untrodden Ground"

1. Washington to Catherine Macaulay Graham, January 9, 1790, W. W. Abbot and Dorothy Twohig, eds., *The Papers of George Washington, Presidential Series*, vol. 4 (Charlottesville: University Press of Virginia, 1993), 551–54.

2. A rich literature exists concerning the political uses of symbolism. See Clifford Geertz, *Negara: The Theatre State in Nineteenth-century Bali* (Princeton: Princeton University Press, 1980); Clifford Geertz, "Centers, Kings, and Charisma: Reflections on the Symbolics of Power," in *Culture and Its Creators*, Joseph Ben-David and Terry Nichols Clark, eds. (Chicago: University of Chicago Press, 1977); Lynn Hunt, *Politics, Culture and Class in the French Revolution* (Berkeley: University of California Press, 1984); David I. Kertzer, *Ritual, Politics, and Power* (New Haven: Yale University Press, 1988); Mona Ozouf, *Festivals and the French Revolution* (Cambridge: Harvard University Press, 1988); and Roy Strong, *Art and Power, Renaissance Festivals, 1450–1650* (Berkeley: University of California Press, 1984).

3. Many historians have described the American ideas of popular sovereignty and representation as "governing fictions." The constructed quality of these ideas made it essential that the political leaders who wanted to see the new national government succeed would need to find ways to make these concepts relevant and pertinent to a newly sovereign public. See Clifford Geertz, "Centers, Kings, and Charisma: Reflections on the Symbolics of Power," in *Culture and Its Creators*, Joseph Ben-David and Terry Nichols Clark, eds. (Chicago: University of Chicago Press, 1977), and Edmund S. Morgan, *Inventing the People: The Rise of Popular Sovereignty in England and America* (New York: W.W. Norton, 1988).

4. Although citizenship was defined very narrowly during the 1790s and included only white men with property, the republican political culture of presidential ceremony and partisan organizations reached a much wider audience than just the nation's official citizenry. Men without property, young men, African Americans, and women of all ages were involved in presidential ceremony either as observers or as presenters. For this reason, my understanding of citizenship extends beyond the right to vote. For a more broadly defined conception of citizenship, see Rosemarie Zagarri, *Revolutionary Backlash: Women and Politcs in the Early American Republic* (Philadelphia: University of Pennsylvania Press, 2007), 7–8.

5. For a "corrective" to the emphasis on presidents in understanding early American politics, see Jeffrey L. Pasley, Andrew Robertson, and David Waldstreicher, eds., *Beyond the*

Founding Fathers: New Approaches to the Political History of the Early Republic (Chapel Hill: University of North Carolina Press, 2004).

6. Washington, and many in the public and in the Congress, borrowed liberally from European monarchical traditions, including those of the Tudors, Stuarts, and Hanoverians in England, and the Hapsburgs and Bourbons on the continent. For a history of these practices, see David M. Bergeron, *English Civic Pageantry, 1558-1642* (London: Edward Arnold Publishers, 1971); Mary Hill Cole, *The Portable Queen: Elizabeth I and the Politics of Ceremony* (Amherst: University of Massachusetts Press, 1999); Linda Colley, *Britons: Forging the Nation, 1707-1837* (New Haven: Yale University Press, 1992); and Roy Strong, *Art and Power, Renaissance Festivals, 1450-1650* (Berkeley: University of California Press, 1984).

7. Because the early political system relied heavily on letter writing in order to get work done, this study emphasizes the writings of not only Jefferson, but Washington, Monroe, and their political associates. See Michael Warner, *The Letters of the Republic: Publication and the Public Sphere in Eighteenth-century America* (Cambridge: Harvard University Press, 1990). On the establishment of Jeffersonian democracy, see Sean Wilentz, *The Rise of American Democracy: Jefferson to Lincoln* (New York: W. W. Norton, 2005), 40-140.

8. On Washington's presidential policies, see Joseph J. Ellis, *His Excellency: George Washington* (New York: Alfred A. Knopf, 2004), 203-14, 225-30, 236-37.

9. On Jefferson's presidential philosophy, see Joyce Appleby, *Capitalism and a New Social Order: The Republican Vision of the 1790s* (New York: New York University Press, 1984), 53, 103-4; Joseph J. Ellis, *Founding Brothers: The Revolutionary Generation* (New York: Alfred A. Knopf, 2000), 13-14, 145, 156.

10. On the role of first ladies and other Washington women in the establishment of a political culture, see Catherine Allgor's *Parlor Politics: In Which the Ladies of Washington Help Build a City and a Government* (Charlottesville: University Press of Virginia, 2000) and *A Perfect Union: Dolley Madison and the Creation of the American Nation* (New York: Henry Holt and Company, 2006).

11. Kathleen O. Potter, *The Federalist's Vision of Popular Sovereignty in the New American Republic* (New York: LFB Scholarly Publishing LLC, 2002), 11, 30, 50.

12. On popular sovereignty as a fiction, see Edmund S. Morgan, *Inventing the People: The Rise of Popular Sovereignty in England and America* (New York: W. W. Norton, 1988), 13-15. For a challenge to this approach, see Jack N. Rakove, *Original Meanings: Politics and Ideas in the Meaning of the Constitution* (New York: Alfred A. Knopf, 1997), 384n16, and Christian G. Fritz, *American Sovereigns: The People and America's Constitutional Tradition before the Civil War* (Cambridge: Cambridge University Press, 2008).

13. On the affordability of newspaper postage, see Richard R. John, *Spreading the News: The American Postal System from Franklin to Morse* (Cambridge: Harvard University Press, 1995).

14. *New-York Daily Gazette*, April 29, 1789; republished in the *Providence Gazette and Country Journal* (Rhode Island), May 9, 1789.

15. *New-Jersey Journal* (Elizabethtown), November 11, 1789.

16. Jeffrey L. Pasley, *"The Tyranny of Printers": Newspaper Politics in the Early American Republic* (Charlottesville: University Press of Virginia, 2001), 165-66.

17. While other studies have documented ceremonial culture within the early republic, they have failed to make the linkage between these activities and political outcomes. See Joanne Freeman, *Affairs of Honor: National Politics in the New Republic* (New Haven: Yale University Press, 2001); Simon P. Newman, *Parades and Politics of the Street:*

Festive Culture in the Early American Republic (Philadelphia: University of Pennsylvania Press, 1997); and David Waldstreicher, *In the Midst of Perpetual Fetes: The Making of American Nationalism, 1776-1820* (Chapel Hill: University of North Carolina Press, 1997).

18. On the republican rules of politics, see M. J. Heale, *The Presidential Quest: Candidates and Images in American Political Culture, 1787-1852* (London: Longman, 1982), 1-22, and Joanne Freeman, *Affairs of Honor: National Politics in the New Republic* (New Haven: Yale University Press, 2001).

1—"Ceremonies, Endless Ceremonies"

1. George Washington to Edward Rutledge, May 5, 1789, in John C. Fitzpatrick, ed., *The Writings of George Washington*, vol. 30 (Washington: Government Printing Office, 1939), 309.

2. North Carolina and Rhode Island did not approve the Constitution until November 26, 1789, and May 29, 1790, respectively. See Douglas Southall Freeman, *George Washington, a Biography: Patriot and President*, vol. six (New York: Charles Scribner's Sons, 1954), 143, 246, 268.

3. On the "republican court" of Washington's presidency, see Catherine Allgor, *Parlor Politics: In Which the Ladies of Washington Help Build a City and a Government* (Charlottesville: University Press of Virginia, 2000), 20, 74, 99-100; Joseph J. Ellis, *His Excellency: George Washington* (New York: Alfred A. Knopf, 2004), 184-185; Joanne Freeman, *Affairs of Honor: National Politics in the New Republic* (New Haven: Yale University Press, 2001), 6; and David Waldstreicher, *In the Midst of Perpetual Fetes: The Making of American Nationalism, 1776-1820* (Chapel Hill: University of North Carolina Press, 1997), 119-121.

4. On royal progresses, triumphal arches, and entries, see Mary Hill Cole, *The Portable Queen: Elizabeth I and the Politics of Ceremony* (Amherst: University of Massachusetts Press, 1999), 13-19, and David M. Bergeron, *English Civic Pageantry, 1558-1642* (London: Edward Arnold Publishers, 1971), 11-121. On the origins of "God save the King," see Linda Colley, *Britons: Forging the Nation, 1707-1837* (New Haven: Yale University Press, 1992), 43-44.

5. On the monarchy's presence in the colonies before the revolution, see David Waldstreicher, *In the Midst of Perpetual Fetes: The Making of American Nationalism, 1776-1820* (Chapel Hill: University of North Carolina Press, 1997), 20; Richard L. Bushman, *King and People in Provincial Massachusetts* (Chapel Hill: University of North Carolina Press, 1985), 14-17; Jerrilyn Greene Marston, *King and Congress: The Transfer of Political Legitimacy, 1774-1776* (Princeton: Princeton University Press, 1987), 13-14, 25; and Brendan McConville, *The King's Three Faces: The Rise and Fall of Royal America, 1688-1776* (Chapel Hill: University of North Carolina Press, 2006).

6. On the monarchy's presence in the colonies during the 1770s, see Waldstreicher, *In the Midst of Perpetual Fetes*, 30-31, 46, and Colley, *Britons*, 136-37.

7. See William Maclay's April 25, 1789 diary entry, contained in Kenneth R. Bowling and Helen E. Veit, eds., *Documentary History of the First Federal Congress of the United States of America*, vol. IX (Baltimore: The Johns Hopkins University Press, 1988), 5.

8. Washington first asserted his preferences on presidential ceremony on May 10, 1789, when he issued a query to John Adams and others. See Dorothy Twohig, ed., *The Papers of George Washington*, Presidential Series, vol. 2 (Charlottesville: University Press of Virginia, 1987), 245-47.

9. See Ellis, *His Excellency: George Washington*, 184–85, and Waldstreicher, *In the Midst of Perpetual Fetes*, 119–21.

10. Stanley Elkins and Eric McKittrick, *The Age of Federalism: The Early American Republic, 1788–1800* (New York: Oxford University Press, 1993), 34.

11. Ellis, *His Excellency: George Washington*, 117. For a discussion of Washington as a national symbol, see Barry Schwartz, *George Washington: The Making of an American Symbol* (New York: The Free Press, 1987).

12. Elkins and McKittrick, *The Age of Federalism*, 33.

13. Linda Grant De Pauw, ed., *Documentary History of the First Federal Congress of the United States of America, 1789–1791*, vol. I (Baltimore: The Johns Hopkins University Press, 1972), 3. Sol Bloom, *History of the Formation of the Union under the Constitution* (Washington, D.C.: U.S. Government Printing Office, 1943), 220–21.

14. New York became the eleventh state to ratify the Constitution on July 26, 1788. North Carolina and Rhode Island did not approve the Constitution until much later, on November 26, 1789, and May 29, 1790, respectively. See Freeman, *George Washington*, vol. six, 143, 246, 268.

15. Bloom, *History of the Formation of the Union under the Constitution*, 145–46. Elkins and McKittrick, *The Age of Federalism*, 33.

16. In a letter to Benjamin Lincoln, Washington referred to the "multiplicity of applications" for a variety of positions, and his desire to remain unencumbered by any specific commitments. Among the most popular requests were for the position of revenue collector at customs houses. See Washington to Lincoln, March 11, 1789, in Dorothy Twohig, ed., *The Papers of George Washington*, Presidential Series, vol. 1 (Charlottesville: University Press of Virginia, 1987), 383.

17. On the republican rules of politics, see Freeman, *Affairs of Honor*, and M. J. Heale, *The Presidential Quest: Candidates and Images in American Political Culture, 1787–1852* (London: Longman, 1982), 1–22. On Washington's reticence, see Ellis, *His Excellency: George Washington*, 182–84.

18. David McCullough, *John Adams* (New York: Simon and Schuster, 2001), 394.

19. Freeman, *Affairs of Honor*, 2–3.

20. De Pauw, ed., *Documentary History of the First Federal Congress*, vol. I, 5.

21. De Pauw, ed., *Documentary History of the First Federal Congress*, vol. I, 3–59, and Linda Grant De Pauw, ed., *Documentary History of the First Federal Congress of the United States of America, 1789–1791*, vol. III (Baltimore: The Johns Hopkins University Press, 1977), 3–79.

22. De Pauw, ed., *Documentary History of the First Federal Congress*, vol. I, 7 and vol. III, 7.

23. De Pauw, ed., *Documentary History of the First Federal Congress*, vol. I , 7–8.

24. The Congressional certificates announcing Washington's and Adams's elections read, in part: "That the Senate and House of Representatives of the United States, being convened in the City and State of New-York, the sixth day of April . . . for the sole purpose of receiving, opening, and counting the votes of the Electors, did . . . open all the certificates, and count all the votes of the Electors for a President and for a Vice President." See De Pauw, ed., *Documentary History of the First Federal Congress*, vol. I, 10.

25. Twohig, ed., *The Papers of George Washington*, vol. 2, 54–55. Page Smith, *John Adams, 1784–1826*, vol. II (Garden City, New York: Doubleday and Company, Inc., 1962), 742.

26. Twohig, ed., *The Papers of George Washington*, vol. 2, 56.

27. The April 30, 1789, edition of the *American Herald and the Worcester Recorder*

(Massachusetts) reported on Washington's notification, while the May 7, 1789, edition of the *New-Hampshire Recorder, and the Weekly Advertiser* (Keene) reported on Adams's.

28. Reflecting a desire for geographical balance in the planning of the inauguration, the House committee consisted of Egbert Benson of New York, Frederick Muhlenberg of Pennsylvania, and Samuel Griffin of Virginia, while the Senate committee included John Langdon of New Hampshire, William Johnson of Connecticut, and William Few of Georgia. De Pauw, ed., *Documentary History of the First Federal Congress*, vol. I, 3, 12, and vol. III, 3, 19.

29. De Pauw, ed., *Documentary History of the First Federal Congress*, vol. I, 16–17, and vol. III, 23.

30. De Pauw, ed., *Documentary History of the First Federal Congress*, vol. I, 16–17, and vol. III, 23.

31. *Boston Independent Chronicle*, April 16, 1789, reprinted in the *Daily Advertiser* (New York), May 4, 1789, and the *Vermont Gazette* (Bennington), May 4, 1789.

32. *Osborne's New-Hampshire Spy* (Portsmouth), May 4, 1789; *New-Hampshire Recorder*, May 7, 1789; and *Vermont Gazette*, May 11, 1789.

33. McCullough, *John Adams*, 394–95. In its May 2 to May 6, 1789 edition, the *Gazette of the United States* (New York) praised Washington, Adams, and other members of Congress who supported American manufacturers by wearing "homespun clothes" to the inaugural festivities.

34. Adams's arrival in New York City received widespread coverage in the *Middlesex Gazette* (Middletown, Connecticut), May 2, 1789; the *Weekly Monitor* (Litchfield, Connecticut), May 4, 1789; the *American Herald and Worcester Recorder*, May 8, 1789; the *Vermont Gazette*, May 11, 1789; and the *New-Hampshire Recorder*, May 14, 1789.

35. Adams's reception in Congress and his address were reported in *Freeman's Journal* (Philadelphia), April 29, 1789; *Worcester Magazine*, April 30, 1789; *United States Chronicle: Political, Commercial, and Historical* (Providence, Rhode Island), April 30, 1789; and *Norwich Packet and Country Journal* (Connecticut), May 8, 1789. See also De Pauw, ed., *Documentary History of the First Federal Congress*, vol. I, 21.

36. Adams was not sworn in as vice president until June 3, 1789, when the entire U.S. Senate received the oath as well. See De Pauw, ed., *Documentary History of the First Federal Congress*, vol. I, 58–59.

37. Donald Jackson and Dorothy Twohig, eds., *The Diaries of George Washington*, vol. V (Charlottesville: University Press of Virginia, 1979), 445.

38. On the partisan ramifications of these rituals, see Simon P. Newman, "'Principles or Men?' George Washington and the Political Culture of National Leadership, 1776–1801," *Journal of the Early Republic*, Vol. 12 (1992), 477–507.

39. Toasting played a significant role in the celebrations occurring during Washington's northern and southern tours of 1789 and 1791. By the time of Monroe's presidential tours, this practice was employed exclusively in the South. On the civic and gentlemanly functions of toasting, see Peter Thompson, "'The Friendly Glass': Drink and Gentility in Colonial Pennsylvania," *Pennsylvania Magazine of History and Biography*, Vol. CXIII (1989), 549–73.

40. Washington's preinaugural journey received intensive coverage from newspapers in larger cities such as Baltimore, Philadelphia, New York, Boston, and New Haven as well as smaller ones like Newport, Pennsylvania; Litchfield, Connecticut; and Cumberland, Maine. These reports encouraged the participation of those citizens living along the procession's route, as well as the involvement of those who lived farther away.

41. Twohig, ed., *The Papers of George Washington*, vol. 2, 60–61.

42. Twohig, ed., *The Papers of George Washington*, vol. 2, 59–60.

43. For a collection of the speeches delivered to and from Washington during his preinaugural journey, including those issued after he visited, see Twohig, ed., *The Papers of George Washington*, vol. 2, 59–113.

44. *Vermont Gazette*, May 11, 1789.

45. European monarchs, particularly the English Tudors and Stuarts, frequently employed triumphal arches when they made royal entries into a city or town, including the national capital. These arches announced their governing values and principles, as well as symbolizing their standing and authority. See Cole, *The Portable Queen*, and Bergeron, *English Civic Pageantry*.

46. Accounts of Washington's Philadelphia visit were published in the *New-York Packet*, May 1, 1789; the *Worcester Magazine*, May 6, 1789; the *New-Jersey Journal* (Elizabethtown), May 6, 1789; the *New-Haven Gazette, and Connecticut Magazine*, May 7, 1789; the *Newport Herald* (Pennsylvania), May 7, 1789; and the *Independent Chronicle, and Universal Advertiser* (Boston), May 8, 1789.

47. By using his artistic talents to help illustrate the nation's regard for its leader, Peale participated in a well-established artistic tradition. Leonardo da Vinci played a similar role welcoming Louis XII into Milan. See Roy Strong, *Art and Power, Renaissance Festivals, 1450–1650* (Berkeley: University of California Press, 1984), 45.

48. James Thomas Flexner, *George Washington and the New Nation (1783–1793)* (Boston: Little, Brown and Company, 1970), 175.

49. Among the newspapers covering his dramatic reception in Trenton were: the *New-York Daily Gazette*, May 1, 1789; *Pennsylvania Mercury, and Universal Advertiser* (Philadelphia), May 2, 1789; *Independent Chronicle, and Universal Advertiser*, May 8, 1789; and *American Mercury* (Hartford), May 11, 1789. See also Fitzpatrick, ed., *The Writings of George Washington*, vol. 30, 291.

50. *Daily Advertiser*, April 30, 1789; *New-York Packet*, May 1, 1789; *New-York Daily Gazette*, May 1, 1789. These accounts of the Trenton visit were widely reprinted in newspapers throughout the North.

51. *New-Jersey Journal*, April 29, 1789; *Pennsylvania Packet, and Daily Advertiser* (Philadelphia), May 5, 1789. See also Twohig, ed., *The Papers of George Washington*, vol. 2, 114.

52. Flexner, *George Washington and the New Nation*, 178–79.

53. Jackson and Twohig, eds., *The Diaries of George Washington*, vol. V, 447.

54. For pictorial images of Washington's journey and landing into New York City, see Brooks McNamara, *Day of Jubilee: The Great Age of Public Celebrations in New York, 1788–1909* (New Brunswick, N.J.: Rutgers University Press, 1997), 22–23.

55. The anthem "God save the King" was a recent addition to the British monarchy's ceremonial repertoire, having been written in 1745 to emphasize the crown's relationship to the Protestant church. Its presence in the American inauguration of 1789 illustrates the way monarchical practices traveled across the Atlantic and were adopted in the colonies, even as late as the mid-1700s. See Colley, *Britons*, 43–44. For the lyrics to the American version, see Flexner, *George Washington and the New Nation*, 179.

56. Flexner, *George Washington and the New Nation*, 180.

57. *Pennsylvania Mercury*, April 30, 1789. Similar descriptions of Washington's arrival were published in the *Pennsylvania Packet*, April 30, 1789; the *United States Chronicle*, April 30, 1789; the *New-York Journal*, April 30, 1789; the *Salem Mercury*, May 5, 1789; the *New-Hampshire Gazette*, May 6, 1789; and the *Cumberland Gazette* (Portland), May 8, 1789.

58. Twohig, ed., *The Papers of George Washington*, vol. 2, 114, as quoted in *Memoir of Life of Eliza S. M. Quincy*, 50–51.

59. *Pennsylvania Packet*, May 7, 1789. Similar comments were published in the *Federal Gazette and Philadelphia Evening Post*, May 5, 1789, and reprinted in the *Independent Chronicle and Universal Advertiser* (Boston), May 8, 1789.

60. *Boston Gazette*, May 11, 1789.

61. De Pauw, ed., *Documentary History of the First Federal Congress*, vol. I, 26 and vol. III, 32–33.

62. Bowling and Veit, eds., *Documentary History of the First Federal Congress*, vol. IX, 8.

63. Newspapers provided detailed coverage of the inaugural planning, including this controversy. For the final resolution of these arrangements, see the *New-York Packet*, May 1, 1789; *New-York Daily Gazette*, May 1, 1789; *Federal Gazette*, May 1, 1789; *Pennsylvania Mercury*, May 2, 1789; *Osborne's New-Hampshire Spy*, May 4, 1789; *Herald of Freedom, and the Federal Advertiser* (Boston), May 5, 1789; and *New-York Journal*, May 7, 1789.

64. De Pauw, ed., *Documentary History of the First Federal Congress*, vol. III, 33.

65. Adams's opposition to the oath occurring in the House of Representatives may come from his understanding of the British Parliament. The monarch's opening address to Parliament is delivered in the upper house, the House of Lords, while the lower house, the House of Commons, intentionally assembled on the periphery. See Ilse Hayden, *Symbol and Privilege: The Ritual Context of British Royalty* (Tucson: University of Arizona Press, 1987), 31, and Julian Paget, *The Pageantry of Britain* (London: Michael Joseph, 1979), 41, 45–46.

66. De Pauw, ed., *Documentary History of the First Federal Congress*, vol. III, 34.

67. De Pauw, ed., *Documentary History of the First Federal Congress*, vol. III, 39.

68. Since 1777, Livingston had served as the Chancellor of New York, a lifetime judicial position that ranked second only to the state's governor. In addition to presiding over the state's equity cases (mortgage, guardianship, insolvency, insanity, divorce) in the Chancery Court, the chancellor also had responsibility for administering the oath of office in the state of New York. See George Dangerfield, *Chancellor Robert R. Livingston of New York, 1746–1813* (New York: Harcourt, Brace and Company, 1960), 93, 185, 186, 242, 445.

69. De Pauw, ed., *Documentary History of the First Federal Congress*, vol. I, 24–25.

70. Flexner, *George Washington and the New Nation*, 185.

71. The House members on the escort committee were Egbert Benson of New York, Fisher Ames of Massachusetts, and Daniel Carroll of Maryland, and the Senate members were Richard Henry Lee of Virginia, Ralph Izard of South Carolina, and Tristram Dalton of Massachusetts. See Twohig, ed., *The Papers of George Washington*, vol. 2, 156, and De Pauw, ed., *Documentary History of the First Federal Congress*, vol. I, xxiii, and vol. III, xxvii–xxviii.

72. Washington's inauguration received extensive coverage in the nation's newspapers. See *Gazette of the United States*, April 29 to May 2, 1789; *Daily Advertiser*, May 1, 1789; *New-York Daily Gazette*, May 1, 1789; *Federal Gazette*, May 2, 1789; *Connecticut Courant* (Hartford), May 4, 1789; *Pennsylvania Packet*, May 4, 1789; *Independent Gazetteer* (Philadelphia), May 4, 1789; *Newport Mercury* (Rhode Island), May 4, 1789; *Connecticut Journal* (New Haven), May 6, 1789; *Norwich Packet and the Country Journal*, May 8, 1789; *American Herald and Worcester Recorder*, May 8, 1789; the *Independent Chronicle and Universal Advertiser*, May 8, 1789; the *Boston Gazette*, May 11, 1789; and the *Weekly Monitor*, May 11, 1789. See also Twohig, ed., *The Papers of George Washington*, vol. 2, 154, and Freeman, *George Washington*, vol. six, 189.

73. Flexner, *George Washington and the New Nation*, 186.

74. De Pauw, ed., *Documentary History of the First Federal Congress*, vol. I, 29. On the introduction of this proposal in the House of Representatives, see also the *Middlesex Gazette*,

May 2, 1789; the *Salem Mercury*, May 5, 1789; and *Osborne's New-Hampshire Spy*, May 12, 1789.

75. For a pictorial engraving of Washington receiving the oath, see McNamara, *Day of Jubilee*, 25. For a written description, see Flexner, *George Washington and the New Nation*, 187.

76. Flexner, *George Washington and the New Nation*, 187, and De Pauw, ed., *Documentary History of the First Federal Congress*, vol. I, 30.

77. This statement, posed to the crowd after Washington received the oath and permitting them to affirm his new status, reproduced a ritual found in British coronations, in which the audience in Westminster Abbey answers the question of whether they will obey the new queen by responding, "God Save Queen Elizabeth." See Paget, *The Pageantry of Britain*, 133.

78. *Federal Gazette*, May 2, 1789; *New-York Weekly Museum*, May 2, 1789.

79. Twohig, ed., *The Papers of George Washington*, vol. 2, 155, and Flexner, *George Washington and the New Nation*, 187. The decision of both Houses of Congress to stand during Washington's speech seems to be a uniquely American practice, rather than a ritual borrowed from the king's opening of parliament, particularly since the monarch was not permitted to enter the House of Commons. See Paget, *The Pageantry of Britain*, 41.

80. Twohig, ed., *The Papers of George Washington*, vol. 2, 152–53.

81. The entire speech, as delivered, is available in De Pauw, ed., *Documentary History of the First Federal Congress*, vol. I, 30–33. It was also widely reprinted in the newspapers that covered the inauguration. Washington's decision to eschew a salary was highlighted in a separate article in the *Albany Journal* (New York), May 4, 1789.

82. De Pauw, ed., *Documentary History of the First Federal Congress*, vol. I, 32.

83. Bowling and Veit, eds., *Documentary History of the First Federal Congress*, vol. IX, 11.

84. Flexner, *George Washington and the New Nation*, 187.

85. Twohig, ed., *The Papers of George Washington*, vol. 2, 155, and De Pauw, ed., *Documentary History of the First Federal Congress*, vol. I, 33, and vol. III, 43.

86. For the elaborate schedule of the inaugural fireworks, see the *New-York Journal and Weekly Register*, April 30, 1789. See also Twohig, ed., *The Papers of George Washington*, vol. 2, 155–56. The first Inaugural Ball did not occur until March 4, 1809, when Dolley Madison introduced this feminine practice to mark the beginning of her husband's presidency. See Allgor, *Parlor Politics*, 71.

87. For the House of Representatives' address, and Washington's reply, see *Gazette of the United States*, May 6 to May 9, 1789. These speeches were widely reprinted in northern newspapers. Madison was the obvious choice to write the House of Representatives' response because he had participated in the writing of Washington's inaugural address. See Twohig, ed., *The Papers of George Washington*, vol. 2, 152–53.

88. Maclay's detailed diary serves as a significant source for the early Senate debates. See Bowling and Veit, eds., *Documentary History of the First Federal Congress*, vol. IX, 16.

89. Bowling and Veit, eds., *Documentary History of the First Federal Congress*, vol. IX, 16.

90. Bowling and Veit, eds., *Documentary History of the First Federal Congress*, vol. IX, 18–19.

91. De Pauw, ed., *Documentary History of the First Federal Congress*, vol. I, 37–38, 48–49.

92. Washington's careful behavior as president was consistent with his lifelong concern with appropriate conduct. At the age of fourteen, Washington copied the 110 items that comprised the "Rules of Civility and Decent Behaviour in Company and Conversation"

as a way of guiding his youthful conduct. See Charles Moore, ed., *George Washington's Rules of Civility and Decent Behaviour in Company and Conversation* (Boston: Houghton Mifflin Company, 1926), 3–21.

93. William Maclay, who had dubbed Washington the "Great Man," provided a tart account of Washington's inauguration, including his appearance. See Bowling and Veit, eds., *Documentary History of the First Federal Congress*, vol. IX, 13, and Smith, *John Adams*, 749.

94. These sartorial choices were widely praised in newspapers as evidence of "a national spirit [that] distinguishes and adorns the present age." See *Pennsylvania Packet*, May 13, 1789; *Herald of Freedom*, May 12, 1789; and *Boston Gazette*, May 18, 1789.

95. Twohig, ed., *The Papers of George Washington*, vol. 2, 157.

96. Fisher Ames to George Richards Minot, May 3, 1789. W. B. Allen, ed., *Works of Fisher Ames*, vol. I (Indianapolis: Liberty Classics, 1983), 568.

97. Washington issued "Queries on a line of conduct to be pursued by the president" on May 10, 1789. See Twohig, *The Papers of George Washington*, vol. 2, 245–247.

98. This debate was reported in the *Daily Advertiser*, May 6, 1789; the *New-York Packet*, May 7, 1789; and the *Independent Chronicle and Universal Advertiser*, May 14, 1789.

99. May 8, 1789 entry, Diary of William Maclay, in Bowling and Veit, eds., *Documentary History of the First Federal Congress*, vol. IX, 27.

100. Bowling and Veit, eds., volumx IX, 28.
101. Bowling and Veit, eds., volumx IX, 28.
102. Bowling and Veit, eds., volumx IX, 28.
103. Bowling and Veit, eds., volumx IX, 28.
104. Bowling and Veit, eds., volumx IX, 28.
105. Bowling and Veit, eds., volumx IX, 28–29.
106. Bowling and Veit, eds., volumx IX, 29.
107. Bowling and Veit, eds., volumx IX, 30.
108. Bowling and Veit, eds., volumx IX, 31.

109. On Adams's philosophical vision, see Joseph J. Ellis, *Founding Brothers: The Revolutionary Generation* (New York: Alfred A. Knopf, 2000), 14, 167–69. On Adams's tortured relationship concerning the role of monarchy in American politics, see Louise Burnham Dunbar, *A Study of "Monarchical" Tendencies in the United States from 1776 to 1801*, vol. X, no. 1 (Urbana: University of Illinois Studies in the Social Sciences, 1922), 119.

110. May 9, 1789 entry, Diary of William Maclay, in Bowling and Veit, eds., *Documentary History of the First Federal Congress*, vol. IX, 32.

111. For the May 11 debate in the House of Representatives, see *Gazette of the United States*, May 9 to 13, 1789.

112. Not only was Madison leading the House through the debate on import duties, he also helped to pen Washington's inaugural address and the House of Representatives' response to it. See Twohig, ed., *The Papers of George Washington*, vol. 2, 152–53.

113. *The Debates and Proceedings in the Congress of the United States*, 331–34.

114. For the entire May 11 discussion, see *The Debates and Proceedings in the Congress of the United States* (Washington, D.C.: Gales and Seaton, 1834–1856), 331–34, 337.

115. May 14, 1789 entry, Diary of William Maclay, in Bowling and Veit, eds., *Documentary History of the First Federal Congress*, vol. IX, 36–37.

116. May 14, 1789 entry, Diary of William Maclay, in Bowling and Veit, eds., *Documentary History of the First Federal Congress*, vol. IX, 37.

117. *New-York Daily Gazette*, May 12, 1789.

118. For the April 8 oath, see De Pauw, ed., *Documentary History of the First Federal Congress*, vol. III, 16. For the June 2 oath, see De Pauw, ed., *Documentary History of the First Federal Congress*, vol. III, 79. For the June 3 oath, see De Pauw, ed., *Documentary History of the First Federal Congress*, vol. I, 59.

2—"To Preserve the Dignity and Respect"

1. *New-York Daily Gazette*, May 4, 1789; *New-York Packet*, May 5, 1789; *Independent Gazetteer* (Philadelphia), May 6, 1789; *Pennsylvania Packet* (Philadelphia), May 6, 1789; *Pennsylvania Mercury and Universal Advertiser* (Philadelphia), May 7, 1789; *Herald of Freedom, and Federal Advertiser* (Boston), May 8, 1789; *Connecticut Courant* (Hartford), May 11, 1789; *Cumberland Gazette* (Portland), May 14, 1789; *United States Chronicle: Political, Commercial, and Historical* (Providence), May 14, 1789.

2. For the entire query, see George Washington to John Adams, May 10, 1789, in Dorothy Twohig, ed., *The Papers of George Washington*, Presidential Series, vol. 2 (Charlottesville: University Press of Virginia, 1987), 245–47.

3. Between 1558 and 1603, Queen Elizabeth I made annual progresses during her reign as queen in which she promoted an image of an accessible monarch who ruled over all of England, not just London. Mary Hill Cole, *The Portable Queen: Elizabeth I and the Politics of Ceremony* (Amherst: University of Massachusetts Press, 1999), 1–3.

4. See Twohig, ed., *The Papers of George Washington*, vol. 2, 247.

5. The presidential title debate preoccupied the House of Representatives and particularly the Senate from May 5 to May 14, with the House discussion of May 11 marking the pivotal defeat of an embellished title. For the House debate, see *The Debates and Proceedings in the Congress of the United States*, 331–34, 337, and for the Senate proceedings, see William Maclay's diary, in Kenneth R. Bowling and Helen E. Veit, eds., *Documentary History of the First Federal Congress of the United States of America*, vol. IX (Baltimore: The Johns Hopkins University Press, 1988), 27–32, 36–37.

6. George Washington to James Madison, May 12, 1789, in Twohig, ed., *The Papers of George Washington*, vol. 2, 282.

7. Despite the speed associated with modern presidential appointments, Washington did not formally nominate his cabinet and the judicial branch until the fall of 1789, six months into his presidency, because the cabinet offices and the judiciary had to be established through legislation first. Alexander Hamilton was nominated to be secretary of the treasury on September 11, 1789, while John Jay was nominated to be chief justice of the Supreme Court on September 24, 1789. See Douglas Southall Freeman, *George Washington, a Biography: Patriot and President*, vol. six (New York: Charles Scribner's Sons, 1954), 207, and Dorothy Twohig, ed., *The Papers of George Washington*, Presidential Series, vol. 4 (Charlottesville: University Press of Virginia, 1993), 19, 75.

8. George Washington to John Jay, May 11, 1789, in Twohig, ed., *The Papers of George Washington*, vol. 2, 270. Prior to 1789, Jay had distinguished himself in foreign affairs. He had helped to negotiate the Treaty of Paris in 1783, and since 1784, he had been serving as the foreign secretary in the Confederation government. See Samuel Flagg Bemis, ed., *The American Secretaries of State and their Diplomacy*, vol. I (New York: Cooper Square Publishers, 1963)., 190–285.

9. Some histories have omitted Robert Livingston as one of Washington's five respondents. For the complete list, see Twohig, ed., *The Papers of George Washington*, vol.

2, 247n. For the written comments of Livingston, Hamilton, and Adams, see Twohig, ed., *The Papers of George Washington*, vol. 2, 192–95, 211–14, and 312–14, respectively.

10. See questions 1, 3, and 4 in the May 10 query. Twohig, ed., *The Papers of George Washington*, vol. 2, 245.

11. Question 6 in May 10 query. Twohig, ed., *The Papers of George Washington*, vol. 2, 246.

12. Question 5 in May 10 query. Twohig, ed., *The Papers of George Washington*, vol. 2, 245.

13. Question 7 in May 10 query. Twohig, ed., *The Papers of George Washington*, vol. 2, 246.

14. Question 8 in May 10 query. Twohig, ed., *The Papers of George Washington*, vol. 2, 246.

15. Question 9 in May 10 query. Twohig, ed., *The Papers of George Washington*, vol. 2, 246.

16. Twohig, ed., *The Papers of George Washington*, vol. 2, 247.

17. Although Jay's response has not been located, Washington recorded its existence and then bundled it with the "sentiments" of Adams and Hamilton. See Twohig, ed., *The Papers of George Washington*, vol. 2, 314n. Jay also corresponded with Washington on matters of housing and entertainment. On April 14, 1789, Jay offered Washington the use of his New York City home, and on November 30, 1789, the Washingtons invited the Jays to the theater. See Henry P. Johnstone, ed., *The Correspondence and Public Papers of John Jay*, vol. III (New York: Bert Franklin, 1890), 366–67, 380.

18. While no letter from Madison has been located, it is not clear Madison even sent one. During the first months of his presidency, Washington met regularly with Madison to seek his advice and help on such matters as the inaugural address and Congressional-executive interactions. Washington's cabinet had not been appointed and Madison served as a de facto aide/minister to the president. Given their frequent contact, it is possible Madison shared his opinions in person. Unlike Washington's other correspondents, Madison probably saw little political reason to produce a detailed public record on the necessity of presidential ceremony. See Charles F. Hobson and Robert A. Rutland, eds., *The Papers of James Madison*, vol. 12 (Charlottesville: University Press of Virginia, 1979), 157–58. For examples of Washington's reliance on Madison, see Twohig, ed., *The Papers of George Washington*, vol. 2, 152–54; and Dorothy Twohig, ed., *The Papers of George Washington*, Presidential Series, vol. 3 (Charlottesville: University Press of Virginia, 1989), 387, 405.

19. Livingston to Washington, May 2, 1789, in Twohig, ed., *The Papers of George Washington*, vol. 2, 193.

20. Twohig, ed., *The Papers of George Washington*, vol. 2, 194.

21. James Thomas Flexner, *George Washington and the New Nation (1783–1793)* (Boston: Little, Brown and Company, 1970), 187.

22. Livingston had been selected to preside over Washington's inauguration because one of his responsibilities as the state's chancellor was to administer the oath of office in the state of New York. See George Dangerfield, *Chancellor Robert R. Livingston of New York, 1746–1813* (New York: Harcourt, Brace and Company, 1960), 242.

23. Harold C. Syrett, ed., *The Papers of Alexander Hamilton*, vol. V (New York: Columbia University Press, 1962), 335.

24. Syrett, ed., *The Papers of Alexander Hamilton*, vol. V, 336.

25. Syrett, ed., *The Papers of Alexander Hamilton*, vol. V, 336.

26. Syrett, ed., *The Papers of Alexander Hamilton*, vol. V, 336–37.

27. Charles Francis Adams, ed., *The Works of John Adams, Second President of the United States*, vol. VIII (Boston: Little, Brown and Company, 1853), 491.

28. Adams, ed., *The Works of John Adams*, vol. VIII, 491.

29. Adams, ed., *The Works of John Adams*, vol. VIII, 492.

30. Adams, ed., *The Works of John Adams*, vol. VIII, 493.

31. On Washington's ceremonial schedule, see Stephen Decatur, Jr., *Private Affairs of George Washington, From the Records and Accounts of Tobias Lear, Esquire, his Secretary* (Boston: Houghton Mifflin Company, 1933), 39, 73–74. See also Twohig, ed., *The Papers of George Washington*, vol. 2, 247–49n, and Flexner, *George Washington and the New Nation*, 196, 200.

32. Washington dispatched William Heth to Mount Vernon to deliver a letter to Martha Washington and to make arrangements to bring her to New York City. Heth presented the letter on May 2 and wrote to Washington on May 3. Twohig, ed., *The Papers of George Washington*, vol. 2, 204.

33. Twohig, ed., *The Papers of George Washington*, vol. 2, 205n. Upon the death of her son, John Custis, in 1781, George and Martha Washington had unofficially adopted his two younger children, Eleanor and George, who resided in the presidential mansions during Washington's two terms. See Flexner, *George Washington and the New Nation*, 33, and Helen Bryan, *Martha Washington: First Lady of Liberty* (New York: John Wiley and Sons, 2002), 254, 255, and 257.

34. While Catherine Allgor's work on the political role of early presidential spouses deals briefly with Martha Washington and Abigail Adams, her primary emphasis is the political culture of Washington that began with Jefferson's presidency in 1801. See Catherine Allgor, *Parlor Politics: In Which the Ladies of Washington Help Build a City and a Government* (Charlottesville: University Press of Virginia, 2000).

35. Martha Washington described the presidential barge in a June 8, 1789 letter to her niece, Fanny Bassett Washington. See Joseph Fields, ed., *"Worthy Partner": The Papers of Martha Washington* (Westport, Ct.: Greenwood Press, 1994), 215.

36. Betty Boyd Caroli, *First Ladies* (New York: Oxford University Press, 1987), 3.

37. Caroli, *First Ladies*, 4.

38. The Washingtons later moved to a larger house at 39–41 Broadway because the Cherry Street residence proved too small. See Decatur, Jr., *Private Affairs of George Washington*, 117, 118.

39. Washington received written housing invitations from James McHenry, Elias Boudinot, Robert Morris, and John Jay, all of which he politely declined. For these letters, see Twohig, ed., *The Papers of George Washington*, vol. 2, 3, 24–25, 32–33, and Johnstone, ed., *The Correspondence and Public Papers of John Jay*, vol. III, 366–67. New York Governor George Clinton was particularly persistent, sending a second one on April 23, even though Washington had already declined his March 10 invitation. See Dorothy Twohig, ed., *The Papers of George Washington*, Presidential Series, vol. 1 (Charlottesville: University Press of Virginia, 1987), 378–79, and vol. 2, 118–19.

40. See George Washington to James McHenry, April 1, 1789, in Twohig, ed., *The Papers of George Washington*, vol. 2, 3.

41. George Washington to James Madison, March 30, 1789, in John C. Fitzpatrick, ed., *The Writings of George Washington*, vol. 30 (Washington, D.C.: U.S. Government Printing Office, 1939), 254–56.

42. Twohig, ed., *The Papers of George Washington*, vol. 2, 248n. De Pauw, ed., *Documentary History of the First Federal Congress*, vol. I, 16–17, and Linda Grant DePauw,

Documentary History of the First Federal Congress of the United States of America, 1789-1791, vol. III (Baltimore: The Johns Hopkins University Press, 1977), 23.

43. Stanley Elkins and Eric McKittrick, *The Age of Federalism: The Early American Republic, 1788-1800* (New York: Oxford University Press, 1993), 172.

44. Decatur, Jr., 43.

45. Decatur, Jr., 44.

46. This description comes from Decatur, Jr., *Private Affairs of George Washington*, 44.

47. See Fields, ed., *"Worthy Partner,"* xxvi.

48. Decatur, Jr., *Private Affairs of George Washington*, 106-7, 137-38. Caroli, *First Ladies*, 7.

49. Twohig, ed., *The Papers of George Washington*, vol. 2, 247n.

50. Twohig, ed., vol. 2, 248n.

51. Decatur, Jr., *Private Affairs of George Washington*, 56, 92. Freeman, *Affairs of Honor*, 45-46. Washington repeatedly mentioned his morning horseback rides in his diary. See Donald Jackson and Dorothy Twohig, eds., *The Diaries of George Washington*, vols. V and VI (Charlottesville: University Press of Virginia, 1979).

52. Decatur, Jr., *Private Affairs of George Washington*, 52.

53. Decatur, Jr., 26, 96-98.

54. *Gazette of the United States*, May 9 to 13, 1789; *Middlesex Gazette* (Middletown, Connecticut), May 16, 1789.

55. Decatur, Jr., 73-74.

56. Watson, John F., *Annals of Philadelphia and Pennsylvania in the olden time*, vol. I (Philadelphia: Elijah Thomas, 1857), 578.

57. Allgor, *Parlor Politics*, 20.

58. Letter to Fanny Bassett Washington, October 23, 1789, in Fields, ed., *"Worthy Partner,"* 220.

59. Her desire to return to Mount Vernon was expressed in a letter to Mercy Otis Warren, December 26, 1789. Fields, ed., *"Worthy Partner,"* 223.

60. The term *republican court*, originally coined by Abigail Adams, has been used by contemporaries and historians to describe the complex social interactions that occurred during the presidencies of Washington and Adams. The term has been used as a positive description, as well as an epithet by political opponents who saw the "republican court" as aristocratic and a threat to republican government. For recent historians, the phrase connotes a social space that permitted the political participation of women as well as men. While "republican court" is useful in describing drawing rooms and levees, it excludes the more accessible parts of Washington's social calendar, such as his tours and his open visiting hours. On Adams's origination of the term, see Elizabeth Ellet, *The Court Circles of the Republic* (Hartford: Hartford Publishing Company, 1869), 19. For historical accounts of the republican court, see Rufus Wilmot Griswold, *The Republican Court; or, American Society in the Days of Washington* (New York: D. Appleton and Company, 1867). See also Allgor, *Parlor Politics*, 20, 74, 99-100, and Freeman, *Affairs of Honor*, 6, as well as the unpublished papers by David S. Shields and Fredrika J. Teute.

61. Congress had established Philadelphia as the nation's temporary capital until 1800, when the permanent capital would be situated somewhere along the Potomac River. Washington himself chose the specific site on January 24, 1791. See Elkins and McKittrick, *The Age of Federalism*, 172, and Decatur, Jr., *Private Affairs of George Washington*, 40, 153.

62. Decatur, Jr., 158.

63. Decatur, Jr., 177, 179, 249, 290.

64. Although we think of interior decorating as a feminine concern, in the eighteenth century upper-class men focused on such matters. See Richard L. Bushman, *The Refinement of America: Persons, Houses, Cities* (New York: Alfred A. Knopf, 1992), 441.

65. Originally appearing in the *Gazette of the United States* (New York) on May 6, 1789; this posting was reprinted on numerous occasions in newspapers throughout New York, Philadelphia, and New England.

66. *New-York Daily Gazette*, May 7, 1789. This commentary was reprinted in the *Connecticut Courant*, May 11, 1789; *Federal Gazette, and Philadelphia Evening Post*, May 12, 1789; *Middlesex Gazette*, May 16, 1789; and *Boston Gazette*, May 18, 1789.

67. Mark A. Mastromarino, ed., *The Papers of George Washington*, Presidential Series, vol. 6 (Charlottesville: University Press of Virginia, 1996), 399n4. Decatur, Jr., *Private Affairs of George Washington*, 159.

68. Washington to Tobias Lear, September 5, 1790, in Mastromarino, ed., *The Papers of George Washington*, vol. 6, 397.

69. In the September 5 letter, Washington summarized who comprised his family. See Mastromarino, ed., *The Papers of George Washington*, vol. 6, 397.

70. While Decatur has Washington leaving New York on August 30, Elkins and McKittrick mention August 12 instead. On his departure from New York, see Decatur, Jr., *Private Affairs of George Washington*, 150, and Elkins and McKittrick, *The Age of Federalism*, 172. For his arrival in Philadelphia, see Mastromarino, ed., *The Papers of George Washington*, vol. 6, 399n2.

71. Washington to Lear, November 14, 1790, in Mastromarino, ed., *The Papers of George Washington*, vol. 6, 653.

72. Mastromarino, ed., *The Papers of George Washington*, vol. 6, 690n4 Decatur, Jr., *Private Affairs of George Washington*, 161.

73. Washington to Lear, September 26, 1791, in John C. Fitzpatrick, ed., *The Writings of George Washington*, vol. 31 (Washington, D.C.: U.S. Government Printing Office, 1939), 376.

74. See Dorothy Twohig, Mark A. Mastromarino, and Jack D. Warren, eds., *The Papers of George Washington*, Presidential Series, vol. 5 (Charlottesville: University Press of Virginia, 1996), 192–93, and Mastromarino, ed., *The Papers of George Washington*, vol. 6, 578n2.

75. On staffing needs, see Washington to Lear, September 20, 1790, in Mastromarino, ed., *The Papers of George Washington*, vol. 6, 481–83. See also Decatur, Jr., *Private Affairs of George Washington*, 12–13, 22–23, 93, 103, 121, 203, 214.

76. Decatur, Jr., *Private Affairs of George Washington*, 32, 39.

77. Peter Kolchin, *American Slavery, 1619–1877* (New York: Hill and Wang, 1993), 78.

78. Henry Wieneck, *An Imperfect God: George Washington, His Slaves, and the Creation of America* (New York: Farrar, Straus, and Giroux, 2003), 313.

79. Kolchin, *American Slavery*, 78.

80. Lear to Washington, April 5, 1791, and Washington to Lear, April 12, 1791, in Mark A. Mastromarino, ed., *The Papers of George Washington*, Presidential Series, vol. 8, 67–68n3; 84–86.

81. Lear to Washington, April 24, 1791, in Mastromarino, ed., *The Papers of George Washington*, vol. 8, 129–33, 133n4, 134n5, and Decatur, Jr., *Private Affairs of George Washington*, 225.

82. Joseph Ellis argues that the American republic succeeded, in part, because the

Notes to Pages 49–52 **193**

founding generation avoided confronting the controversial issue of slavery. See Joseph J. Ellis, *Founding Brothers: The Revolutionary Generation* (New York: Alfred A. Knopf, 2000), 17–18.

83. For a comprehensive account of both his New England and his southern tours, see Washington's writings, particularly his diary. Jackson and Twohig, eds., *The Diaries of George Washington*, vols. V and VI. Washington's diary is missing for the period of his preinaugural tour. See also Twohig et al., eds., *The Papers of George Washington*, vols. 4, 5, and 6 (Charlottesville: University Press of Virginia, 1993, 1996).

84. North Carolina and Rhode Island did not approve the Constitution until November 26, 1789, and May 29, 1790, respectively. See Freeman, *George Washington*, vol. six, 143, 246, 268.

85. *Gazette of the United States*, October 14, 1789; *Federal Gazette*, October 16, 1789; *Salem Mercury*, October 20, 1789; and *Newport Mercury* (Rhode Island), October 21, 1789.

86. *Connecticut Gazette* (New London), October 23, 1789.

87. *Gazette of the United States*, October 21, 1789; *Pennsylvania Packet, and Daily Advertiser* (Philadelphia), October 24, 1789.

88. *Gazette of the United States*, October 14, 1789. This interpretation of the president's visit was widely reprinted. See the *Federal Gazette*, October 16, 1789; the *Independent Gazetteer*, October 16, 1789; *United States Chronicle*, October 22, 1789. On Fenno's efforts in producing a nationalist newspaper, see Jeffrey L. Pasley, *"The Tyranny of Printers": Newspaper Politics in the Early American Republic* (Charlottesville: University Press of Virginia, 2001), 51–60.

89. By September 26, 1789, the Senate had confirmed Washington's four-member cabinet. See Elkins and McKittrick, *The Age of Federalism*, 52.

90. Washington made these entries on October 5, 6, 7, and 8, 1789. Donald Jackson and Dorothy Twohig, eds., *The Diaries of George Washington*, vol. V (Charlottesville: University Press of Virginia, 1979), 452–53, 454, 456.

91. Jackson and Twohig, eds., *The Diaries of George Washington*, vol. V, 460.

92. Flexner, *George Washington and the New Nation*, 229.

93. *Herald of Freedom*, October 27, 1789; *Independent Chronicle and the Universal Advertiser* (Boston), October 29, 1789.

94. For the addresses delivered to and from Washington, see Twohig, ed., *The Papers of George Washington*, vol. 4, 198–277.

95. Prior to embarking on his tour, Washington wrote to his sister, Betty Washington, on October 12, 1789, describing an "epidemical cold" spreading through the northeast. Twohig, ed., *The Papers of George Washington*, vol. 4, 162.

96. Twohig, ed., *The Papers of George Washington*, vol. 4, 162–63n2.

97. The *Providence Gazette* (Rhode Island), November 7, 1789, and the *United States Chronicle*, November 12, 1789, reported on the spread of influenza into the eastern states.

98. Twohig, ed., *The Papers of George Washington*, vol. 4, 237n.

99. Twohig, ed., *The Papers of George Washington*, vol. 4, 280n2.

100. These paintings can be found in Twohig, ed., *The Papers of George Washington*, vol. 4, 286–89, 290–91.

101. Washington's own account of this struggle with Hancock can be found in his diary entries for October 24 and 25. See Jackson and Twohig, eds., *The Diaries of George Washington*, vol. V, 473–77. See also Twohig, ed., *The Papers of George Washington*, vol. 4, 228–29, and Flexner, *George Washington and the New Nation*, 230,

102. For a more sympathetic account of Governor Hancock's incapacitation, see the *Essex*

Journal (Newburyport, Massachusetts), October 28, 1789; *Independent Chronicle*, October 29, 1789; *New-Hampshire Gazette, and General Advertiser* (Portsmouth), October 29, 1789.

103. *Gazette of the United States*, November 14, 1789; *Independent Gazetteer*, November 19, 1789; *Connecticut Courant*, November 23, 1789. See also Jackson and Twohig, eds., *The Diaries of George Washington*, vol. V, 487, 491, and 497.

104. Mastromarino, ed., *The Papers of George Washington*, vol. 6, 280n.

105. *Connecticut Courant*, August 18, 1789. See also Mastromarino, ed., *The Papers of George Washington*, vol. 6, 281n.

106. *Newport Mercury*, August 23, 1790. See also Mastromarino, ed., *The Papers of George Washington*, vol. 6, 281n2, 283–87, 299–303.

107. *Providence Gazette*, August 21, 1790.

108. *Providence Gazette*, August 21, 1790.

109. *Boston Gazette*, August 23, 1790.

110. See Mastromarino, ed., *The Papers of George Washington*, vol. 6, 305n4, and Freeman, *George Washington, a Biography: Patriot and President*, 275.

111. See Washington's March 16, 1791, letter to David Humphreys in Jack D. Warren, Jr., ed., *The Papers of George Washington*, Presidential Series, vol. 7 (Charlottesville: University Press of Virginia, 1998), 584.

112. During the summer of 1791, Secretary of State Jefferson and Congressman Madison embarked on their own trip, traveling through New York State and New England. See Tobias Lear to George Washington, June 19–20, 1791, in Mastromarino, ed., *The Papers of George Washington*, vol. 8, 279.

113. Warren, Jr., ed., *The Papers of George Washington*, vol. 7, 473n.

114. Washington's surprising anonymity in the South highlighted crucial differences in the economic and social organization of these two regions. The South was primarily an agricultural region, and its population organized itself into scattered, self-contained units ranging from small farms to vast plantations dominated by the landowner. The North arranged itself into an interdependent cluster of towns, villages, and hamlets that required print communication networks to facilitate the exchange of information. Numerous newspapers flourished in the northern states out of necessity, while in the southern states, sharing information was not vital to the region's economic survival. See Stephanie McCurry, *Masters of Small Worlds: Yeoman Households, Gender Relations, and the Political Culture of the Antebellum South Low Country* (New York: Oxford University Press, 1995), and William J. Gilmore, *Reading Becomes a Necessity of Life: Material and Cultural Life in Rural New England, 1780–1835* (Knoxville: University of Tennessee Press, 1989).

115. For example, between 1789 and 1791, South Carolina and North Carolina had six newspapers combined, while New York City alone had six and Boston had seven. See Clarence S. Brigham, *History and Bibliography of American Newspapers, 1690–1820*, vols. I and II (Worcester, Mass.: American Antiquarian Society, 1947). On Washington's unexpected arrivals, see Flexner, *George Washington and the New Nation*, 287–88.

116. *Dunlap's American Daily Advertiser* (Philadelphia), April 21, 1791.

117. Washington's diaries were filled with disparaging comments regarding the shoddy accommodations available in the North and especially the South. These observations are particularly persuasive coming from a man reputed to have slept in as many places as Washington had. See Donald Jackson and Dorothy Twohig, eds., *The Diaries of George Washington*, vols. V and VI (Charlottesville: University Press of Virginia, 1979).

118. For Washington's description of this incident, see his April 20, 1791 diary entry

in Jackson and Twohig, eds., *The Diaries of George Washington*, vol. VI, 115, 116n.

119. By contrast, Washington's New England tour was roughly 550 miles based on the author's modern mileage estimates. For the southern tour total, see Flexner, *George Washington and the New Nation*, 289.

120. The poor southern roads were particularly hard on the team of horses that traveled with the president. See Mastromarino, ed., *The Papers of George Washington*, vol. 8, 23–24n.

121. In a March 28, 1790, letter to David Stuart, Washington commented on the "jealousies . . . poisoning the minds of the Southern people" and the general need to unite Americans around their national, rather than regional, interests. See Twohig, Mastromarino, and Warren, eds., *The Papers of George Washington*, vol. 5, 286–87.

122. *Middlesex Gazette*, May 21, 1791; *City Gazette and Daily Advertiser* (Charleston), May 24, 1791. See also Jackson and Twohig, eds., *The Diaries of George Washington*, vol. VI, 128n, 136–37n.

123. *City Gazette and Daily Advertiser*, May 14, 1791. Trumbull completed the painting, entitled *George Washington before the Battle of Trenton*, and delivered a copy of it to the city of Charleston in 1792. This painting is available at the National Portrait Gallery's exhibition site entitled: "George and Martha Washington: Portraits from the Presidential Years."

124. *City Gazette and Daily Advertiser*, May 14, 1791.

125. *Gazette of the United States*, June 22, 1791. Jackson and Twohig, eds., *The Diaries of George Washington*, vol. VI, 163.

126. On the rituals associated with a royal progress, see Cole, *The Portable Queen*, 122, 124, 125.

127. This discussion has benefited from Clifford Geertz, *Negara: The Theatre State in Nineteenth-century Bali* (Princeton: Princeton University Press, 1980), and Clifford Geertz, "Centers, Kings, and Charisma: Reflections on the Symbolics of Power," in *Culture and Its Creators*, Joseph Ben-David and Terry Nichols Clark, eds. (Chicago: University of Chicago Press, 1977).

128. Catherine Macaulay Graham (1731–1791), also known as Catherine Macaulay, wrote the eight-volume *The History of England from the Accession of James to that of the Brunswick Line*, published between 1763 and 1783. Macaulay Graham visited Mount Vernon in June 1785, and afterwards, she and Washington exchanged ten letters on a variety of matters, including the state of republican government in America. See Bridget Hill, *The Republican Virago: The Life and Times of Catherine Macaulay, Historian* (Oxford: Clarendon Press, 1992), 26–39, 126–27.

129. Washington to Catherine Macaulay Graham, January 9, 1790, in Twohig, ed., *The Papers of George Washington*, vol. 4, 551–54.

130. Washington to Catherine Macaulay Graham, July 19, 1791, Mastromarino, ed., *The Papers of George Washington*, vol. 8, 357–58.

131. Washington to David Humphreys, July 20, 1791, Mastromarino, ed., *The Papers of George Washington*, vol. 8, 359.

132. Elkins and McKittrick, *The Age of Federalism*, 257, 282, 288.

133. Ellis, *Founding Brothers*, 22, 60.

134. Originally published in Freneau's *Jersey Chronicle* (Mount Pleasant) and then reprinted in the *New York Argus* on December 26, 1795. See also J. A. Carrroll and M. W. Ashworth, *George Washington, First in Peace*, vol. 7 (New York: Charles Scribner's Sons, 1957), 321n.

135. Dr. David Stuart, a physician by training and a planter by profession, was a member of the extended Washington-Custis family. He was married to Eleanor Calvert Custis, the widow of John Parke Custis, a son of Martha Washington. After her son's death in 1781, George and Martha Washington raised his two younger children. Later, Washington named Stuart as one of three commissioners to launch the new capital in Washington, D.C. See Flexner, *George Washington and the New Nation*, 33, 327, and Bryan, *Martha Washington*, 254, 255, 263.

136. Washington to David Stuart, July 26, 1789. Twohig, ed., *The Papers of George Washington*, vol. 3, 322–23.

137. Washington to David Stuart, June 15, 1790. Twohig, Mastromarino, and Warren, eds., *The Papers of George Washington*, vol. 5, 526.

138. Washington to David Stuart, June 15, 1790. Twohig, Mastromarino, and Warren, eds., *The Papers of George Washington*, vol. 5, 527.

139. Elkins and McKittrick, *The Age of Federalism*, 266.

140. *The Diary, or Loudon's Register* (New York), March 6, 1793. *Federal Gazette*, March 6, 1793. *Gazette of the United States*, March 6, 1793. *National Gazette* (Philadelphia), March 6, 1793.

141. David Waldstreicher, *In the Midst of Perpetual Fetes: The Making of American Nationalism, 1776–1820* (Chapel Hill: University of North Carolina Press, 1997), 154, 155, 192; Simon P. Newman, *Parades and Politics of the Street: Festive Culture in the Early American Republic* (Philadelphia: University of Pennsylvania Press, 1997), 60.

142. *Dunlap's American Daily Advertiser* (Philadelphia), March 6, 1793; *American Mercury* (Hartford), March 6, 1797; *Gazette of the United States*, March 7, 1797; *Massachusetts Mercury* (Boston), March 7, 1797.

143. Freeman, *Affairs of Honor*, 14–15.

144. Joyce Appleby, *Capitalism and a New Social Order: The Republican Vision of the 1790s* (New York: New York University Press, 1984), 70–71, 73–74.

145. Carrroll, J. A., and M. W. Ashworth, *George Washington, First in Peace* (New York: Charles Scribner's Sons, 1957), vol. 7, 227, 414, 427, 430–31, 434.

146. Ellis, *Founding Brothers*, 186–88.

147. The Twelfth Amendment to the Constitution resolved this problem by creating separate ballots for the presidential and vice presidential candidates.

148. Ellis, *Founding Brothers*, 156.

149. David McCullough, *John Adams* (New York: Simon and Schuster, 2001), 468.

150. McCullough, *John Adams*, 470.

151. *The Diary*, March 6, 1797.

152. *Claypoole's American Daily Advertiser*, March 6, 1797; *Philadelphia Gazette and Universal Daily Advertiser*, March 6, 1797.

153. On Abigail Adams's role as first spouse, see Lynne Withey, *Dearest Friend: A Life of Abigail Adams* (New York: The Free Press, 1981), 213, 249, and Caroli, *First Ladies*, 8, 9.

154. Elkins and McKittrick, *The Age of Federalism*, 590–92; Ellis, *Founding Brothers*, 190–91.

155. James Morton Smith, *Freedom's Fetters: The Alien and Sedition Laws and American Civil Liberties* (Ithaca: Cornell University Press, 1956), 270.

156. Smith, *Freedom's Fetters*, 270–71.

157. Smith, *Freedom's Fetters*, 271, 271n75.

3—"We Deal in Ink Only"

1. A rich literature exists on the transition from Federalist politics and the ascent of Jefferson's Democratic-Republicans. See Sean Wilentz, *The Rise of American Democracy: Jefferson to Lincoln* (New York: W.W. Norton, 2005); John Ferling, *Adams vs. Jefferson: The Tumultuous Election of 1800* (New York: Oxford University Press, 2004); Edward J. Larson, *A Magnificent Catastrophe: The Tumultuous Election of 1800: America's First Presidential Campaign* (New York: Free Press, 2007); Joseph J. Ellis, *Founding Brothers: The Revolutionary Generation* (New York: Alfred A. Knopf, 2000); Joseph J. Ellis, *American Sphinx: The Character of Thomas Jefferson* (New York: Alfred A. Knopf, 1997); Stanley Elkins and Eric McKittrick, *The Age of Federalism: The Early American Republic, 1788-1800* (New York: Oxford University Press, 1993); Joyce Appleby, *Capitalism and a New Social Order: The Republican Vision of the 1790s* (New York: New York University Press, 1984); Daniel Sisson, *The American Revolution of 1800* (New York: Alfred A. Knopf, 1974); Noble E. Cunningham, Jr., *The Jeffersonian Republicans: The Formation of Party Organization, 1789-1801* (Chapel Hill: University of North Carolina Press, 1957), and *The Jeffersonian Republicans in Power: Party Operations, 1801-1809* (Chapel Hill: University of North Carolina Press, 1963).

2. Jefferson demonstrated a mastery of the rules of republican politics, many of which he pioneered. First, a national candidate demonstrated his worthiness to hold office by denying any interest in the position. Second, letters from a national candidate to his allies were not private, but instead contained ideas to be disseminated, without publicly mentioning the source. Third, allies and surrogates took action on behalf of the national candidate, through legislation, pamphlets, or newspaper pieces, again disguising their political connections. See Joanne B. Freeman, *Affairs of Honor: National Politics in the New Republic* (New Haven: Yale University Press, 2001), 114, 116, 118, 140, and M. J. Heale, *The Presidential Quest: Candidates and Images in American Political Culture, 1787-1852* (London: Longman, 1982), 1-22.

3. Elkins and McKittrick, *The Age of Federalism*, 288, 290.

4. The Twelfth Amendment to the Constitution, ratified in 1804, rectified this problem.

5. Jefferson to Benjamin Rush, January 22, 1797, in Barbara B. Oberg, ed., *The Papers of Thomas Jefferson*, vol. 29 (Princeton: Princeton University Press, 2002), 275.

6. The Senate had confirmed Washington's four-member cabinet by September 26, 1789, although Jefferson did not assume his duties until March 21, 1790. See Elkins and McKittrick, *The Age of Federalism*, 52, and Dorothy Twohig, ed., *The Papers of George Washington*, Presidential Series, vol. 5 (Charlottesville: University Press of Virginia, 1996), 302n.

7. Ellis, *American Sphinx*, 116.

8. Ellis, *American Sphinx*, 98-105.

9. Jefferson's accusations of corruption and intrigue seemed to sometimes border on the paranoid. This approach to republican politics was common in the 1790s, as the nation's leaders struggled to faithfully fulfill the Constitution's mandate. See Ellis, *American Sphinx*, 131-33.

10. Ellis, *Founding Brothers*, 48-50.

11. Jefferson to George Washington, September 9, 1792, in John Catanzariti, ed., *The Papers of Thomas Jefferson*, vol. 24 (Princeton: Princeton University Press, 1990), 352.

12. Catanzariti, ed., *The Papers of Thomas Jefferson*, vol. 24, 353.

13. Catanzariti, ed., *The Papers of Thomas Jefferson*, vol. 24, 26.

14. Notes of a Conversation with George Washington, February 7, 1793, in John Catanzariti, ed., *The Papers of Thomas Jefferson*, vol. 25 (Princeton: Princeton University Press, 1992), 153–55. See also his Notes on a Conversation with George Washington from December 27, 1792, in Catanzariti, ed., *The Papers of Thomas Jefferson*, vol. 24, 793–94n.

15. Cunningham, *The Jeffersonian Republicans: The Formation of Party Organization, 1789-1801*, 24. For further reactions to the Democratic-Republican attacks, see the *Gazette of the United States* (New York), June 23 and June 27, 1792.

16. Notes of Agenda to Reduce the Government to True Principles, July 11, 1792, in Catanzariti, ed., *The Papers of Thomas Jefferson*, vol. 24, 215.

17. On his involvement in these resolutions, see his Notes on the Giles Resolution, March 2, 1793, and his letter to Thomas Mann Randolph, Jr., March 3, 1793, in Catanzariti, ed., *The Papers of Thomas Jefferson*, vol. 25, 311–12, 313–14. See also Joseph J. Ellis, *American Creation: Triumphs and Tragedies at the Founding of the Republic* (New York: Alfred A. Knopf, 2007), 184–86, and Cunningham, *The Jeffersonian Republicans*, 50–54.

18. Ellis, *American Sphinx*, 122–23.

19. Jefferson to Lafayette, June 16, 1792, in Catanzariti, ed., *The Papers of Thomas Jefferson*, vol. 24, 85–86; and Jefferson to Brissot de Warville, May 8, 1793, in Catanzariti, ed., *The Papers of Thomas Jefferson*, vol. 25, 679. Freeman, *Affairs of Honor*, 124.

20. Jefferson relied on his sons-in-law, Thomas Mann Randolph and John Wayles Eppes, as political confidants and surrogates, particularly Randolph, who was the husband of Jefferson's eldest daughter, Martha. The Randolphs lived closer to Monticello than the Eppeses, permitting Jefferson to form a close relationship with Randolph. Because of the need for political discretion, family members became trusted allies during the electoral struggles of the 1790s. Sons-in-law were of particular importance to the first six presidents because only John Adams produced a male heir. For Jefferson and Monroe, who had daughters, their sons-in-law filled the political role a son might have. Washington and Madison did not have children of their own, and Adams's son became the sixth president of the United States. See Ellis, *American Sphinx*, 134–36, and Ellis, *Founding Brothers*, 169. Jefferson to Thomas Mann Randolph, June 2, 1793, in John Catanzariti, ed., *The Papers of Thomas Jefferson*, vol. 26, 169, and Jefferson to Thomas Mann Randolph, January 7, 1793, in Catanzariti, ed., *The Papers of Thomas Jefferson*, vol. 25, 30.

21. Notes on a Conversation with George Washington, May 23, 1793, in Catanzariti, ed., *The Papers of Thomas Jefferson*, vol. 26, 101–2.

22. Notes on a Conversation with George Washington, August 6, 1793, in Catanzariti, ed., *The Papers of Thomas Jefferson*, vol. 26, 628.

23. On the importance of political gossip and the channels for disseminating it, see Freeman, *Affairs of Honor*, 66–91.

24. Notes on Conversations with John Beckley and George Washington, June 7, 1793, in Catanzariti, ed., *The Papers of Thomas Jefferson*, vol. 26, 219–20, and 220n. Freeman, *Affairs of Honor*, 22, 130.

25. See Catanzariti, ed., *The Papers of Thomas Jefferson*, vol. 26, 220n.

26. Ferling, *Adams vs. Jefferson*; Cunningham, *The Jeffersonian Republicans*, 97, 132, 198, 212.

27. Notes on a Conversation with Tench Coxe, December 27, 1797, in Barbara B. Oberg, ed., *The Papers of Thomas Jefferson*, vol. 29 (Princeton: Princeton University Press, 2002), 596.

28. Notes on Conversations with Abraham Baldwin, John Brown, and John Hunter,

March 11, 1798, in Barbara B. Oberg, ed., *The Papers of Thomas Jefferson*, vol. 30 (Princeton: Princeton University Press, 2003), 172–73.

29. Wilentz, *The Rise of American Democracy*, 52, and Elkins and McKittrick, *The Age of Federalism*, 282.

30. Jefferson to Thomas Mann Randolph, Jr., March 3, 1793, in Catanzariti, ed., *The Papers of Thomas Jefferson*, vol. 25, 314.

31. See Heale, *The Presidential Quest*, 1–22.

32. Wilentz, *The Rise of American Democracy*, 53–54, 61.

33. Ellis, *American Creation*, 189–90.

34. Ellis, *Founding Brothers*, 136, 145, 170.

35. Notes of Cabinet Meeting Edmond Charles Genet, August 20, 1793, in Catanzariti, ed., *The Papers of Thomas Jefferson*, vol. 26, 730–32. Ellis, *American Creation*, 190–91, Wilentz, *The Rise of American Democracy*, 59–60.

36. Jefferson to James Madison, August 11, 1793, in Catanzariti, ed., *The Papers of Thomas Jefferson*, vol. 26, 652.

37. For a history of the Society of Cincinnati, see Minor Myers, *Liberty without Anarchy: A History of the Society of Cincinnati*, (Charlottesville: University Press of Virginia, 1983).

38. Jefferson to James Madison, December 28, 1794, in Catanzariti, ed., *The Papers of Thomas Jefferson*, vol. 28 (Princeton: Princeton University Press, 2000), 228.

39. Jefferson to William Branch Giles, December 17, 1794, in Catanzariti, ed., *The Papers of Thomas Jefferson*, vol. 28 (Princeton: Princeton University Press, 2000), 219.

40. Ellis, *American Creation*, 195–96; Wilentz, *The Rise of American Democracy*, 62–65.

41. Jefferson submitted his resignation letter on July 31, 1793, but extended his tenure until the end of the year, at Washington's request. See Jefferson to George Washington, July 31, 1793, in Catanzariti, ed., *The Papers of Thomas Jefferson*, vol. 26, 593–94, and Jefferson to George Washington, December 31, 1793, in John Catanzariti, ed., *The Papers of Thomas Jefferson*, vol. 27 (Princeton: Princeton University Press, 1997), 656. Wilentz, *The Rise of American Democracy*, 72.

42. On Washington's retirement and the first partisan presidential election, see Wilentz, *The Rise of American Democracy*, 73, and Ellis, *American Sphinx*, 164. On Washington's retirement and the implications of his decision to eschew a third term, see Ellis, *Founding Brothers*, 122–28.

43. Ellis, *Founding Brothers*, 179–84.

44. Jefferson to James Madison, January 1, 1797, in Oberg, ed., *The Papers of Thomas Jefferson*, vol. 29, 248.

45. Jefferson to James Madison, January 22, 1797, in Oberg, ed., *The Papers of Thomas Jefferson*, vol. 29, 271.

46. Jefferson to James Madison, January 22, 1797, in Oberg, ed., *The Papers of Thomas Jefferson*, vol. 29, 271.

47. Jefferson to Thomas Mann Randolph, January 22, 1797, and Jefferson to George Wythe, January 22, 1797, in Oberg, ed., *The Papers of Thomas Jefferson*, vol. 29, 273–74, 275–76.

48. On the role of newspapers as partisan organs, see Jeffrey L. Pasley, *"The Tyranny of Printers": Newspaper Politics in the Early American Republic* (Charlottesville: University Press of Virginia, 2001), and Freeman, *Affairs of Honor*, 182–84.

49. Archibald Stuart (1757–1832) served as a lawyer and a judge in Virginia, having studied law with Jefferson in the early 1780s. He embraced the Republican party in the early 1790s and became a reliable supporter of Jefferson and Madison in Virginia politics. See

John A. Garraty and Mark C. Carnes, eds., *American National Biography*, vol. 21 (New York: Oxford University Press, 1999), 64–65. Jefferson to Archibald Stuart, May 14, 1799, in Oberg, ed., *The Papers of Thomas Jefferson*, vol. 31 (Princeton: Princeton University Press, 2004), 110.

50. Richard R. John, *Spreading the News: The American Postal System from Franklin to Morse* (Cambridge: Harvard University Press, 1995), 31.

51. Cunningham, *The Jeffersonian Republicans*, 19, 24.

52. Cunningham, *The Jeffersonian Republicans in Power*, 253–54.

53. This newspaper was not successfully launched. Jefferson to Tench Coxe, May 21, 1799, in Oberg, ed., *The Papers of Thomas Jefferson*, vol. 31, 113, 114n.

54. Jefferson to James Madison, March 29, 1798, in Oberg, ed., *The Papers of Thomas Jefferson*, vol. 30, 227.

55. Jefferson to James Madison, September 21, 1795, in Catanzariti, ed., *The Papers of Thomas Jefferson*, vol. 28, 476.

56. Jefferson to Edmund Pendleton, April 22, 1799, in Oberg, ed., *The Papers of Thomas Jefferson*, vol. 31, 97.

57. Edmund Pendleton of Virginia (1721–1803) distinguished himself as one of America's leading lawyers during and after the American Revolution. Like many of Jefferson's supporters, Pendleton became increasingly dismayed by Federalist policies and outspoken in his support for the Republican cause. See Garraty and Carnes eds., *American National Biography*, vol. 17, 275–77.

58. In addition to Charles Pinckney, Edmund Pendleton and John Page had defected from the Federalist party.

59. Jefferson to Charles Pinckney, October 29, 1799, in Oberg, ed., *The Papers of Thomas Jefferson*, vol. 31, 227, 228n.

60. See Charles Pinckney (1757–1824) in Garraty and Carnes, eds., *American National Biography*, vol. 17, 533–36. On his efforts during the 1800 presidential election, see Wilentz, *The Rise of American Democracy*, 91–92.

61. Joseph J. Ellis generously refers to this burgeoning gap between Jefferson's claims and his actions as a "cultivated tolerance for inconsistency." See *American Sphinx*, 122.

62. On Mazzei, see Garraty and Carnes, eds., *American National Biography*, vol. 14, 803–4.

63. Jefferson to Philip Mazzei, April 24, 1796, in Oberg, ed., *The Papers of Thomas Jefferson*, vol. 29, 82.

64. See Ellis, *Founding Brothers*, 141, 145.

65. Mazzei initially disseminated this letter to a French newspaper, where the *Minerva*'s editor, Noah Webster, eventually obtained it. Oberg, ed., *The Papers of Thomas Jefferson*, vol. 29, 74–75n.

66. For Jefferson's efforts to manage the Mazzei controversy, see his letters to John Carey and James Madison, November 10, 1796, and August 3, 1797, respectively, and Madison's reply to Jefferson on August 5, 1797, in Oberg, ed., vol. 29, 205, 489, 505.

67. While Jefferson's reaction to the U.S. Post Office might seem excessive, partisan postmasters could wield considerable influence as letters and newspapers passed through offices. See Freeman, *Affairs of Honor*, 144–45.

68. Jefferson to James Madison, November 22, 1799, in Oberg, ed., vol. 31, 241.

69. Jefferson to Tadeusz Kosciuszko, February 21, 1799, in Oberg, ed., vol. 31, 52.

70. Elkins and McKittrick, *The Age of Federalism*, 719.

71. Wilentz, *The Rise of American Democracy*, 78

72. As quoted in Elkins and McKittrick, *The Age of Federalism*, 590–91. For the full text of these four laws, see James Morton Smith, *Freedom's Fetters: The Alien and Sedition Laws and American Civil Liberties* (Ithaca: Cornell University Press, 1967), 435–42.

73. Kentucky and Virginia passed these resolutions on November 13 and December 24, 1798, respectively. See Elkins and McKittrick, *The Age of Federalism*, 719.

74. For the background history of the Kentucky Resolutions, including the draft and adopted versions, see Oberg, ed., *The Papers of Thomas Jefferson*, vol. 30, 529–35.

75. Elkins and McKittrick, *The Age of Federalism*, 720 and 902n72.

76. Conveniently for the Republicans, the English Parliament had recently passed their own version of the Alien and Sedition Acts, consisting of the Alien Act in 1793, the Treasonable Practices Act in 1795, and the Seditious Meetings Act in 1795. See Elkins and McKittrick, *The Age of Federalism*, 712.

77. Wilentz, *The Rise of American Democracy*, 81–82.

78. Jefferson disguised his involvement by generating a very small paper trail on these resolutions and by relying on a political surrogate from a state other than Virginia to introduce them. His role remained largely unknown, although articles published in 1814 and 1821 mentioned his involvement. Jefferson's authorship became widely known during the nullification controversy of 1832 because the late president's ideas in these resolutions were regarded as a justification of secession. See Oberg, ed., *The Papers of Thomas Jefferson*, vol. 30, 529–30.

79. Jefferson to John Wise, February 12, 1798, in Oberg, ed., *The Papers of Thomas Jefferson*, vol. 30, 98.

80. Jefferson to James Madison, December 17, 1796, and January 1, 1797, in Oberg, ed., *The Papers of Thomas Jefferson*, vol. 29, 223, 247.

81. Jefferson to James Thomson Callender, October 6, 1799, in Oberg, ed., *The Papers of Thomas Jefferson*, vol. 31, 201.

82. Jefferson to Henry Remsen, October 14, 1799. Jefferson also repeated this argument in letters to Charles Pinckney and Philip Nicholas on October 29 and November 2, 1799, respectively. See Oberg, ed., *The Papers of Thomas Jefferson*, vol. 31, 211, 227, 232.

83. Jefferson to Thomas Mann Randolph, May 7, 1800, in Oberg, ed., *The Papers of Thomas Jefferson*, vol. 31, 561.

84. Jefferson to John Page, January 24, 1799, in Oberg, ed., *The Papers of Thomas Jefferson*, vol. 30, 641. Page had served in the U.S. Congress from 1789 until 1797, when he lost his reelection. He ran for the Virginia House of Delegates, not the U.S. Congress, in 1800, where he was successfully elected. See Garraty and Carnes, eds., *American National Biography*, vol. 16, 902–3.

85. President Washington wrote to Thomas Jefferson on August 23, 1792, and Alexander Hamilton on August 26, 1792, in an effort to calm the growing political tensions between the two men. Rather than producing the truce that Washington sought, his letters launched a volley of replies from both men that merely heightened the tensions between them. For Washington's letters, see Christine Sternberg Patrick, ed., *The Papers of George Washington*, Presidential Series, vol. 11 (Charlottesville: University of Virginia Press, 2002), 28–32 and 38–40.

86. Washington wrote his last letter to Jefferson on July 6, 1794. They saw each other for the last time at Adams's presidential inauguration on March 4, 1797. See Ellis, *Founding Brothers*, 267n44 and Elkins and McKittrick, *The Age of Federalism*, 528. For a further elaboration of their rift, see Ellis, *Founding Brothers*, 140–45.

87. Jefferson to James Monroe, July 10, 1796, in Oberg, ed., *The Papers of Thomas Jefferson*, vol. 29, 147.

88. Jefferson to Archibald Stuart, January 4, 1797, in Oberg, ed., *The Papers of Thomas Jefferson*, vol. 29, 252.

89. Jefferson to James Madison, January 8, 1797, in Oberg, ed., *The Papers of Thomas Jefferson*, vol. 29, 255.

90. Jefferson to William Bache, February 2, 1800, in Oberg, ed., *The Papers of Thomas Jefferson*, vol. 31, 354.

91. Jefferson to Thomas Pinckney, April 12, 1793, in Catanzariti, ed., *The Papers of Thomas Jefferson*, vol. 25, 536. On February 14 and March 12, 1799, Jefferson reiterated this notion of returning to the "true principles" of the Constitution and to the "spirit of 1776" in letters to Edmund Pendleton and Thomas Lomax. See Oberg, ed., *The Papers of Thomas Jefferson*, vol. 31, 36, 77.

92. For an overview of Jefferson's philosophical ideas on government, see Ellis, *American Sphinx*, 97–115.

93. In 1800, Gerry favored reelecting Adams and Jefferson as president and vice president. When the moderate wing of the Federalist Party collapsed, Gerry became a Jeffersonian Republican. See George A. Billias, *Elbridge Gerry: Founding Father and Republican Statesman* (New York: McGraw-Hill Book Company, 1976), 302–3.

94. Jefferson to Elbridge Gerry, January 26, 1799, in Oberg, ed., *The Papers of Thomas Jefferson*, vol. 30, 646–47.

95. Jefferson to Gideon Granger, August 13, 1800, in Oberg, ed., *The Papers of Thomas Jefferson*, vol. 32, 95–96. Granger, a Jeffersonian Republican from Connecticut, had been an unsuccessful candidate for Congress in 1798. Granger came to hold political office, not in Congress, but as Jefferson's postmaster general of the United States. See Garraty and Carnes, eds., *American National Biography*, vol. 9, 400–1.

96. Jefferson and Burr each received seventy-three electoral votes; Adams had sixty-five and his running mate, Charles C. Pinckney, had sixty-four. Although most people recognized that Jefferson was intended to be the presidential candidate, Burr refused to concede this point, forcing the election into the House of Representatives for resolution. In the interim, Burr even began to suggest that he would accept the presidency if the vote in the House of Representatives went in that direction. The winning president needed nine votes; Jefferson received ten on the thirty-sixth ballot. On the electoral and congressional vote totals, see Elkins and McKittrick, *The Age of Federalism*, 741, 749. On Burr's preferences, see Oberg, ed., *The Papers of Thomas Jefferson*, vol. 32, 400n. On the "two" presidential elections of 1800, see Wilentz, *The Rise of American Democracy*, 90.

97. For the voting results, see Oberg, ed., *The Papers of Thomas Jefferson*, vol. 32, 578n, and Elkins and McKittrick, *The Age of Federalism*, 749. On Hamilton's pivotal role in persuading members of the House of Representatives to support Jefferson over Burr, see Ellis, *Founding Brothers*, 41–43, and Wilentz, *The Rise of American Democracy*, 93–94.

98. On the 1800 Congressional election results, see Wilentz, *The Rise of American Democracy*, 98.

99. Jefferson to Spencer Roane, September 6, 1819, as quoted in Sisson, *The American Revolution of 1800*, 11, and Wilentz, *The Rise of American Democracy*, 97.

100. Jefferson to John Wayles Eppes, April 21, 1800, in Oberg, ed., *The Papers of Thomas Jefferson*, vol. 32, 531.

101. In 1792, Congress passed a law making March 4 the date of the presidential inauguration. The Twentieth Amendment to the Constitution, ratified in 1933, later

changed the inaugural date to January 3. See Edward Stanwood, *A History of the Presidency* (Boston: Houghton, Mifflin and Company, 1904), 36–38.

102. Jefferson to Thomas Randolph, January 22, 1797, in Oberg, ed., *The Papers of Thomas Jefferson*, vol. 29, 274.

103. Jefferson to James Madison, January 30, 1797, in Oberg, ed., *The Papers of Thomas Jefferson*, vol. 29, 281.

104. Jefferson to Volney, April 9, 1797, Oberg, ed., *The Papers of Thomas Jefferson*, vol. 29, 352.

105. Jefferson to John Marshall, March 2, 1801, in Oberg, ed., *The Papers of Thomas Jefferson*, vol. 33, 119.

106. John Marshall to Jefferson, March 2, 1801, in Oberg, ed., *The Papers of Thomas Jefferson*, vol. 33, 120.

107. With the exception of Washington's first inauguration, the newspaper coverage for subsequent ones was briefer and less widely reprinted. In addition, the reports reflected the increasing partisanship of the events themselves. For a range of opinions concerning Jefferson's inauguration, see *American Citizen and General Advertiser* (New York), March 5, 1801; *Gazette of the United States*, March 5, 1801; and the *Evening Post* (New York), March 7, 1801.

108. For descriptions of Jefferson's first inauguration, see Editorial Note, in Oberg, ed., *The Papers of Thomas Jefferson*, vol. 33, 134–35. See also Noble E. Cunningham, Jr., *The Process of Government under Jefferson* (Princeton: Princeton University Press, 1978) 10; Ferling, *Adams vs. Jefferson*, 200–6; and Ellis, *American Sphinx*, 169–70.

109. First Inaugural Address, March 4, 1801, in Oberg, ed., *The Papers of Thomas Jefferson*, vol. 33, 150.

110. First Inaugural Address, March 4, 1801, in Oberg, ed., *The Papers of Thomas Jefferson*, vol. 33. 151. See also Jefferson to Elbridge Gerry, January 26, 1799, in Oberg, ed., *The Papers of Thomas Jefferson*, vol. 30, 645–50.

111. Ferling, *Adams vs. Jefferson*, 206.

112. Everett S. Brown, ed., *William Plumer's Memorandum of Proceedings in the United States Senate, 1803–1807* (New York: MacMillan Company, 1923), 211, 550.

113. Brown, ed., *William Plumer's Memorandum*, 193.

114. Merrill D. Peterson, *Thomas Jefferson and the New Nation: A Biography* (New York: Oxford University Press, 1970), 727.

115. Samuel Harrison Smith's July 5, 1801 letter to his sister, Mary Ann Smith, appears in Margaret Bayard Smith's *The First Forty Years of Washington Society in the Family Letters of Margaret Bayard Smith*, Galliard Hunt, ed. (New York: Frederick Ungar Publishing Co., 1965), 30–31.

116. Catherine Allgor has written extensively on the feminine world of entertaining and politics in the new Washington capital. See *Parlor Politics: In Which the Ladies of Washington Help Build a City and a Government* (Charlottesville: University Press of Virginia, 2000), and *A Perfect Union: Dolley Madison and the Creation of the American Nation* (New York: Henry Holt and Company, 2006).

117. Betty Boyd Caroli, *First Ladies* (New York: Oxford University Press, 1987), 12.

118. Margaret Bayard Smith's May 28, 1801 letter to her sister, Maria Bayard, in Hunt, ed., *The First Forty Years of Washington Society*, 29.

119. Peterson, *Thomas Jefferson and the New Nation*, 731.

120. Peterson, *Thomas Jefferson and the New Nation*, 732.

121. Peterson, *Thomas Jefferson and the New Nation*, 732.

122. As quoted in William C. Dowling, *Literary Federalism in the Age of Jefferson: Joseph Dennie and The Port Folio, 1801–1812* (Columbia: University of South Carolina Press, 1999), 30–31.

123. For a range of partisan views on Madison's inauguration, see the *Evening Post*, March 7, 1809; *Poulson's American Daily Advertiser* (Philadelphia), March 7, 1809; the *Public Advertiser* (New York), March 7, 1809; and the *Repertory* (Boston), March 7, 1809.

124. Irving Brant, *The Fourth President: A Life of James Madison* (London: Eyre and Spottiswoode, 1970), 403.

125. For an elaboration of the feminine world of politics and entertaining, see Catherine Allgor's works, *Parlor Politics* and *A Perfect Union*.

126. Caroli, *First Ladies*, 14.

127. Caroli, *First Ladies*, 14–16.

4—Desperately Seeking "Good Feelings"

1. U.S. Government, *Inaugural Addresses of the Presidents of the United States* (Washington, D.C.: U.S. Government Printing Office, 1961), 35.

2. There are numerous primary and secondary sources that have discussed Monroe's tours, with the 1817 trip receiving the bulk of the attention. Several contemporary sources published the newspaper accounts and the welcoming addresses from the tours. These include: *A narrative of a tour of observation, made during the summer of 1817, by James Monroe, president of the United States, through the north-eastern and north-western departments of the Union* (Philadelphia: S. A. Mitchell and H. Ames, 1818), and Richard Radcliffe, ed., *The President's Tour: A Collection of Addresses made to James Monroe, esq. President of the United States* (New Ipswich: Salmon Wilder, 1822).

Samuel P. Waldo published three books on Monroe's tours, beginning with the northern tour and then including updates of the subsequent tours. These are: *The Tour of James Monroe, President of the United States, in the year 1817* (Hartford: F. D. Bolles and Company, 1818), *The Tour of James Monroe, President of the United States, through the Northern and Eastern States, in 1817; His Tour in the Year 1818; together with a Sketch of his Life* (Hartford: Silas Andrus, 1819), and *The Tour of James Monroe*, (Hartford: F. D. Bolles and Company, 1820).

A recently published documentary history covers the northern, southern, and abortive Chesapeake tours. See Daniel Preston, ed., *The Papers of James Monroe: A Documentary History of the Presidential Tours of James Monroe, 1817, 1818, and 1819*, vol. I (Westport, Connecticut: Greenwood Press, 2003).

Among secondary sources, two recent Monroe biographies address the tours, as does David Waldstreicher's *In the Midst of Perpetual Fetes: The Making of American Nationalism, 1776–1820* (Chapel Hill: University of North Carolina Press, 1997), 296, 298–302, 338–39. See Harry Ammon, *James Monroe: The Quest for National Identity* (Charlottesville: University Press of Virginia, 1990), 369–79, 437–38, and Noble E. Cunningham, Jr., *The Presidency of James Monroe* (Lawrence: University Press of Kansas, 1996), 31–40, 71–75.

3. Beyond its widespread circulation during Monroe's northern tour, this phrase has also been employed by historians as a shorthand description of Monroe's two-term presidency. See George Dangerfield's *The Era of Good Feelings* (New York: Harcourt, Brace and World, 1952), 95, and Ammon, *James Monroe*, 366, 380. Both books embrace this phrase and then discredit it. Some recent histories have reversed this phrase, referring to the partisan discontent

during Monroe's presidency as the "era of bad feelings" or the "era of good and bad feelings." See Sean Wilentz, *The Rise of American Democracy: Jefferson to Lincoln* (New York: W. W. Norton, 2005), 181, and Daniel Walker Howe, *What Hath God Wrought: The Transformation of America, 1815–1848* (New York: Oxford University Press, 2007), respectively.

4. Donald R. Hickey, *The War of 1812: A Forgotten Conflict* (Urbana: University of Illinois Press, 1989).

5. Stanley Elkins and Eric McKittrick, *The Age of Federalism: The Early American Republic, 1788–1800* (New York: Oxford University Press, 1993). Joseph J. Ellis, *Founding Brothers: The Revolutionary Generation* (New York: Alfred A. Knopf, 2000).

6. For a detailed account of the Hartford Convention, see James M. Banner, Jr., *To the Hartford Convention: The Federalists and the Origins of Party Politics in Massachusetts, 1789–1815* (New York: Alfred A. Knopf, 1970). For a firsthand account of its work, see Samuel G. Goodrich, *Recollections of a Lifetime*, vol. II (New York: Miller, Orton and Mulligan, 1857), 9–61.

7. Wilentz, *The Rise of American Democracy*, 173–75.

8. Samuel Eliot Morison, *Harrison Gray Otis, 1765–1848: The Urbane Federalist* (Boston: Houghton Mifflin Company, 1969), 395.

9. At the state level, the Federalists remained competitive in Massachusetts, Connecticut, Delaware, and Maryland into the late 1810s and early 1820s. See Shaw Livermore, *The Twilight of Federalism: The Disintegration of the Federalist Party, 1815–1830* (Princeton: Princeton University Press, 1962), 265, and Richard Hofstadter, *The Idea of a Party System: The Rise of Legitimate Opposition in the United States, 1780–1840* (Berkeley: University of California Press, 1969), 200.

10. Hickey, *The War of 1812*.

11. John L. Larson, *Internal Improvement: National Public Works and the Promise of Popular Government in the Early United States* (Chapel Hill: University of North Carolina Press, 2001).

12. Monroe's First Inaugural Address, March 4, 1817. U.S. Government, *Inaugural Addresses of the Presidents of the United States*, 32–34.

13. On the American System, see Robert V. Remini, *Henry Clay: Statesman for the Union* (New York: W.W. Norton and Company, 1991), 225–33.

14. On Monroe's vision of managing partisan discord through one-party government, see Hofstadter, *The Idea of a Party System*, 22–23, 194–203.

15. Monroe first acquired Washington as a mentor when he enlisted in the Third Virginia Infantry under his command. Monroe fought in the battles of Trenton and Monmouth, sustaining wounds at Trenton. Monroe's military aspirations were thwarted when he was unable to raise a regiment to command, despite a glowing recommendation from Washington. Monroe acquired Governor Thomas Jefferson as a lifelong fiend and mentor when he returned to the College of William and Mary to study law in 1780. The 37-year-old Jefferson served as the 22-year-old Monroe's law professor, conducting a freewheeling tutorial that included the Virginia statutes, as well as political and legal philosophy. During Monroe's long career in public service, he would emulate Jefferson's career by serving as minister to France, governor of Virginia, and secretary of state. On Monroe's early career, see Ammon, *James Monroe*, 7–14, 28, 29–40.

16. Joyce Appleby, *Inheriting the Revolution: The First Generation of Americans* (Cambridge: The Belknap Press of Harvard University Press, 2000).

17. Monroe's greatest partisan blunder came during his stint as Washington's minister to France between 1794 and 1796. Washington envisioned Monroe's appointment

as a bipartisan gesture intended to assuage his Republican critics; instead, it became a diplomatic embarrassment. Monroe, departing from the administration's policy of neutrality, expressed pro-Revolutionary sentiments to the delegates in Paris, forcing Washington to recall him. See Ammon, *James Monroe*, 114–25.

18. James Madison advanced this argument in *Federalist #10*.

19. Joseph J. Ellis dubbed Monroe a "second-tier member of the Virginia dynasty." See *Founding Brothers*, 146.

20. William Wirt, *The Letters of the British Spy* (Chapel Hill: University of North Carolina Press, 1970), 174.

21. Christopher Hughes, Jr. (1786–1849) was a young diplomat from Baltimore who had served as a secretary to the Treaty of Ghent peace delegation. See John A. Garraty and Mark C. Carnes, eds., *American National Biography*, vol. 11 (New York: Oxford University Press, 1999), 421.

22. Hughes to Monroe, April 13, 1816, James Monroe Papers, Library of Congress, reel 6, series I.

23. Although the author of the convention report remained anonymous, it was widely assumed that Otis had written it. In addition, when the Treaty of Ghent was announced, Otis was in Washington with two of his convention colleagues to present the Federalists' recommendations. Banner, *To the Hartford Convention*, 324, 347, and Morison, *Harrison Gray Otis*, 353.

24. Hughes to Monroe, April 13, 1816, James Monroe Papers, Library of Congress, reel 6, series I.

25. On Otis's plans to revive the Federalist Party through Monroe's visit, see Morison, *Harrison Gray Otis*, 402–3.

26. Mason to Gore, January 25, 1817, in G. J. Clark, ed., *Memoirs of Jeremiah Mason* (Boston: Boston Law Book Company, 1917), 144.

27. Jeremiah Mason of New Hampshire (1768–1848); Christopher Gore of Massachusetts (1758–1827); Daniel Webster of New Hampshire and later Massachusetts (1782–1852). See *Biographical Directory of the American Congress*, 1455, 2027, and Garraty and Carnes, eds., *American National Biography*, vol. 9, 298, respectively.

28. Webster to Mason, June 28, 1817, in Charles M. Wiltse, ed., *The Papers of Daniel Webster: Correspondence*, vol. I (Hanover: University Press of New England, 1974), 211.

29. Data compiled from *Biographical Directory of the American Congress*, 86–91.

30. Robert V. Remini, *Daniel Webster: The Man and his Time* (New York: W. W. Norton and Company, 1997), 143, 144, 148, 150.

31. Joseph Gardner Swift, *The Memoirs of General Joseph Gardner Swift, LL.D, U.S.A.* (Worcester, Mass.: F. S. Blanchard and Co., 1890), 150.

32. Monroe to Jefferson, April 23, 1817, in Stanislaus M. Hamilton, ed., *The Writings of James Monroe*, vol. VI (New York: G.P. Putnam's Sons, 1891), 22.

33. Monroe to Jefferson, July 27, 1817, in Hamilton, ed., *The Writings of James Monroe*, vol. VI, 26–29.

34. Thomas P. Govan, *Nicholas Biddle: Nationalist and Public Banker, 1786–1844* (Chicago: University of Chicago Press, 1959), 19.

35. Biddle to Monroe, April 10, 1817, James Monroe Papers, New York Public Library, reel 3.

36. Biddle to Monroe, April 10, 1817, James Monroe Papers, New York Public Library, reel 3.

37. Biddle to Monroe, April 10, 1817, James Monroe Papers, New York Public Library, reel 3.

38. The rate was one cent for papers traveling less than 100 miles and one and a half cents for papers traveling over 100 miles. Richard R. John, *Spreading the News: The American Postal System from Franklin to Morse* (Cambridge: Harvard University Press, 1995), 36.

39. See *Columbian Centinel* (Boston) and *New-Hampshire Gazette* (Portsmouth).

40. Otis to Monroe, April 22, 1817, The Otis Papers, The Massachusetts Historical Society.

41. Monroe to Otis, April 28, 1817, The Otis Papers, The Massachusetts Historical Society.

42. *Columbian Centinel*, June 4, 1817.

43. *Columbian Centinel*, June 4, 1817.

44. William M. Meigs, *The Life of Charles Jared Ingersoll* (Philadelphia: J. B. Lippincott Company, 1897), 117.

45. *American Beacon* (Norfolk, Virginia), July 8, 1817.

46. Mason was also the son of General John Mason of Georgetown and the older brother of Senator James Murray Mason of Virginia. See Robert W. Young, *Senator James Murray Mason: Defender of the Old South* (Knoxville: University of Tennessee Press, 1998).

47. Suzanne Ellery Greene, *Baltimore: An Illustrated History* (Woodland Hills, Calif.: Windsor Publications, 1980), 70, 73.

48. *Niles' Weekly Register*, June 7, 1817.

49. *Niles' Weekly Register*, June 7, 1817.

50. Reported in the *National Intelligencer* (Washington, D.C.), June 5, 1817.

51. *The Baltimore Patriot and Mercantile Advertiser*, June 2, 1817.

52. *Niles' Weekly Register* (Baltimore), June 7, 1817.

53. *True American* (Philadelphia), reprinted in the *Columbian Centinel*, June 11, 1817.

54. Monroe to Jackson, June 2, 1817, in John Spencer Bassett, ed., *The Correspondence of Andrew Jackson*, vol. 2 (Washington, D.C.: Carnegie Institution of Washington, 1927), 296.

55. Russell F. Weigley, ed., *Philadelphia: A 300-year History* (New York: W. W. Norton and Company, 1982), 127, 138.

56. Weigley, ed., *Philadelphia*, 168.

57. Weigley, ed., *Philadelphia*, 205, 218, 242.

58. *United States Gazette* (Philadelphia), June 6, 1817.

59. Weigley, ed., *Philadelphia*, 177; John F. Watson, *The Annals of Philadelphia and Pennsylvania in the Olden Time*, vol. I (Philadelphia: Elijah Thomas, 1845), 414; and Gideon Burton, *Reminiscences of Gideon Burton* (Cincinnati: Press of George P. Houston, 1895), 122.

60. Minor Myers, *Liberty without Anarchy: A History of the Society of Cincinnati* (Charlottesville: University Press of Virginia, 1983).

61. June 6, 1817 speeches contained in *Niles' Weekly Register*, June 14, 1817.

62. June 7, 1817 speech contained in *Niles' Weekly Register*, June 28, 1817.

63. Ammon, *James Monroe*, 13–14.

64. Swift, *Memoirs*, 148.

65. An analysis of military leadership during the War of 1812 can be found in William B. Skelton, "High Army Leadership in the Era of the War of 1812: The Making and Remaking of the Officer Corps," *The William and Mary Quarterly* (April 1994), 253–74.

66. William Bradford founded the *New-York Gazette* in 1725. Despite Bradford's desire to remain neutral, the *Gazette* subsequently played a prominent role in the celebrated John Peter Zenger case of 1735. See "William Bradford," in John A. Garraty and Mark C. Carnes, eds., *American National Biography*, vol. 3 (New York: Oxford University Press, 1999), 365.

67. *New-York Gazette and General Advertiser*, June 10, 1817.

68. Reflecting the increasing irrelevance of political labels, Radcliff was a Federalist and an ardent opponent of Republican DeWitt Clinton, who nonetheless broke with his party to support the War of 1812. Radcliff later became a follower of Martin Van Buren and his Bucktail coalition. "Jacob Radcliff," in Garraty and Carnes, *American National Biography*, vol. 18, 56–57.

69. June 11, 1817 address, reprinted in *Niles' Weekly Register*, June 28, 1817.

70. *New-York Gazette and General Advertiser*, June 11, 1817.

71. *National Intelligencer*, June 17, 1817.

72. In the 1820 census, New York City's population surpassed 123,000. Christine Stansell, *City of Women: Sex and Class in New York, 1789–1890* (Urbana: University of Illinois Press, 1987), 4.

73. Edwin G. Burrows and Mike Wallace, *Gotham: A History of New York City to 1898* (New York: Oxford University Press, 1999), 374–76.

74. *National Intelligencer*, June 19, 1817, and June 24, 1817, and *Connecticut Gazette* (New London), June 25, 1817.

75. *The Recorder* (Boston), June 24, 1817, *American Periodical Series*, reel 97.

76. Later in Monroe's first term, controversy raged concerning the direction of West Point. While Monroe wanted a school for career officers and the West Point faculty stressed a scientific curriculum, the acting superintendent, Captain Alden Partridge, believed that military discipline should be the academy's focus. John C. Calhoun, Monroe's secretary of war, also advocated the establishment of additional military academies throughout the nation. Although Monroe's vision prevailed, Partridge did not surrender quietly, forcing the Army to institute court martial proceedings against him. See Appleby, *Inheriting the Revolution*, 36–38.

77. *Connecticut Gazette*, June 25, 1817. On Green, see Isaiah Thomas, *The History of Printing in America*, vol. I (Albany: Joel Munsell Printer, 1874), 188.

78. *Connecticut Gazette*, June 25, 1817.

79. As reported in *Niles' Weekly Register*, July 12, 1817.

80. Mann to his family, July 18, 1817, Horace Mann Papers, Massachusetts Historical Society.

81. Henry Mayer, *All on Fire: William Lloyd Garrison and the Abolition of Slavery* (New York: St. Martin's Press, 1998), 35.

82. Eliza Noel Pintard Davidson, *Letters from John Pintard to his Daughter, 1816–1833*, vol. I (New York: New-York Historical Society, 1940), 65–66.

83. David Cobb to Charles W. Hare, June 30, 1817, David Cobb Papers, Massachusetts Historical Society.

84. July 15, 1817 entry, Sarah Connell Ayer, *Diary of Sarah Connell Ayer* (Portland, Maine: Lefavor-Tower Company, 1910), 224.

85. *New-York Gazette and General Advertiser*, June 18, 1817.

86. *New-Hampshire Gazette*, July 15, 1817. On the *Gazette*'s history, see Thomas, *The History of Printing in America*, vol. II, 94–95.

87. *New-York Gazette and General Advertiser*, June 19, 1817.

88. *The National Intelligencer*, June 17, 1817, reprinted in the *Richmond Enquirer*, June 20, 1817.

89. Thomas, *The History of Printing in America*, vol. I, 188.

90. From the *Virginia Herald* (Fredericksburg), reprinted in the *Charleston Courier*, June 24, 1817.

91. *New York Evening Post*, June 5, 1817.

92. *Niles' Weekly Register*, June 21, 1817.

93. *Niles' Weekly Register*, June 21, 1817.

94. Mason to King, June 26, 1817, in *Memoir of Jeremiah Mason*, 155.

95. King to Mason, July 4, 1817, in Charles R. King, ed., *The Life and Correspondence of Rufus King*, vol. II (New York: G. P. Putnam's Sons, 1900), 76.

96. Mason to Gore, June 18, 1817, in *Memoir of Jeremiah Mason*, 152.

97. Charles A. Place, *Charles Bulfinch, Architect and Citizen* (Boston: Houghton Mifflin, 1925), 203.

98. *Columbian Centinel*, June 7, 1817.

99. Adams to Benjamin Waterhouse, June 18, 1817, in Preston, ed., *The Papers of James Monroe*, vol. I, 101.

100. Adams to Monroe, July 1817, in Preston, ed., *The Papers of James Monroe*, vol. I, 198.

101. Ammon, *James Monroe*, 361, and Paul C. Nagel, *John Quincy Adams: A Public Life, A Private Life* (New York: Alfred A. Knopf, 1997), 245.

102. General Henry A. S. Dearborn was the son of Major General Henry Dearborn, one of the commanding officers during the War of 1812. Joseph Story was a Supreme Court justice. He also served on the Committee of Arrangements in his hometown of Salem, Massachusetts, when Monroe visited on July 8. On Dearborn, see Allen Johnson and Dumas Malone, eds., *Dictionary of American Biography*, vol. III (New York: Charles Scribner's Sons, 1931), 176–77. On Story, see Garraty and Carnes, eds., *American National Biography*, vol. 12, 711–13.

103. Swift, *Memoirs*, 159.

104. Banner, *To the Hartford Convention*, 22, 31, 50, 190–92.

105. Gore to Mason, June 22, 1817, in *Memoir of Jeremiah Mason*, 153.

106. *The National Intelligencer*, July 8, 1817.

107. Preston, ed., *The Papers of James Monroe*, vol. I, 190.

108. *Columbian Centinel*, July 5, 1817.

109. *Columbian Centinel*, July 5, 1817.

110. Preston, ed., *The Papers of James Monroe*, vol. I, 197.

111. *Columbian Centinel*, July 5, 1817.

112. Caleb H. Snow, *A History of Boston, The Metropolis of Massachusetts* (Boston: Abel Bowen, 1828), 329–31.

113. Place, *Charles Bulfinch*, 242.

114. *National Intelligencer*, July 8, 1817.

115. Banner, *To the Hartford Convention*, 13.

116. *Niles' Weekly Register*, July 12, 1817.

117. Preston, ed., *The Papers of James Monroe*, vol. I, 230–31.

118. Elizabeth Kortright Monroe was regarded as a highly fashionable, if somewhat reserved and formal, first lady. While in France, she received high praise for her stylishness in the nickname "La Belle Americaine." See W. P. Cresson, *James Monroe* (Chapel Hill: University of North Carolina Press, 1946), 205. See also Carrie Rebora Barratt and Ellen G. Miles, *Gilbert Stuart* (New York: The Metropolitan Museum of Art and New Haven: Yale University Press, 2004), 310.

119. Barratt and Miles, *Gilbert Stuart*, 310, 312.

120. Len Travers, *Celebrating the Fourth: Independence Day and the Rites of Nationalism in the Early Republic* (Amherst: University of Massachusetts Press, 1997).

121. Like Abraham Bishop in New Haven, Dearborn possessed political influence in

Boston as a federal political appointee, named to this post by President Madison in 1812. See David Waldstreicher and Stephen R. Grossbart, "Abraham Bishop's Vocation; or, The Mediation of Jeffersonian Politics," *Journal of the Early Republic* (Winter 1998): 617–58.

122. The pro-Federalist Boston press did not publish either address. Instead, *Niles' Weekly Register* reprinted them on July 19, 1817, and July 26, 1817, respectively.

123. Preston, ed., *The Papers of James Monroe*, vol. I, 197, 224, 226.

124. Preston, ed., *The Papers of James Monroe*, vol. I, 226. Although appointed to this position on March 6, 1817, John Quincy Adams did not return to the United States from his diplomatic posting in England until August 6, 1817. See Ammon, *James Monroe*, 361, and Nagel, *John Quincy Adams*, 236.

125. M. A. De Wolfe Howe, ed., *The Articulate Sisters: Passages from Journals and Letters of the Daughters of Josiah Quincy* (Cambridge: Harvard University Press, 1946), 21.

126. *Columbian Centinel*, July 9, 1817.

127. Howe, ed., *The Articulate Sisters*, 20.

128. Sullivan to Monroe, July 10, 1817, James Monroe Papers, Library of Congress, reel 6, series I.

129. Wiltse, ed., *The Papers of Daniel Webster*, 211n, and Remini, *Daniel Webster*, 171.

130. Hopkinson to Webster, November 20, 1817, in Wiltse, ed., *The Papers of Daniel Webster*, 214.

131. "Joseph Hopkinson," in Garraty and Carnes, *American National Biography*, vol. 11, 192.

132. Leverett Saltonstall (1783–1845), in *Who Was Who in America, Historical Volume, 1607–1896* (Chicago: A. N. Marquis Company, 1963), 532.

133. Abbot to Saltonstall, July 23, 1817, Saltonstall Papers, Box 5 (1817), Massachusetts Historical Society. On King Herod the Great, see *The New Catholic Encyclopedia*, second edition, vol. 6 (Detroit: Thomson Gale, 2003), 801–3.

134. "Benjamin Russell," in Garraty and Carnes, *American National Biography*, vol. 19, 87–88.

135. *Columbian Centinel*, July 12, 1817.

136. *Columbian Centinel*, July 23, 1817.

137. From the *Richmond Enquirer*, July 18, 1817, reprinted in the *Columbian Centinel*, July 26, 1817.

138. From the *Richmond Enquirer*, July 29, 1817, reprinted in the *Columbian Centinel*, August 6, 1817.

139. *Columbian Centinel*, September 13, 1817.

140. *Columbian Centinel*, September 20, 1817.

141. For the northern tour's itinerary, see Preston, ed., *The Papers of James Monroe*, vol. I, xvii, 7–8.

142. Monroe to Jefferson, July 27, 1817, in Hamilton, ed., *The Writings of James Monroe*, vol. VI, 27.

143. Monroe to Jefferson, July 27, 1817, in Hamilton, ed., *The Writings of James Monroe*, vol. VI, 27–28.

144. Monroe to Jefferson, July 27, 1817, in Hamilton, ed., *The Writings of James Monroe*, vol. VI, 28.

145. Jefferson to Gallatin, June 16, 1817, in Andrew A. Lipscomb and Albert E. Bergh, eds., *The Writings of Thomas Jefferson*, vol. XV (Washington, D.C.: The Thomas Jefferson Memorial Association, 1905), 135.

146. Monroe to Jefferson, July 27, 1817, in Hamilton, ed., *The Writings of James Monroe*, vol. VI, 27.

147. Meigs, *The Life of Charles Jared Ingersoll*, 117.

148. See Wirt, *The Letters of the British Spy*, 174.

149. Monroe to Hay, August 5, 1817, "Letters of James Monroe, 1812–1817," *Bulletin of the New York Public Library*, vol. VI (New York: Astor Lenox and Tilden Foundations, 1902), 228–29.

150. *The Hampshire Gazette and Public Advertiser* (Northampton, Massachusetts), July 30, 1817.

151. *The Exeter Watchman*, reprinted in the *Federal Republican and Baltimore Telegraph*, September 2, 1817.

152. Mason to King, July 24, 1817, in King, ed., *The Life and Correspondence of Rufus King*, 79.

153. Mason to King, July 24, 1817, in King, ed., *The Life and Correspondence of Rufus King*, 80.

154. Crawford to Gallatin, October 27, 1817, in Adams, ed., *The Writings of Albert Gallatin*, vol. II (Philadelphia: J. B. Lippincott and Co., 1879), 55.

155. Clay to Russell, August 18, 1817, Jonathan Russell Papers, Massachusetts Historical Society.

156. Remini, *Henry Clay*, 150–51.

157. Wirt disguised himself as the "British spy" in a series of newspaper essays published in 1803. He wrote of Monroe: "Nature has given him a mind neither rapid nor rich. . . . But to compensate him for this, he is endued with a spirit of generous and restless emulation, a judgment solid, strong and clear, and a habit of application, which no difficulties can shake." See Wirt, *The Letters of the British Spy*, 174.

158. King to Mason, November 30, 1817, in King, ed., *The Life and Correspondence of Rufus King*, 82.

159. Nagel, *John Quincy Adams*, 146–47; Ammon, *James Monroe*, 361.

160. Ammon, *James Monroe*, 360–61.

161. Harold Kirker, *The Architecture of Charles Bulfinch* (Cambridge: Harvard University Press, 1969), 321–22.

162. Place, *Charles Bulfinch*, 242–43. Talbot Hamlin, *Benjamin Henry Latrobe* (New York: Oxford University Press, 1955), 476–80.

163. Biddle became a target of much of the criticism against the Bank of the United States during Jackson's 1832 campaign against its rechartering. See Wilentz, *The Rise of American Democracy*, 364–66.

164. Jeffrey M. Dorwart, *Fort Mifflin of Philadelphia* (Philadelphia: University of Pennsylvania Press, 1998), 96.

165. Abigail Adams to Richard Rush, July 14, 1817, in Preston, ed., *The Papers of James Monroe*, vol. I, 235–36.

166. Hofstadter, *The Idea of a Party System*.

167. Monroe to Madison, May 12, 1822, in Preston, ed., *The Papers of James Monroe*, vol. I, 775.

168. Monroe to Madison, May 12, 1822, in Preston, ed., *The Papers of James Monroe*, vol. I, 775.

169. Madison to Monroe, May 18, 1822, in Gaillard Hunt, ed., *The Writings of James Madison*, vol. IX (New York: G. P. Putnam's Sons, 1908), 97.

170. Hunt, ed., *The Writings of James Madison*, vol. IX, 97.

171. Hunt, ed., *The Writings of James Madison*, vol. IX, 97.

172. Jefferson to Gallatin, October 29, 1822, in Adams, ed., *The Writings of Albert Gallatin*, vol. II, 259.

173. Monroe's two tours inspired a spate of political journeys, most notably the Marquis de Lafayette's visit of 1824–1825, but also those of younger politicians such as Henry Clay, Andrew Jackson, and Daniel Webster. On Lafayette's tour, see Edgar Ewing Brandon, ed., *Lafayette, Guest of the Nation: A Contemporary Account of the Triumphal Tour of General Lafayette*, 3 vols. (Oxford: Oxford Historical Press, 1950); Stanley J. Idzerda, et al., *Lafayette: Hero of Two Worlds* (Flushing, New York: Queens Museum, 1989); Lloyd S. Kramer, *Lafayette in Two Worlds: Public Cultures and Personal Identities in the Age of Revolutions* (Chapel Hill: University of North Carolina Press, 1996); Anne C. Loveland, *Emblem of Liberty: The Image of Lafayette in the American Mind* (Baton Rouge: Louisiana State University Press, 1971); and Sylvia Neely, *Lafayette and the Liberal Ideal, 1814–1824: Politics and Conspiracy in an Age of Reaction* (Carbondale: Southern Illinois University Press, 1991). See also Fletcher M. Green, "On Tour with President Andrew Jackson," *The New England Quarterly* (March–December 1963), 209–28; Remini, *Henry Clay*, 353–54, 356–57, 442–43, 538–39, 630–41; and Remini, *Daniel Webster*, 388–93.

174. This idea is also advanced in Ralph Ketcham, *Presidents above Party: The First American Presidency, 1789–1829* (Chapel Hill: University of North Carolina Press, 1984), 129; Ammon, *James Monroe*, 380; and Harry L. Watson, *Liberty and Power: The Politics of Jacksonian America* (New York: Hill and Wang, 1990), 59, 72.

175. On the establishment of the Second American party system, see Richard P. McCormick, *The Second American Party System: Party Formation in the Jacksonian Era* (Chapel Hill: University of North Carolina Press, 1966); Robert V. Remini, *Andrew Jackson and the Course of American Freedom, 1822–1832* (New York: Harper and Row Publishers, 1981); Michael F. Holt, *The Rise and Fall of the American Whig Party: Jacksonian Politics and the Onset of the Civil War* (New York: Oxford University Press, 1999).

176. Holt, *The Rise and Fall of the American Whig Party*, 2–3, 7.

177. *Who Was Who in America, Historical Volume, 1607–1896*, 484.

178. *Who Was Who in America, Historical Volume, 1607–1896*, 362.

179. Holt, *The Rise and Fall of the American Whig Party*, 97.

5—"The Success and Stability of Our Republican Institutions"

1. The issue of Missouri statehood became controversial with the introduction of the Tallmadge Amendment in February 1819, which attempted to gradually emancipate slaves in Missouri. Although unsuccessful, this amendment exposed the growing rift between North and South over slavery's expansion. See Harry L. Watson, *Liberty and Power: The Politics of Jacksonian America* (New York: Hill and Wang, 1990), 70–72.

2. For biographies of these four men, see Chase C. Mooney, *William H. Crawford, 1772–1834* (Lexington: University Press of Kentucky, 1974); Robert V. Remini, *Andrew Jackson and the Course of American Empire* (New York: Harper and Row, 1977); Robert V. Remini, *Henry Clay: Statesman for the Union* (New York: W. W. Norton, 1991); and Charles M. Wiltse, *John C. Calhoun: Nationalist, 1782–1828* (Indianapolis: The Bobbs-Merrill Company, 1944).

3. The northern tour lasted four months and covered 2,000 miles, while the southern tour lasted six months and covered 2,600 miles. For the itineraries of the northern, southern, and Chesapeake tours, see Daniel Preston, ed., *The Papers of James Monroe:*

A Documentary History of the Presidential Tours of James Monroe, 1817, 1818, and 1819, vol. I (Westport, Conn.: Greenwood Press, 2003), xvii, xxii, 7–8, 519, 553. On Monroe's "disappearance," see *National Intelligencer* (Washington, D.C.), June 12, 1819.

4. Although Andrew Jackson served in the Revolutionary War, James Monroe was the last president to have played a role in the development and ratification of the U.S. Constitution.

5. There is a rich literature on memory and commemoration, particularly related to the Civil War. See David W. Blight, *Race and Reunion: The Civil War in American Memory* (Cambridge: Belknap Press of Harvard University Press, 2001), and *Beyond the Battlefield: Race, Memory and the American Civil War* (Amherst: University of Massachusetts Press, 2002). See also Alice Fahs and Joan Waugh, eds., *Memory of the Civil War in American Culture* (Chapel Hill: University of North Carolina Press, 2004).

6. Preston, ed., *The Papers of James Monroe*, vol. I, 519.

7. For details on Monroe's visit to Annapolis, see the Annapolis-based *Maryland Gazette and Political Intelligencer* for June 4 and June 18, 1818.

8. *American Beacon and Commercial Diary* (Norfolk, Virginia), June 6, 1818.

9. John Lauritz Larson, *Internal Improvement: National Public Works and the Promise of Popular Government in the Early United States* (Chapel Hill: University of North Carolina Press, 2001), 164–66; Thomas C. Parramore, *Norfolk: The First Four Generations* (Charlottesville: University Press of Virginia, 1994), 147–48.

10. *American Beacon and Commercial Diary*, June 13, 1818.

11. *American Beacon and Commercial Diary*, June 9, 1818.

12. Remini, *Andrew Jackson and the Course of American Empire*, 180.

13. For a detailed examination of the Seminole War, see chapters 22 and 23 of Remini's *Andrew Jackson and the Course of American Empire*.

14. Remini, *Andrew Jackson and the Course of American Empire*, 367.

15. Noble E. Cunningham, Jr., *The Presidency of James Monroe* (Lawrence: University Press of Kansas, 1996), 61.

16. Remini, *Henry Clay*, 165.

17. Remini, *Henry Clay*, 165.

18. Andrew Jackson to Rachel Jackson, January 25, 1819, Miscellaneous Manuscripts, Gilder Lehrman Collection, Pierpoint Morgan Library.

19. Remini, *Henry Clay*, 165.

20. Cunningham, *The Presidency of James Monroe*, 68–69.

21. In 1831, Jackson discovered that it was his vice president, Calhoun, who had led the administration's efforts against him. Jackson's rift with Calhoun occurred during the Peggy Eaton controversy and resulted in Martin Van Buren's accession to the vice presidency. See Mooney, *William H. Crawford*, 180–81, and "John H. Eaton," in John A. Garraty and Mark C. Carnes, eds., *American National Biography*, vol. 7 (New York: Oxford University Press, 1999), 262.

22. Harry Watson, *Liberty and Power*,

23. See Anita S. Goodstein, *Nashville, 1780–1860: From Frontier to City* (Gainesville: University of Florida Press, 1989), 5, and Remini, *Henry Clay*, 15.

24. Drew Gilpin Faust, *James Henry Hammond and the Old South: A Design for Mastery* (Baton Rouge: Louisiana State University Press, 1982), 3, 41–43.

25. Kenneth S. Greenberg, *Honor and Slavery: Lies, Duels, Noses, Masks, Dressing as a Woman, Gifts, Strangers, Humanitarianism, Death, Slave Rebellions, The Proslavery Argument, Baseball, Hunting, and Gambling in the Old South* (Princeton: Princeton University Press, 1996).

26. Although toasting had occurred during Washington's northern and southern tours, by the time of Monroe's tours, this practice was found exclusively in the South, further evidence of growing regionalism in the country.

27. Faust, *James Henry Hammond and the Old South*, 18.

28. Mooney, *William H. Crawford*, 10–11.

29. Wiltse, *John C. Calhoun*, 85, and Remini, *Henry Clay*, 55, 295.

30. Remini, *Andrew Jackson and the Course of American Empire*, 38, 142, 184–86.

31. Cunningham, *The Presidency of James Monroe*, 181.

32. Douglas R. Egerton, *Gabriel's Rebellion: The Virginia Slave Conspiracies of 1800 and 1802* (Chapel Hill: University of North Carolina Press, 1993), 74–75.

33. For this report, see Robert L. Meriwether, ed., *The Papers of John C. Calhoun*, vol. III (Columbia: University of South Carolina Press, 1969), 461–72.

34. Robert J. Brugger, *Maryland: A Middle Temperament, 1634–1980* (Baltimore: Johns Hopkins University Press, 1988), 200, 202.

35. See Preston, ed., *The Papers of James Monroe*, vol. I, xvii, xxii.

36. *Raleigh Register*, April 23, 1819. "William Kennedy," *Who Was Who in America, Historical Volume, 1607–1896* (Chicago: A. N. Marquis Company, 1963), 291. On the Blount family, see Remini, *Andrew Jackson and the Course of American Empire*, 50–51.

37. *Charleston Courier*, April 28, 1819. "Thomas Lee," *Who Was Who in America, Historical Volume*, 310. "William Drayton," Garraty and Carnes, eds., *American National Biography*, vol. 6, 892–93.

38. *Carolina Centinel* (New Bern, North Carolina), April 17, 1819.

39. *Carolina Centinel*, April 17, 1819.

40. *Carolina Centinel*, April 17, 1819.

41. Hugh T. Lefler and Albert R. Newsome, *The History of a Southern State: North Carolina* (Chapel Hill: University of North Carolina Press, 1973), 69.

42. *National Intelligencer*, April 22, 1819.

43. Lefler and Newsome, *The History of a Southern State*, 314, 321.

44. *Richmond Enquirer*, April 20, 1819.

45. Lefler and Newsome, *The History of a Southern State*, 334, 336, 384.

46. Lefler and Newsome, *The History of a Southern State*, 311.

47. *Carolina Centinel*, May 1, 1819.

48. Walter Edgar, *South Carolina, A History* (Columbia: University of South Carolina Press, 1998), 271, 273, 275, 276.

49. John Lofton, *Denmark Vesey's Revolt: The Slave Plot that Lit the Fuse to Fort Sumter* (Kent: Kent State University Press, 1964), 27, 39, 44, 96, 108.

50. "Francois Andre Michaux's Travel's West of the Allegheny Mountains, 1802," in Reuben Gold Thwaites, ed., *Early Western Travels, 1748–1846*, vol. 3 (Cleveland: Arthur H. Clark Company, 1904), 118–20.

51. *Charleston Courier*, April 27, 1819.

52. *Charleston Courier*, April 28, 1819.

53. *Columbian Museum and Savannah Daily Gazette*, May 22, 1819.

54. See Stephens to Monroe, March 31 and April 17, 1819, James Monroe Papers, New York Public Library, reel 3.

55. *Charleston Courier*, April 26, 1819.

56. See Geddes to Monroe on April 24, 1819. James Monroe Papers, Library of Congress, reel 7, series 1.

57. *Charleston Courier*, April 28, 1819.

58. *Charleston Courier*, April 29, 1819.

59. Cunningham, *The Presidency of James Monroe*, 105.

60. Although covering a later period than this study, William and Jane Pease's *The Web of Progress* (Oxford: Oxford University Press, 1985) compares Charleston and Boston between 1828 and 1843.

61. "Thomas Pinckney," in Garraty and Carnes, eds., *American National Biography*, vol. 17, 539–40. "Charles Cotesworth Pinckney," in Garraty and Carnes, eds., *American National Biography*, vol. 17, 536–38.

62. *Charleston Courier*, April 27, 1819.

63. Monroe to Hay, May 2, 1819, James Monroe Papers, New York Public Library, reel 3.

64. Amanda Johnson, *Georgia as Colony and State* (Atlanta: Cherokee Publishing Company, 1970), 211, 230, 231, 232.

65. George M. Gilmer, *Sketches of Some of the First Settlers of Upper Georgia* (Americus, Georgia: Americus Book Company, 1926), 201.

66. Greenberg, *Honor and Slavery*, xi, xii, 81.

67. Johnson, *Georgia as Colony and State*, 192.

68. Crawford to Monroe, April 27, 1819, James Monroe Papers, New York Public Library, reel 3.

69. *Augusta Chronicle*, May 17, 1819.

70. Alexander A. Lawrence, *James Moore Wayne, Southern Unionist* (Chapel Hill: University of North Carolina Press, 1943), 27–28.

71. *Richmond Enquirer*, June 15, 1819.

72. *National Intelligencer*, June 12, 1819.

73. *Niles' Weekly Register* (Baltimore), June 26, 1819.

74. Johnson, *Georgia as Colony and State*, 192.

75. *Western Monitor* (Lexington, Kentucky), June 22, 1819.

76. Remini, *Andrew Jackson and the Course of American Empire*, 342–43.

77. Goodstein, *Nashville, 1780–1860*, 21, 22, 24, 25.

78. "Samuel Hogg" and "William B. Lewis," in *Who Was Who in America, Historical Volume*, 255 and 314.

79. On Bronaugh and Grundy, see Remini, *Andrew Jackson and the Course of American Empire*, 321; and "Felix Grundy," in Garraty and Carnes, eds., *American National Biography*, vol. 9, 688–89.

80. See "John H. Eaton," in Garraty and Carnes, eds., *American National Biography*, vol. 7, 261–63. For a discussion of the Eaton affair, see Catherine Allgor, *Parlor Politics: In Which the Ladies of Washington Help Build a City and a Government* (Charlottesville: University Press of Virginia, 2000), 190–238.

81. Richard C. Wade, *The Urban Frontier: Pioneer Life in Early Pittsburgh, Cincinnati, Lexington, Louisville, and St. Louis* (Chicago: University of Chicago Press, 1959).

82. *National Intelligencer*, June 30, 1819.

83. *The Clarion and Tennessee State Gazette* (Nashville), June 15, 1819.

84. *The Clarion and Tennessee State Gazette*, June 15, 1819.

85. Preston, ed., *The Papers of James Monroe*, vol. I, 553, 680–81.

86. On Clay's life, see Remini, *Henry Clay: Statesman for the Union*.

87. Pope to Monroe, March 1, 1819, James Monroe Papers, Library of Congress, reel 7, series 1.

88. H. McMurtrie, *Sketches of Louisville and Its Environs* (Louisville: S. Penn, 1819), 111.

89. For accounts of journeys down the Ohio River into Kentucky, see Timothy Flint, *Recollections of the Last Ten Years in the Valley of the Mississippi* (New York: DaCapo Press, 1968); and "Cuming's Sketch of a Tour to the Western Country, 1807–1809," in Thwaites, ed., *Early Western Travels, 1784–1846*, vol. 5.

90. "Amos Kendall," in Garraty and Carnes, eds., *American National Biography*, vol. 12, 555–57.

91. *Argus of Western America* (Frankfort), June 18, 1819.

92. *Richmond Enquirer*, July 20, 1819.

93. *Richmond Enquirer*, July 20, 1819.

94. *Richmond Enquirer*, July 23, 1819.

95. *Richmond Enquirer*, July 23, 1819.

96. Flint, *Recollections of the Last Ten Years*, 68.

97. *National Intelligencer*, July 24, 1819.

98. On Clay's travels, see James F. Hopkins, ed., *The Papers of Henry Clay*, vol. 2 (Lexington, University of Kentucky Press, 1959), 692–93, 697.

99. Clay to Gales, Jr., July 19, 1819, in Hopkins, ed., *The Papers of Henry Clay*, 700–1.

100. Hopkins, ed., *The Papers of Henry Clay*, 701.

101. *Richmond Enquirer*, August 3, 1819.

102. Crawford to Monroe, July 2, 1819, James Monroe Papers, Library of Congress, reel 7, series 1.

103. Preston, ed., *The Papers of James Monroe*, vol. I, 553.

104. *American Beacon and Commercial Diary*, April 3, 1819.

105. *Augusta Chronicle*, May 14, 1819.

106. *Kentucky Gazette* (Lexington), reprinted in the *Weekly Messenger* (Russellville, Ky.), April 24, 1819.

107. *Kentucky Republican* (Hopkinsville), reprinted in the *American Beacon*, June 28, 1819.

108. *Kentucky Gazette*, April 23, 1819.

109. Because of the Twelfth Amendment to the Constitution, which distinguished between the presidential and vice presidential candidates, along with the taint surrounding Aaron Burr as Jefferson's vice president, this office was no longer regarded as the steppingstone to the presidency as it had been in earlier administrations. Instead, the secretary of state was now viewed as the heir apparent, having led to Madison and Monroe's elevation to the presidency. In this configuration, Monroe's putative successor was Secretary of State John Quincy Adams of Massachusetts, who remained the sole practitioner of an older form of national politics, believing that his accomplishments in this position would result in his accession as chief magistrate.

110. From Monroe's remarks delivered in Beaufort, South Carolina, May 8, 1819, in Preston, ed., *The Papers of James Monroe*, vol. I, 629.

Conclusion

1. Gaillard Hunt, ed., *The First Forty Years of Washington Society in the Family Letters of Margaret Bayard Smith* (New York: Frederick Ungar Publishing Co., 1965), 294.

2. Robert V. Remini, *Andrew Jackson and the Course of American Freedom, 1822–1832*, vol. II (New York: Harper and Row Publishers, 1981), 178.

3. Remini, *Andrew Jackson and the Course of American Freedom*, 174–79.

4. There is a rich literature on memory and commemoration related to the

nation's founding. See Sarah J. Purcell, *Sealed with Blood: War, Sacrifice, and Memory in Revolutionary America* (Philadelphia: University of Pennsylvania Press, 2002), and Michael Kammen, *A Season of Youth: The American Revolution and the Historical Imagination* (New York: Alfred A. Knopf, 1978).

5. Calhoun had not been able to generate enough support as a presidential candidate, and he put himself forward as a nominee for vice president instead, serving under Adams from 1825 to 1829 and then Jackson from 1829 to 1832. See Charles M. Wiltse, *John C. Calhoun, 1782-1828* (Indianapolis: Bobbs-Merrill Company, 1944), 283-84.

6. Robert V. Remini, *Henry Clay: Statesman for the Union* (New York: W. W. Norton, 1991), 249.

7. Sean Wilentz, *The Rise of American Democracy: Jefferson to Lincoln* (New York: W. W. Norton, 2005), 254-311; Richard P. McCormick, *The Second American Party System: Party Formation in the Jacksonian Era* (Chapel Hill: University of North Carolina Press, 1966), 3, 13.

8. McCormick, *The Second American Party System*, 14.

9. On Clay's decision to support Adams, see Remini, *Henry Clay*, chapter 15.

10. Remini, *Andrew Jackson and the Course of American Freedom*, 108.

11. Robert V. Remini, *Andrew Jackson and the Course of American Empire, 1767-1821*, vol. I (New York: Harper and Row Publishers, 1977), 113.

12. On Crawford's poor health and his death in 1832, see Chase C. Mooney, *William H. Crawford, 1772-1834* (Lexington: University Press of Kentucky, 1974), 241, 302, 303, 341.

13. Michael F. Holt, *The Rise and Fall of the American Whig Party: Jacksonian Politics and the Onset of the Civil War* (New York: Oxford University Press, 1999), 10.

14. Holt, *The Rise and Fall of the Whig Party*, 17.

15. Holt, *The Rise and Fall of the Whig Party*, 27.

16. *Who Was Who in America, Historical Volume, 1607-1896* (Chicago: A. N. Marquis Company, 1963).

17. *Who Was Who in America, Historical Volume, 1607-1896*, 362.

18. See the region-by-region analysis in McCormick's *The Second American Party System*.

19. McCormick, *The Second American Party System*, 29.

20. McCormick, *The Second American Party System*, 30.

21. On the Erie Canal, see Carol Sheriff, *The Artificial River: The Erie Canal and the Paradox of Progress, 1817-1862* (New York: Hill and Wang, 1996).

22. "De Witt Clinton," Garraty and Carnes, eds., *American National Biography*, vol. 5 (Oxford: Oxford University Press, 1999), 77-80.

23. See Robert V. Remini, *Daniel Webster: The Man and his Time* (New York: W. W. Norton and Company, 1997), 178-87.

24. Remini, *Daniel Webster*, 247-52. For these addresses, see Daniel Webster, *The Orations on Bunker Hill Monument, the Character of Washington, and the Landing at Plymouth* (New York: American Book Company, 1894).

25. On Lafayette's tour, see Edgar Ewing Brandon, ed., *Lafayette, Guest of the Nation: A Contemporary Account of the Triumphal Tour of General Lafayette*, 3 vols. (Oxford: Oxford Historical Press, 1950); Stanley J. Idzerda, ed., *Lafayette: Hero of Two Worlds* (Flushing, New York: Queens Museum, 1989); Lloyd S. Kramer, *Lafayette in Two Worlds: Public Cultures and Personal Identities in the Age of Revolutions* (Chapel Hill: University of North Carolina Press, 1996); Anne C. Loveland, *Emblem of Liberty: The Image of Lafayette*

in the American Mind (Baton Rouge: Louisiana State University Press, 1971); and Sylvia Neely, *Lafayette and the Liberal Ideal, 1814-1824: Politics and Conspiracy in an Age of Reaction* (Carbondale: Southern Illinois University Press, 1991).

26. Remini, *Daniel Webster*, 247-52; Remini, *Henry Clay*, 254.

27. Mooney, *William H. Crawford*, 292.

28. Robert V. Remini, *Andrew Jackson and the Course of American Democracy, 1833-1845* (New York: Harper and Row Publishers, 1984), 60-83, and Fletcher M. Green, "On Tour with President Andrew Jackson," *The New England Quarterly* (March-December 1963): 209-28.

29. Remini, *Daniel Webster*, 388-93.

30. Remini, *Henry Clay*, 353-54, 356-57, 442-43, 538-39, 630-41.

31. Joseph J. Ellis, *Founding Brothers: The Revolutionary Generation* (New York: Alfred A. Knopf, 2000), 225, 248.

32. Harry Ammon, *James Monroe: The Quest for National Identity* (Charlottesville: University Press of Virginia, 1990), 572.

33. Paul C. Nagel, *John Quincy Adams: A Public Life, A Private Life* (New York: Alfred A. Knopf, 1997), 311-12.

Bibliography

Primary Sources
Manuscripts

Gilder Lehrman Collection, Pierpoint Morgan Library, New York City:
  Miscellaneous Manuscripts—James Monroe, Andrew Jackson

Library of Congress, Washington, D.C.:
  Manuscript Division
  Andrew Jackson Papers
  Thomas Jefferson Papers
  James Monroe Papers

Massachusetts Historical Society, Boston, Massachusetts:
  David Cobb Papers
  Horace Mann Papers
  Harrison Gray Otis Papers
  Saltonstall Papers

New-York Historical Society, New York City:
  Albert Gallatin Papers
  Miscellaneous Manuscripts—Charles Jared Ingersoll

New York Public Library, New York City:
  James Monroe Papers

Newspapers
CONNECTICUT

American Mercury (Hartford)
Connecticut Courant (Hartford)
Connecticut Gazette (New London)
Connecticut Journal (New Haven)

220 Bibliography

Middlesex Gazette (Middletown)
New-Haven Gazette, and Connecticut Magazine
Norwich Packet, and Country Journal
Weekly Monitor (Litchfield)
Windham Herald

Georgia

Augusta Chronicle
Columbian Museum and Savannah Daily Gazette

Kentucky

Argus of Western America (Frankfort)
Kentucky Gazette (Lexington)
Kentucky Republican (Hopkinsville)
Weekly Messenger (Russellville)
Western Monitor (Lexington)

Maine

Cumberland Gazette (Portland)

Maryland

Baltimore Patriot and Mercantile Advertiser
Federal Republican and Baltimore Telegraph
Maryland Gazette and Political Intelligencer (Annapolis)
Niles' Weekly Register (Baltimore)

Massachusetts

American Herald and Worcester Record
Boston Gazette, and the Country Journal
Boston Independent Chronicle
Columbian Centinel (Boston)
Essex Journal (Newburyport)
Hampshire Gazette and Public Advertiser (Northampton)
Herald of Freedom, and the Federal Advertiser (Boston)
Independent Chronicle and Universal Advertiser (Boston)
Massachusetts Mercury (Boston)
The Recorder (Boston)
The Repertory (Boston)
Salem Mercury
Worcester Magazine, and Massachusetts Spy

New Hampshire

Exeter Watchman
New-Hampshire Gazette, and General Advertiser (Portsmouth)
New-Hampshire Recorder, and Weekly Advertiser (Keene)
Osborne's New-Hampshire Spy (Portsmouth)

New Jersey

New-Jersey Journal (Elizabethtown)

New York

Albany Journal
American Citizen and General Advertiser (New York)
Daily Advertiser (New York)
The Diary, or Loudon's Register (New York)
Gazette of the United States (New York)
New-York Daily Gazette
New York Evening Post
New York Gazette and General Advertiser
New-York Journal, and Weekly Register
New-York Packet
New-York Weekly Museum
Public Advertiser (New York)

North Carolina

Carolina Centinel (New Bern)
Raleigh Register

Pennsylvania

Carlisle Gazette, and Western Repository of Knowledge
Dunlap's American Daily Advertiser (Philadelphia)
Federal Gazette, and Philadelphia Evening Post
Freeman's Journal (Philadelphia)
Gazette of the United States (Philadelphia)
General Advertiser and Political, Commercial, Agricultural and Literary Journal (Philadelphia)
Independent Gazetteer (Philadelphia)
Mail, or Claypoole's American Daily Advertiser (Philadelphia)
National Gazette (Philadelphia)
Newport Herald
Pennsylvania Mercury, and Universal Advertiser (Philadelphia)
Pennsylvania Packet, and Daily Advertiser (Philadelphia)
Philadelphia Gazette and Universal Daily Advertiser

Poulson's American Daily Advertiser (Philadelphia)
True American (Philadelphia)
United States Gazette (Philadelphia)

RHODE ISLAND

Newport Mercury
Providence Gazette and Country Journal
United States Chronicle: Political, Commercial, and Historical (Providence)

SOUTH CAROLINA

Charleston Courier
City Gazette and Daily Advertiser (Charleston)
South Carolina Independent Gazette, and Georgetown Chronicle

TENNESSEE

Clarion and Tennessee State Gazette (Nashville)

VERMONT

Vermont Gazette (Bennington)
Vermont Journal (Windsor)

VIRGINIA

American Beacon and Commercial Diary (Norfolk)
Richmond Enquirer
Virginia Herald (Fredericksburg)

WASHINGTON, D.C.

National Intelligencer

Published Works

Abbot, W. W., and Dorothy Twohig, eds. *The Papers of George Washington, Presidential Series,* 13 vols. Charlottesville: University Press of Virginia, 1987–1993.

Adams, Charles Francis, ed. *Memoirs of John Quincy Adams, comprising portions of history diary from 1795 to 1848,* 12 vols. Philadelphia: J.B. Lippincott, 1874–1877.

Adams, Charles Francis, ed. *The Works of John Adams, Second President of the United States,* 10 vols. Boston: Little, Brown, 1850–1856.

Adams, Charles Francis, ed. *The Writings of Albert Gallatin,* 3 vols. Philadelphia: J.B. Lippincott, 1879.

Allen, W. B., ed. *Works of Fisher Ames,* 2 vols. Indianapolis: Liberty Classics, 1983.

Appleby, Joyce, and Terence Ball, eds. *Jefferson: Political Writings*. Cambridge: Cambridge University Press, 1999.
Ayer, Sarah Connell. *Diary of Sarah Connell Ayer*. Portland, Maine: Lefavor-Tower Co., 1910.
Bassett, John Spencer, ed. *The Correspondence of Andrew Jackson*, 7 vols. Washington, D.C.: Carnegie Institution of Washington, 1926–1935.
Boston Directory: containing names of the inhabitants, their occupation, place of business, and dwelling houses. Boston: E. Cotton, 1818.
Brandon, Edgar Ewing, ed. *Lafayette, Guest of the Nation: A Contemporary Account of the Triumphal Tour of General Lafayette*, 3 vols. Oxford: Oxford Historical Press, 1950.
Brown, Everett S., ed. *William Plumer's Memorandum of Proceedings in the United States Senate, 1803–1807*. New York: MacMillan, 1923.
Burton, Gideon. *Reminiscences of Gideon Burton*. Cincinnati: Press of George P. Houston, 1895.
Clark, G. J., ed. *Memoirs of Jeremiah Mason*. Boston: Boston Law Book, 1917.
Davidson, Eliza Noel Pintard. *Letters from John Pintard to his Daughter, 1816–1833*, 4 vols. New York: New-York Historical Society, 1940.
The Debates and Proceedings in the Congress of the United States, 42 vols. Washington, D.C.: Gales and Seaton, 1834–1856.
De Pauw, Linda Grant, et al., eds. *Documentary History of the First Federal Congress of the United States of America, 1789–1791*, 14 vols. Baltimore: The Johns Hopkins University Press, 1972–1995.
Fields, Joseph, ed. *"Worthy Partner": The Papers of Martha Washington*. Westport, Connecticut: Greenwood Press, 1994.
Fitzpatrick, John C., ed. *The Writings of George Washington, 1745–1799*, 39 vols. Washington, D.C.: Government Printing Office, 1931–1944.
Flint, Timothy. *Recollections of the Last Years in the Valley of the Mississippi*. New York: DaCapo Press, 1968.
Ford, Paul Leicester, ed. *The Writings of Thomas Jefferson*, 10 vols. New York: G.P. Putman's Sons, 1892–1899.
Ford, Worthington Chauncey, ed. *The Writings of George Washington*, 14 vols. New York: G. P. Putnam's Sons, 1889–1893.
Gilmer, George M. *Sketches of Some of the First Settlers of Upper Georgia*. Americus, Georgia: Americus Book, 1926.
Goodrich, Samuel G. *Recollections of a Lifetime*, 2 vols. New York: Miller, Orton and Mulligan, 1857.
Graham, Catherine Macaulay. *The History of England from the Accession of James to that of the Brunswick Line*, 8 vols. 1763–1783.
Griswold, Rufus Wilmot. *The Republican Court; or, American Society in the Days of Washington*. New York: D. Appleton, 1867.
Hobson, Charles F., and Robert A. Rutland, eds. *The Papers of James Madison*, vol. 12. Charlottesville: University Press of Virginia, 1979.
Hopkins, James F., ed. *The Papers of Henry Clay*, 10 vols. Lexington: University of Kentucky Press, 1959–1991.
Howe, M. A. De Wolfe, ed. *The Articulate Sisters: Passages from Journals and Letters of the Daughters of Josiah Quincy*. Cambridge: Harvard University Press, 1946.
Hunt, Gaillard, ed. *The First Forty Years of Washington Society in the Family Letters of*

Margaret Bayard Smith. New York: Frederick Ungar Publishing Co., 1965.
Hunt, Gaillard, ed. *The Writings of James Madison*, 10 vols. New York: G. P. Putnam's Sons, 1900–1910.
Jackson, Donald, and Dorothy Twohig, eds. *The Diaries of George Washington*, 6 vols. Charlottesville: University Press of Virginia, 1976–1979.
Johnstone, Henry P., ed. *The Correspondence and Public Papers of John Jay*, 4 vols. New York: Bert Franklin, 1890–1893.
King, Charles R., ed. *The Life and Correspondence of Rufus King*, 6 vols. New York: G. P. Putnam's Sons, 1894–1900.
Lipscomb, Andrew A., and Albert E. Bergh, eds. *The Writings of Thomas Jefferson*, 20 vols. Washington, D.C.: The Thomas Jefferson Memorial Association, 1905.
Maclay, Edgar, ed. *The Journal of William Maclay, United States Senator from Pennsylvania, 1789–1791*. New York: Albert & Charles Boni, 1927.
Massachusetts Historical Society. "Letters of James Monroe," *Proceedings of the Massachusetts Historical Society*, vol. 42. Boston: Massachusetts Historical Society, 1909.
The Massachusetts Register and United States Calendar: for the year our Lord 1817. Boston: West Richardson, and James Loring, 1818.
McMurtrie, H. *Sketches of Louisville and Its Environs*. Louisville: S. Penn, 1819.
Meriwether, Robert L., ed. *The Papers of John C. Calhoun*, 25 vols. Columbia: University of South Carolina Press, 1969.
Michigan Historical Commission. "Historical Notes." *Michigan History Magazine*, vol. XIV. Lansing: Michigan Historical Commission, 1930.
Moore, Charles, ed. *George Washington's Rules of Civility and Decent Behaviour in Company and Conversation*. Boston: Houghton Mifflin, 1926.
A narrative of a tour of observation, made during the summer of 1817, by James Monroe, president of the United States, through the north-eastern and north-western departments of the Union. Philadelphia: S.A. Mitchell and H. Ames, 1818.
New York Public Library. "Letter of James Monroe, 1812–1817," *Bulletin of the New York Public Library*, vol. VI. New York: Astor Lenox and Tilden Foundations, 1902.
Oberg, Barbara B. et al., eds. *The Papers of Thomas Jefferson*, 34 vols. Princeton: Princeton University Press, 1950–2002.
Preston, Daniel, ed. *The Papers of James Monroe: A Documentary History of the Presidential Tours of James Monroe, 1817, 1818, and 1819*, vol. I. Westport, Connecticut: Greenwood Press, 2003.
Quincy, Eliza Susan. *Memoir of the Life of Eliza S. M. Quincy*. Boston: John Wilson and Son, 1861.
Radcliffe, Richard, ed. *The President's Tour: A Collection of Addresses Made to James Monroe, esq. President of the United States*. New Ipswich: Salmon Wilder, 1822.
Richardson, James D., ed. *A Compilation of the Messages and Papers of the Presidents, 1789–1897*. Washington: Government Printing Office, 1896–1899.
Rossiter, Clinton, ed. *The Federalist Papers*. New York: New American Library, 1961.
Smucker, Samuel L., ed. *The Life and Speeches of Daniel Webster*. Philadelphia: Quaker City Publishing House, 1860.
Swift, Joseph Gardner. *The Memoirs of General Joseph Gardner, LL.D, U.S.A.* Worcester, Massachusetts: F.S. Blanchard and Co., 1890.
Syrett, Harold C., ed. *The Papers of Alexander Hamilton*, 27 vols. New York: Columbia University Press, 1961–1987.

Thwaites, Reuben Gold, ed. *Early Western Travels, 1748–1846*, 32 vols. Cleveland: Arthur H. Clark, 1904.
Tyler's Quarterly Historical and Genealogical Magazine. "Letters of James Monroe," vol. V. Richmond, Va 1924.
U.S. Congress. *Letters and Other Writings of James Madison*, 4 vols. Philadelphia: J.B. Lippincott, 1865.
U.S. Government. *Inaugural Addresses of the Presidents of the United States.* Washington, D.C.: U.S. Government Printing Office, 1961.
Waldo, Samuel Putnam. *The Tour of James Monroe.* Hartford: F.D. Bolles, 1820.
Waldo, Samuel Putnam. *The Tour of James Monroe: President of the United States, in the Year 1817.* Hartford: F. D. Bolles, 1818.
Waldo, Samuel Putnam. *The Tour of James Monroe: President of the United States, through the Northern and Eastern States, in 1817; His Tour in the Year 1818; together with a Sketch of his Life.* Hartford: Silas Andrus, 1819.
Watson, John F. *Annals of Philadelphia and Pennsylvania in the olden time: Being a collection of memoirs, anecdotes and incidents of the city and its inhabitants*, 3 vols. Philadelphia: Elijah Thomas, 1857.
Webster, Daniel. *The Orations on Bunker Hill Monument, the Character of Washington, and the Landing at Plymouth.* New York: American Book, 1894.
Wiltse, Charles M., ed. *The Papers of Daniel Webster: Correspondence*, 7 vols. Hanover, N.H.: University Press of New England, 1974–1986.
Wirt, William. *The Letters of the British Spy.* Chapel Hill: University of North Carolina Press, 1970.

Secondary Sources

Allgor, Catherine. *Parlor Politics: In Which the Ladies of Washington Help Build a City and a Government.* Charlottesville: University Press of Virginia, 2000.
Allgor, Catherine. *A Perfect Union: Dolley Madison and the Creation of the American Nation.* New York: Henry Holt, 2006.
Ammon, Harry. *James Monroe: The Quest for National Identity.* Charlottesville: University Press of Virginia, 1990.
Appleby, Joyce. *Capitalism and a New Social Order: The Republican Vision of the 1790s.* New York: New York University Press, 1984.
Appleby, Joyce. *Inheriting the Revolution: The First Generation of Americans.* Cambridge: Belknap Press of Harvard University Press, 2000.
Banner, James M., Jr. *To the Hartford Convention: The Federalists and the Origins of Party Politics in Massachusetts, 1789–1815.* New York: Alfred A. Knopf, 1970.
Barratt, Carrie Rebora, and Ellen G. Miles. *Gilbert Stuart.* New York: Metropolitan Museum of Art, and New Haven: Yale University Press, 2004.
Bemis, Samuel Flagg, ed. *The American Secretaries of State and their Diplomacy*, 19 vols. New York: Cooper Square Publishers, 1963–1980.
Bergeron, David M. *English Civic Pageantry, 1558–1642.* London: Edward Arnold Publishers, 1971.
Billias, George A. *Elbridge Gerry: Founding Father and Republican Statesman.* New York: McGraw-Hill, 1976.
Bloom, Sol. *History of the Formation of the Union under the Constitution.* Washington,

D.C.: U.S. Government Printing Office, 1943.
Brant, Irving. *The Fourth President: A Life of James Madison*. London: Eyre and Spottiswoode, 1970.
Brigham, Clarence S. *History and Bibliography of American Newspapers, 1690–1820*, 2 vols. Worcester, Mass.: American Antiquarian Society, 1947.
Brugger, Robert J. *Maryland: A Middle Temperament, 1634–1980*. Baltimore: Johns Hopkins University Press, 1988.
Bryan, Helen. *Martha Washington: First Lady of Liberty*. New York: John Wiley and Sons, 2002.
Burrows, Edwin G., and Mike Wallace. *Gotham: A History of New York City to 1898*. New York: Oxford University Press, 1999.
Bushman, Richard L. *King and People in Provincial Massachusetts*. Chapel Hill: University of North Carolina Press, 1985.
Bushman, Richard L. *The Refinement of America: Persons, Houses, Cities*. New York: Alfred A. Knopf, 1992.
Cannadine, David, and Simon Price, eds. *Rituals of Royalty: Power and Ceremonial in Traditional Societies*. Cambridge: Cambridge University Press, 1987.
Caroli, Betty Boyd. *First Ladies*. New York: Oxford University Press, 1987.
Carroll, J. A., and M. W. Ashworth. *George Washington, First in Peace*. New York: Charles Scribner's Sons, 1957.
Cole, Mary Hill. *The Portable Queen: Elizabeth I and the Politics of Ceremony*. Amherst: University of Massachusetts Press, 1999.
Colley, Linda. *Britons: Forging the Nation, 1707–1837*. New Haven: Yale University Press, 1992.
Cresson, W. P. *James Monroe*. Chapel Hill: University of North Carolina Press, 1946.
Cunningham, Noble E., Jr. *The Jeffersonian Republicans: The Formation of Party Organization, 1789–1801*. Chapel Hill: University of North Carolina Press, 1957.
Cunningham, Noble E., Jr. *The Jeffersonian Republicans in Power: Party Operations, 1801–1809*. Chapel Hill: University of North Carolina Press, 1963.
Cunningham, Noble E., Jr. *The Presidency of James Monroe*. Lawrence: University Press of Kansas, 1996.
Cunningham, Noble E., Jr. *The Process of Government under Jefferson*. Princeton: Princeton University Press, 1978.
Dangerfield, George. *Chancellor Robert R. Livingston of New York, 1746–1813*. New York: Harcourt, Brace, 1960.
Dangerfield, George. *The Era of Good Feelings*. New York: Harcourt, Brace and World, Inc., 1952.
Davis, Susan G. *Parades and Power: Street Theatre in Nineteenth-Century Philadelphia*. Berkeley: University of California Press, 1988.
Decatur, Stephen, Jr. *Private Affairs of George Washington, From the Records and Accounts of Tobias Lear, Esquire, his Secretary*. Boston: Houghton Mifflin, 1933.
Dorwart, Jeffrey M. *Fort Mifflin of Philadelphia*. Philadelphia: University of Pennsylvania Press, 1998.
Dowling, William C. *Literary Federalism in the Age of Jefferson: Joseph Dennie and The Port Folio, 1801–1812*. Columbia: University of South Carolina Press, 1999.
Dunbar, Louise Burnham. *A Study of "Monarchical" Tendencies in the United States from 1776 to 1801*, vol. X, no. 1. Urbana: University of Illinois Studies in the Social Sciences, 1922.

Edgar, Walter. *South Carolina, A History*. Columbia: University of South Carolina Press, 1998.
Egerton, Douglas R. *Gabriel's Rebellion: The Virginia Slave Conspiracies of 1800 and 1802*. Chapel Hill: University of North Carolina Press, 1993.
Elkins, Stanley, and Eric McKittrick. *The Age of Federalism: The Early American Republic, 1788-1800*. New York: Oxford University Press, 1993.
Ellet, Elizabeth. *The Court Circles of the Republic*. Hartford: Hartford Publishing, 1869.
Ellis, Joseph J. *American Creation: Triumphs and Tragedies at the Founding of the Republic*. New York: Alfred A. Knopf, 2007.
Ellis, Joseph J. *American Sphinx: The Character of Thomas Jefferson*. New York: Alfred A. Knopf, 1997.
Ellis, Joseph J. *Founding Brothers: The Revolutionary Generation*. New York: Alfred A. Knopf, 2000.
Ellis, Joseph J. *His Excellency: George Washington*. New York: Alfred A. Knopf, 2004.
Fahs, Alice, and Joan Waugh, eds. *Memory of the Civil War in American Culture*. Chapel Hill: University of North Carolina Press, 2004.
Faust, Drew Gilpin. *James Henry Hammond and the Old South: A Design for Mastery*. Baton Rouge: Louisiana State University Press, 1982.
Ferling, John. *Adams vs. Jefferson: The Tumultuous Election of 1800*. New York: Oxford University Press, 2004.
Flexner, James Thomas. *George Washington and the New Nation (1783-1793)*. Boston: Little, Brown, 1969.
Freeman, Douglas Southall. *George Washington, a Biography: Patriot and President*, 6 vols. New York: Charles Scribner's Sons, 1954.
Freeman, Joanne. *Affairs of Honor: National Politics in the New Republic*. New Haven: Yale University Press, 2001.
Fritz, Christian G. *American Sovereigns: The People and America's Constitutional Tradition before the Civil War*. Cambridge: Cambridge University Press, 2008.
Geertz, Clifford. "Centers, Kings, and Charisma: Reflections on the Symbolics of Power." In *Culture and Its Creators*, edited by Joseph Ben-David and Terry Nichols Clark. Chicago: University of Chicago Press, 1977.
Geertz, Clifford. *Local Knowledge: Further Essays in Interpretive Anthropology*. New York: Basic Books, 1983.
Geertz, Clifford. *Negara: The Theatre State in Nineteenth-century Bali*. Princeton: Princeton University Press, 1980.
Gilmore, William J. *Reading Becomes a Necessity of Life: Material and Cultural Life in Rural New England, 1780-1835*. Knoxville: University of Tennessee Press, 1989.
Goodstein, Anita S. *Nashville, 1780-1860: From Frontier to City*. Gainesville: University of Florida Press, 1989.
Govan, Thomas P. *Nicholas Biddle: Nationalist and Public Banker, 1786-1844*. Chicago: University of Chicago Press, 1959.
Green, Fletcher M. "On Tour with President Andrew Jackson." *The New England Quarterly* (March-December 1963): 209-28.
Greenberg, Kenneth S. *Honor and Slavery: Lies, Duels, Noses, Masks, Dressing as a Woman, Gifts, Strangers, Humanitarianism, Death, Slave Rebellions, The Proslavery Argument, Baseball, Hunting, and Gambling in the Old South*. Princeton: Princeton University Press, 1996.

Greene, Suzanne Ellery. *Baltimore: An Illustrated History*. Woodland Hills, Calif.: Windsor Publications, 1980.
Hamlin, Talbot. *Benjamin Henry Latrobe*. New York: Oxford University Press, 1955.
Hayden, Ilse. *Symbol and Privilege: The Ritual Context of British Royalty*. Tucson: University of Arizona Press, 1987.
Heale, M. J. *The Making of American Politics, 1750-1850*. London: Longman, 1977.
Heale, M. J. *The Presidential Quest: Candidates and Images in American Political Culture, 1787-1852*. London: Longman, 1982.
Hickey, Donald R. *The War of 1812: A Forgotten Conflict*. Urbana: University of Illinois Press, 1989.
Hill, Bridget. *The Republican Virago: The Life and Times of Catherine Macaulay, Historian*. Oxford: Clarendon Press, 1992.
Hofstadter, Richard. *The Idea of a Party System: The Rise of Legitimate Opposition in the United States, 1780-1840*. Berkeley: University of California Press, 1969.
Holt, Michael F. *The Rise and Fall of the American Whig Party: Jacksonian Politics and the Onset of the Civil War*. New York: Oxford University Press, 1999.
Howe, Daniel Walker. *The Political Culture of the American Whigs*. Chicago: University of Chicago Press, 1979.
Howe, Daniel Walker. *What God Hath Wrought: The Transformation of America, 1815-1848*. New York: Oxford University Press, 2007.
Hunt, Lynn. *Politics, Culture, and Class in the French Revolution*. Berkeley: University of California Press, 1984.
Hunt, Lynn, ed. *The New Cultural History*. Berkeley: University of California Press, 1989.
Idzerda, Stanley J., et al. *Lafayette: Hero of Two Worlds: The Art and Pageantry of His Farewell Tour of America, 1824-1825*. Flushing, New York: The Queens Museum, Hanover: University Press of New England, 1989.
John, Richard R. *Spreading the News: The American Postal System from Franklin to Morse*. Cambridge: Harvard University Press, 1995.
Johnson, Amanda. *Georgia as Colony and State*. Atlanta: Cherokee Publishing, 1970.
Kammen, Michael. *A Season of Youth: The American Revolution and the Historical Imagination*. New York: Alfred A. Knopf, 1978.
Kertzer, David I. *Ritual, Politics and Power*. New Haven: Yale University Press, 1988.
Ketcham, Ralph. *Presidents above Party: The First American Presidency, 1789-1829*. Chapel Hill: University of North Carolina Press, 1984.
Kirker, Harold. *The Architecture of Charles Bulfinch*. Cambridge: Harvard University Press, 1969.
Kolchin, Peter. *American Slavery, 1619-1877*. New York: Hill and Wang, 1993.
Kramer, Lloyd S. *Lafayette in Two Worlds: Public Cultures and Personal Identities in an Age of Revolutions*. Chapel Hill: University of North Carolina Press, 1996.
Larson, Edward J. *A Magnificent Catastrophe: The Tumultuous Election of 1800: America's First Presidential Campaign*. New York: Free Press, 2007.
Larson, John L. *Internal Improvement: National Public Works and the Promise of Popular Government in the Early United States*. Chapel Hill: University of North Carolina Press, 2001.
Lawrence, Alexander A. *James Moore Wayne, Southern Unionist*. Chapel Hill: University of North Carolina Press, 1943.
Lefler, Hugh T., and Albert R. Newsome. *The History of a Southern State: North Carolina*.

Chapel Hill: University of North Carolina Press, 1973.
Livermore, Shaw. *The Twilight of Federalism: The Disintegration of the Federalist Party, 1815–1830*. Princeton: Princeton University Press, 1962.
Lofton, John. *Denmark Vesey's Revolt: The Slave Plot that Lit the Fuse to Fort Sumter*. Kent: Kent State University Press, 1964.
Loveland, Anne C. *Emblem of Liberty: The Image of Lafayette in the American Mind*. Baton Rouge: Louisiana State University Press, 1971.
Marston, Jerrilyn Greene. *King and Congress: The Transfer of Political Legitimacy, 1774–1776*. Princeton: Princeton University Press, 1987.
Mayer, Henry F. *All on Fire: William Lloyd Garrison and the Abolition of Slavery*. New York: St. Martin's Press, 1998.
McConville, Brendan. *The King's Three Faces: The Rise and Fall of Royal America, 1688–1776*. Chapel Hill: University of North Carolina Press, 2006.
McCormick, Richard P. *The Second American Party System: Party Formation in the Jacksonian Era*. Chapel Hill: University of North Carolina Press, 1966.
McCullough, David. *John Adams*. New York: Simon and Schuster, 2001.
McCurry, Stephanie. *Masters of Small Worlds: Yeoman Households, Gender Relations, and the Political Culture of the Antebellum South Low Country*. New York: Oxford University Press, 1995.
McDonald, Forrest. *The Presidency of George Washington*. New York: W.W. Norton, 1974.
McNamara, Brooks. *Day of Jubilee: The Great Age of Public Celebrations in New York, 1788–1909*. New Brunswick, N.J.: Rutgers University Press, 1997.
Meigs, William M. *The Life of Charles Jared Ingersoll*. Philadelphia: J.B. Lippincott, 1897.
Mooney, Chase C. *William H. Crawford, 1772–1834*. Lexington: University Press of Kentucky, 1974.
Morgan, Edmund S. *Inventing the People: The Rise of Popular Sovereignty in England and America*. New York: W.W. Norton, 1988.
Morison, Samuel Eliot. *Harrison Gray Otis, 1765–1848: The Urbane Federalist*. Boston: Houghton Mifflin, 1969.
Myers, Minor. *Liberty without Anarchy: A History of the Society of Cincinnati*. Charlottesville: University Press of Virginia, 1983.
Nagel, Paul C. *John Quincy Adams: A Public Life, A Private Life*. New York: Alfred A. Knopf, 1997.
Neely, Sylvia. *Lafayette and the Liberal Ideal, 1814–1824: Politics and Conspiracy in an Age of Reaction*. Carbondale: Southern Illinois University Press, 1991.
The New Catholic Encyclopedia, 2nd edition, vol. 6. Detroit: Thomson Gale, 2003.
Newman, Simon P. *Parades and Politics of the Street: Festive Culture in the Early American Republic*. Philadelphia: University of Pennsylvania Press, 1997.
Newman, Simon P. "'Principles or Men?' George Washington and the Political Culture of National Leadership, 1776–1801." *Journal of the Early Republic* 12 (1992): 477–507.
Ozouf, Mona. *Festivals and the French Revolution*. Cambridge: Harvard University Press, 1988.
Paget, Julian. *The Pageantry of Britain*. London: Michael Joseph, 1979.
Parramore, Thomas C. *Norfolk: The First Four Generations*. Charlottesville: University Press of Virginia, 1994.
Pasley, Jeffrey L. *"The Tyranny of Printers": Newspaper Politics in the Early American Republic*. Charlottesville: University Press of Virginia, 2001.

Pasley, Jeffrey L., Andrew Robertson, and David Waldstreicher, eds. *Beyond the Founding Fathers: New Approaches to the Political History of the Early Republic.* Chapel Hill: University of North Carolina Press, 2004.
Pease, William, and Jane H. Pease. *The Web of Progress: Private Values and Public Styles in Boston and Charleston, 1828–1843.* Oxford: Oxford University Press, 1985.
Peterson, Merrill D. *The Great Triumvirate: Webster, Clay, and Calhoun.* New York: Oxford University Press, 1987.
Peterson, Merrill D. *The Jefferson Image in the American Mind.* New York: Oxford University Press, 1962.
Peterson, Merrill D. *Thomas Jefferson and the New Nation.* New York: Oxford University Press, 1970.
Place, Charles A. *Charles Bulfinch, Architect and Citizen.* Boston: Houghton Mifflin, 1925.
Potter, Kathleen O. *The Federalist's Vision of Popular Sovereignty in the New American Republic.* New York: LFB Scholarly Publishing LLC, 2002.
Purcell, Sarah J. *Sealed with Blood: War, Sacrifice, and Memory in Revolutionary America.* Philadelphia: University of Pennsylvania Press, 2002.
Rakove, Jack N. *Original Meanings: Politics and Ideas in the Meaning of the Constitution.* New York: Alfred A. Knopf, 1997.
Remini, Robert V. *Andrew Jackson and the Course of American Democracy, 1833–1845.* New York: Harper and Row Publishers, 1984.
Remini, Robert V. *Andrew Jackson and the Course of American Empire, 1767–1821.* New York: Harper and Row Publishers, 1977.
Remini, Robert V. *Andrew Jackson and the Course of American Freedom, 1822–1832.* New York: Harper and Row Publishers, 1981.
Remini, Robert V. *Daniel Webster: The Man and His Time.* New York: W.W. Norton, 1997.
Remini, Robert V. *Henry Clay: Statesman for the Union.* New York: W.W. Norton, 1991.
Rutland, Robert Allen. *James Madison: The Founding Father.* New York: Macmillan, 1987.
Ryan, Mary P. *Cradle of the Middle Class: The Family in Oneida County, New York, 1790–1865.* Cambridge: Cambridge University Press, 1981.
Ryan, Mary P. "Party Formation in the United States Congress, 1789 to 1796: A Quantitative Analysis." *William and Mary Quarterly* 28 (October 1971): 523–42.
Schudson, Michael. *The Good Citizen: A History of American Civic Life.* New York: Free Press, 1998.
Schwartz, Barry. *George Washington: The Making of an American Symbol.* New York: Free Press, 1987.
Sharp, James Roger. *American Politics in the Early Republic: The New Nation in Crisis.* New Haven: Yale University Press, 1993.
Sheriff, Carol. *The Artificial River: The Erie Canal and the Paradox of Progress, 1817–1862.* New York: Hill and Wang, 1996.
Shields, David S., and Frederika J. Teute. Unpublished Conference Papers on Republican Court, 2005.
Sisson, Daniel. *The American Revolution of 1800.* New York: Alfred A. Knopf, 1974.
Skelton, William B. "High Army Leadership in the Era of the War of 1812: The Making and Remaking of the Officer Corps." *William and Mary Quarterly* 51 (April 1994): 253–74.
Smith, James Morton. *Freedom's Fetters: The Alien and Sedition Laws and American Civil Liberties.* Ithaca: Cornell University Press, 1956.

Smith, Page. *John Adams*, 3 vols. Garden City, N.Y.: Doubleday, 1962.
Snow, Caleb H. *A History of Boston: The Metropolis of Massachusetts*. Boston: Abel Bowen, 1828.
Stansell, Christine. *City of Women: Sex and Class in New York, 1789–1890*. Urbana: University of Illinois Press, 1987.
Stanwood, Edward. *A History of the Presidency*. Boston: Houghton, Mifflin, 1904.
Strong, Roy. *Art and Power, Renaissance Festivals, 1450–1650*. Berkeley: University of California Press, 1984.
Thomas, Isaiah. *The History of Printing in America*, 2 vols. Albany: Joel Munsell, 1874.
Thompson, Peter. "'The Friendly Glass': Drink and Gentility in Colonial Pennsylvania." *Pennsylvania Magazine of History and Biography* CXIII (1989): 549–73.
Travers, Len. *Celebrating the Fourth: Independence Day and the Rites of Nationalism in the Early Republic*. Amherst: University of Massachusetts Press, 1997.
Tulis, Jeffrey. *The Rhetorical Presidency*. Princeton: Princeton University Press, 1987.
Voorsanger, Catherine Hoover, and John K. Howat, eds. *Art and the Empire City: New York, 1825–1861*. Metropolitan Museum of Art, New Haven: Yale University Press, 2000.
Wade, Richard C. *The Urban Frontier: Pioneer Life in Early Pittsburgh, Cincinnati, Lexington, Louisville, and St. Louis*. Chicago: University of Chicago Press, 1959.
Waldstreicher, David. "Federalism, the Style of Politics, and the Politics of Style." In *The Federalists Reconsidered*, edited by Doron Ben-Atar and Barbara B. Oberg. Charlottesville: University Press of Virginia, 1998.
Waldstreicher, David. *In the Midst of Perpetual Fetes: The Making of American Nationalism, 1776–1820*. Chapel Hill: University of North Carolina Press, 1997.
Waldstreicher, David, and Stephen R. Grossbart. "Abraham Bishop's Vocation; or, The Mediation of Jeffersonian Politics." *Journal of the Early Republic* 18 (Winter 1998): 617–58.
Walters, Ronald. *American Reformers, 1815–1860*. New York: Hill and Wang, 1997.
Warner, Michael. *The Letters of the Republic: Publication and the Public Sphere in Eighteenth-century America*. Cambridge: Harvard University Press, 1990.
Watson, Harry L. *Liberty and Power: The Politics of Jacksonian America*. New York: Hill and Wang, 1990.
Weigley, Russell F., ed. *Philadelphia: A 300-year History*. New York: W.W. Norton, 1982.
White, Shane. "'It was a proud day': African Americans, Festivals and Parades in the North, 1741–1834." *Journal of American History*, 81, no. 1 (1994): 13–50.
Wiebe, Robert H. *The Opening of American Society: From the Adoption of the Constitution to the Eve of Disunion*. New York: Alfred A. Knopf, 1984.
Wieneck, Henry. *An Imperfect God: George Washington, His Slaves, and the Creation of America*. New York: Farrar, Straus, and Giroux, 2003.
Wilentz, Sean. *The Rise of American Democracy: Jefferson to Lincoln*. New York: W. W. Norton, 2005.
Wiltse, Charles M. *John C. Calhoun: Nationalist, 1782–1828*. Indianapolis: Bobbs-Merrill, 1944.
Withey, Lynne. *Dearest Friend: A Life of Abigail Adams*. New York: Free Press, 1981.
Wood, Gordon S. *The Creation of the American Republic, 1776–1787*. New York: W.W. Norton, 1972.
Wood, Gordon S. *The Radicalism of the American Revolution*. New York, Alfred A. Knopf, 1992.

Young, Robert W. *Senator James Murray Mason: Defender of the Old South.* Knoxville: University of Tennessee Press, 1998.

Zagarri, Rosemarie. *Revolutionary Backlash: Women and Politics in the Early Republic.* Philadelphia: University of Pennsylvania Press, 2007.

Biographical Directories

Biographical Directory of the American Congress, 1774-1996. Alexandria, Virginia: Congressional Quarterly, 1997.

Garraty, John A., and Mark C. Carnes, eds. *American National Biography*, 24 vols. New York: Oxford University Press, 1999.

Johnson, Allen, and Dumas Malone, eds. *Dictionary of American Biography*, 20 vols. New York: Charles Scribner's Sons, 1928-1936.

Who Was Who in America, Historical Vol., 1607-1896. Chicago: A.N. Marquis, 1963.

Index

Abbot, William, 124
Adams, Abigail, 5, 45, 60, 61, 115, 121, 131, 190n34, 191n60, 196n153
Adams, John, 14, 15, 16, 24, 25, 28, 29, 31, 32, 33, 37, 38, 40, 42, 43, 45, 62, 65, 73, 74, 115, 121, 187n109, 198n20; Adams-Pinckney presidential ticket, 76, 80, 153, 202n96; as Minister to Great Britain, 31; as president, 5, 38, 59, 60–61, 74, 76, 79, 82, 84, 124, 151; as Vice President, 15, 16, 24, 25, 28, 33, 37, 38, 59; death of, 177; inauguration, 60; Monroe's northern tour, 115, 121; title debate, 24, 30, 31, 32, 33
Adams, John Quincy, 115, 121, 130, 133, 141, 142, 168, 172, 173, 174, 176, 177, 216n109; as president, 177; as Secretary of State, 115, 130, 141, 142, 176; presidential election of 1824, 133, 172–173
Adams-Onis Treaty, 1819, 142
Addresses, Welcoming, 6, 16, 17, 22, 51, 55, 56, 59, 92, 105, 107, 109, 111, 115, 116, 118, 119, 128, 138, 139, 148, 149, 156, 158, 160, 164, 165, 167
Alabama, 137, 157
Alexandria, Virginia, 17, 84
Alien and Sedition Acts, 1798, 61, 77, 78
Ambition, 8, 14, 65, 76, 94, 133, 158, 163, 175, 201n76
American Aurora, 168
American Beacon, 138, 140, 166
American Revolution, 12, 18, 19, 37, 44, 59, 66, 69, 72, 76, 77, 82, 92, 96, 107, 108, 109, 112, 118, 119, 133, 134, 137, 138, 139, 140, 147, 151, 153, 161, 171, 174, 175, 176, 177
"American System," 96, 138, 160, 163–164, 165, 174, 205n13. See also Clay, Henry
Ames, Fisher, 29
Annapolis, Maryland, 135, 138, 139, 213n7. See also Monroe's Chesapeake Tour
Argus of Western America, 164
Aristocracy, 33, 46, 59, 62, 69, 72, 76, 79, 167, 191n60
Articles of Confederation, 39
Attorney General, U.S., 97, 122, 123, 130, 134, 174
Augusta Chronicle, 166–67
Augusta, Georgia, 154, 156
Authority, Federal, 10, 16, 34, 37, 39, 50
Authority, Presidential, 29, 43
Ayer, Sarah Connell, 112

Bache, Dr. William, 81
Baldwin, Abraham, 71. See also Jefferson, Thomas
Baldwin, Luther, 61. See also Sedition Act
Balls, 45, 51, 55, 85, 105, 121, 160
Balls, inaugural, 89, 171, 186n86
Baltimore, Maryland, 17, 100, 104, 105, 106, 107, 113, 177
Baltimore Patriot, 106
Banking, 57, 79, 154
Bank of the United States, 68, 69, 81, 96, 130, 134, 143, 160, 174, 177
Barge, 18, 19, *21*, 44, 55, 149
Battery Park, 19, 52, 109. See also New York City

Beckley, John, 70. See also Jefferson, Thomas
Biddle, Nicholas, 100–101, 103, 107, 130–131, 133, 174, 211n163
Bingham, Mrs. William (Anne), 47, 107
Blounts, Thomas, William, and William A.: 147, 214n36. See also Washington, North Carolina
Boston, 7, 22, 51, 52, 55, 97, 98, 101, 110, 111, 114, 115, 116, 117, 118, 119, 120, 121, 122, 124, 125, 127, 130, 134, 149, 151, 165, 215n60; Monroe's Tour, 116–124, 149, 151, 165; Washington's Tour, 7, 22, 50, 51, 54, 55
Boston Independent Chronicle, 15
Bourn, Sylvanus, 14, 15
Braintree, Massachusetts, 14, 15, 16. See also John Adams
Breckinridge, John C., 78. See also Kentucky Resolutions
Broadcloth, 16, 29
Broadsides, 75
Bronaugh, James, 158, 215n79. See also Jackson, Andrew; Nashville, Tennessee
Brown, John, 71. See also Jefferson, Thomas
Brown University, 111. See also Mann, Horace
Bulfinch, Charles, 115, 118, 130
Burr, Aaron, 76, 82, 84, 216n109

Cabinet, presidential, 43, 51, 65, 69, 70, 72, 73, 74, 81, 94, 122, 131, 137, 140, 141, 142, 176, 188n7, 197n6; Monroe's, 94, 122, 130, 131, 137, 140, 141, 142, 156, 176; Washington's, 51, 65, 68, 69, 70, 72, 73, 81, 188n7, 189n18, 193n89, 197n6, 199n35
Calhoun, John C., 136, 137, 138, 141, 142, 143, 144, *145*, 146, 148, 149, 156, 161, 163, 170, 172, 173, 17, 212n2, 213n21, 217n5; as Adams's vice president, 217n5; as Jackson's vice president, 142, 170, 213n21; as Monroe's Secretary of War, 136, 137, 138, 141, 145, 146, 148, 149, 156, 161, 176, 208n76. See also Planter class

Callender, James Thomson, 80
Campaigning, 175, 177
Candidates, 79, 81, 90, 168, 175, 177
Cannon salutes, 16, 25, 61, 110, 111
Capitol, U.S., 63, 84, 85, 89, 130, 170
Carriages, 21, 25, 37, 60
Carter, Jimmy, 3; inauguration, 1977, 3
Cavalry, 16, 89, 117, 149
Chamberlain, 42
Chancellor, New York State, 24, 25, 38, 41, 185n68, 189n22. See also Livingston, Robert R
Charleston, South Carolina, 55, 137, 147, 148, 149, 150, 151, 152, 153, 165, 215n60
Charleston Courier, 149, 150
Cherokees, 85, 157
Cincinnati, Ohio, 166
Citizens, United States, 4, 5, 6, 7, 8, 9, 10, 11, 13, 16, 17, 22, 25, 29, 33, 34, 35, 36, 37, 40, 42, 50, 51, 54, 55, 56, 59, 60, 62, 81, 82, 83, 85, 90, 91, 92, 94, 95, 97, 106, 109, 111, 112, 114, 127, 133, 149, 164, 169, 171, 189n4
Clark, Brown, 61. See also Sedition Act
Clarke, General John, 154. See also Crawford, William H
Clay, Henry, 94, 96, 125, 129, 130, 131, 133, 134, 137, 138, 141, 142, 143, 144, 160, 161, *162*, 163, 165, 166, 167, 168, 169, 172, 173, 174, 176, 177, 212n2, 215n86, 216n98, 217n9; Clay's 1819 tour, 164–165, 166, 216n98; as Speaker of the House 137, 141, 142, 161, 176; criticisms of Monroe, 129, 130, 137, 161, 163; presidential candidate, 1824, 133, 168, 169, 172, 173; tour, 1847, 177, 212n173. See also Planter class
Clinton, DeWitt, 168, 175–176, 208n68, 217n22
Clinton, George, 21, 52, 175, 190n39
Cobb, David, 112. See also Monroe's northern tour
Colonists, American, 9, 12
Columbian Centinel, 117, 124, 125, 126
Committee of Arrangements, 103, 111, 184; Boston, 50, 115, 116, 117, 118, 124; Southern, 147, 173

Confederation Congress, 138
Congressional elections, 11, 14, 36, 74, 79
Congress, U.S., 5, 11, 12, 13, 14, 16, 27, 28, 29, 30, 31, 33, 34, 35, 36, 39, 40, 42, 43, 44, 48, 51, 58, 60, 61, 62, 68, 74, 77, 80, 82, 84, 94, 98, 100, 131, 138, 140, 141, 142, 156, 174, 176, 183n28, 185n71
Congressmen, 15, 19, 23, 24, 31, 38, 39, 45, 85, 89, 98, 134, 142, 144
Connecticut, 15, 16, 51, 71, 75, 82, 111
Connecticut Gazette, 110, 113
Constitution, U.S., 4, 5, 6, 8, 9, 10, 11, 12, 13, 14, 15, 19, 25, 29, 30, 32, 33, 34, 35, 36, 37, 38, 39, 49, 50, 51, 52, 54, 57, 59, 60, 62, 63, 64, 65, 66, 69, 70, 72, 73, 74, 76, 78, 81, 82, 83, 89, 90, 92, 119, 126, 134, 138, 141, 156, 164, 171; First Amendment, 70, 71, 72, 74, 78, 82, 84;Tenth Amendment, 78, 82; Twelfth Amendment, 196n147, 197n4, 216n109
Constitutional Convention, 12, 66, 70, 175, 177
Constitutional Gazette; and Republican Courier, 74, 200n53. See also Coxe, Tench
Continental Army, 41
Continental Congress, 13, 15
Correspondence: Jefferson's political, 56, 57, 68, 69, 77, 81; role in politics, 180n7
Corruption, 66, 68, 69, 88. See also Jefferson, Thomas
Coxe, Tench, 70, 71, 74
Crawford, William H., 129, 130, 131, 133, 136–137, 138, 141, 142, 143, 144, 145, *155*, 156, 161, 162, 166, 168, 172, 173, 176, 212n2, 217n12; as Monroe's Secretary of Treasury, 129, 136–137, 141, 154, 156, 161, 176; as presidential candidate, 1824, 133, 168, 172. See also Planter class
Creeks, 144, 153, 158
Crowninshield, Benjamin, 138; Secretary of the Navy, 138

Daily Georgian, 156
Dearborn, Henry A. S., 116, 119, 209n102, 209n121

Declaration of Independence, 39, 177
Delaware, 50, 177
Democracy, 27, 72, 88, 171, 175
Democratic Party, 97, 135, 173, 174, 175
Democratic-Republicans, 57, 58, 59, 60, 61, 62, 63, 64, 65, 66, 68, 70, 71, 72, 74, 75, 77, 78, 79, 80, 82, 83, 88, 91, 92, 94, 95, 96, 97, 100, 115, 116, 118, 119, 121, 122, 125, 127, 129, 130, 131, 132, 133, 136, 143, 153, 154, 163, 168, 169, 172, 173, 174, 175, 177, 197n1, 198n15. See also Jefferson, Thomas
Democratic-Republican Societies, 71, 72, 73. See Whiskey Rebellion
Detroit, Michigan, 104
Dinner parties, 16, 17, 37, 39, 41, 42, 43, 45, 49, 51, 55, 56, 59, 60, 62, 85, 86, 89, 105, 106, 117, 121, 125, 138, 147, 151, 156, 157, 160, 161, 164
Drayton, Colonel William, 147, 214n37. See also Charleston, South Carolina

Eaton, John, 158, 160, 173, 215n80. See also Nashville, Tennessee; Jackson, Andrew
Electoral College, 13, 82; electoral votes, 14, 80, 82, 83, 147, 169, 172, 173, 202n96
Electorate, 74, 171, 175
Elizabeth I, 11, 188n3
Elizabeth City, North Carolina, 139, 140
Elizabethtown, New Jersey, 18, *21*
Ellsworth, Oliver, 30
Eppes, John Wayles, 83, 198n20
"Era of Good Feelings," 91, 92, 124–25, 126, 130, 133, 204n3. See also *Columbian Centinel* and Benjamin Russell
Erie Canal, 139, 175–76, 217n21
Europe, 31, 36, 37, 40, 42, 49, 56, 57, 59, 62, 83, 154
Executive branch, 33, 34, 37, 40, 43, 57, 62, 73, 74, 79, 90, 100
Exeter, New Hampshire, 52, 128
Exeter Watchmen, 128

Factions, 8, 64, 65, 72, 79, 96, 97, 132, 153
Federal government, 5, 6, 7, 9, 10, 11, 12,

13, 14, 15, 17, 25, 26, 30, 31, 33, 34, 36, 37, 38, 41, 42, 46, 47, 50, 52, 54, 56, 57, 62, 66, 76, 88, 91, 92, 94, 95, 96, 100, 106, 108, 114, 116, 124, 134, 138, 139, 143, 147, 148, 150, 160, 163, 164, 166, 171
Federal Hall, 25, *26*, 27
Federalists, 57, 58, 59, 61, 62, 63, 64, 65, 66, 67, 69, 71, 72, 74, 75, 76, 77, 78, 79, 80, 81, 82, 83, 85, 88, 89, 91, 92, 94, 95, 96, 97, 98, 100, 101, 103, 107, 114, 115, 116, 117, 118, 119, 121, 122, 123, 124, 125, 126, 127, 128, 129, 130, 131, 132, 133, 134, 144, 153, 168, 169, 171, 173, 174, 175, 177, 205n9
Federalists Papers, 38; #10, 8, 132
Fenno, John, 50. See also *Gazette of the United States*
First Lady (President's Wife), 44, 45, 46, 60, 85, 88, 89, 119, 171, 190n34; debate on title, 44
Flint, Timothy, 165
Florida, 137, 140, 141, 142, 150, 158, 160, 161. See also Seminole War
Foreign affairs, 43, 58, 61, 82
Founding Generation, 9, 92, 94, 96, 133, 134, 138, 156, 168, 169, 17, 172, 175, 176, 177, 178
France, 39, 42, 69, 71, 72, 77, 79, 86, 95; French Revolution, 56, 72, 76, 81; Genet, "Citizen" Edmund, 71, 72, 73; Reign of Terror, 72; XYZ Affair, 75
Frankfort, Kentucky, 164
Fraunces, Samuel, 47. See also Presidential Steward
Fredericksburg, Virginia, 54, 113
Freneau, Philip, 57, 68, 74. See also Democratic-Republican newspapers

Gales, Joseph, 113, 125, 165. See also *National Intelligencer;* William Seaton
Gallatin, Albert, 127, 129, 132. See also Treasury, Secretary of the
Garrison, William Lloyd, 111
Gazette of the United States, 45, 50, 68. See also Fenno, John
Generation, Antebellum, 91, 94, 96, 137, 161, 169, 171, 175, 177, 178. See also

Adams, John Quincy; Calhoun, John C.; Clay, Henry; Clinton, De Witt; Jackson, Andrew; Democratic Party; Whig Party; Second American Party system
Genet, "Citizen" Edmund Charles, 71, 72, 73. See also France
George III, 12, 174
Georgia, 54, 55, 80, 135, 137, 144, 145, 146, 153, 154, 155, 160
Gerry, Elbridge, 82, 84, 202n93
Giles, William Branch, 69, 72. See also Jefferson, Thomas
"God Save the King," 19
Gore, Christopher, 98, *99*, 114, 117, 121, 206n27
Graham, Catherine Macaulay, 56, 57, 195n128
Granger, Gideon, 82, 202n95
Great Britain, 9, 31, 39, 42, 71, 73, 79, 86, 94, 95, 96, 105, 140, 143, 148, 153; British government, 76, 78, 185n65; Hanoverians, 11, 12; House of Commons, 28; in American colonies, 11; Stuart Dynasty, 12; Tudor Dynasty, 12. See also War of 1812
Grundy, Felix, 158, 173, 215n79. See also Nashville, Tennessee; Jackson, Andrew
Gullager, Christian, 52
Gouverneur, Samuel, 146, 157. See also Monroe's Chesapeake and Southern Tours
Gun Salutes, 44, 54

Habsburg Dynasty, 12
Hamilton, Alexander, 37, 38, 40, 42, 43, 51, 57, 62, 65, 66, 67, 68, 69, 70, 71, 72, 73, 74, 75, 79, 81, 126, 153, 188n7, 202n97; accusations of favoring monarchy, 70–71, 79; "An American," 68; as Washington's Secretary of the Treasury, 51, 57, 65, 66, 68–69, 81; break with Jefferson, 201n85; on public credit, 66. See also Federalists
Hampshire Gazette, 128
Hancock, John, 52, 193n101, 1930194n102
Harrodsburg, Kentucky, 166
Hartford, Connecticut, 15, 16, 111

Hartford Convention, 95, 97, 98, 114, 118, 125, 144, 206n23. See also Federalists; Otis, Harrison Gray; War of 1812
Hartford Manufactory, 16, 29
Harvard University, 52, 53, 118, 165
Hay, George, 127, 128, 153, 198n20. See also Monroe, James
Henry IV, King of France, 113
Hogg, Samuel, 158, 215n78. See also Nashville, Tennessee; Jackson, Andrew
Hopkinson, Joseph, 122, 124, 210n131. See also Federalists
Hopkinsville, Kentucky, 165
House of Representatives, U.S., 4, 13, 14, 15, 23, 24, 25 27, 28, 30, 31, 32, 33, 38, 70, 80, 82, 83, 137, 141, 161, 169, 173, 176, 202n96
House, presidential, 15, 24, 27, 37, 44, 47, 48, 190n39; in New York City, 49; in Philadelphia, 47, 48–49; in Washington, DC, 85, 86, 89, 170; White House, 170, 176
Hughes, Christopher, 97, 98, 206n21. See also Monroe, James
Humphreys, David, 57. See also Washington, George
Hunter, John, 71. See also Jefferson, Thomas

Illuminations, 50, 51, 54, 110, 111
Impressment, 94–95. See also War of 1812
Inaugurations, Presidential, 202n101. See also specific president
Independence Day, 42, 45, 58, 85, 119, 176, 177
Indiana, 163
Ingersoll, Charles J., 128
Inns/Lodgings, 54, 55, 106, 107, 110, 117–118, 125, 194n117, 194n118; Conrad and McMunn's, 63, 84; Gadsby's Hotel, 170
Internal improvements, 96, 101, 139, 146, 148, 160, 165. See also American System; Erie Canal; Roads; Steamboats
Irving, Washington, 89. See also Madison, James

Jackson, Andrew, 94, 95, 106, 130, 133, 136, 137, 138, 140, 141, 142, 143, 144, 146, 157, 158, 159, *160*, 161, 162, 163, 164, 165, 168, 169, 172, 173, 174, 177, 212n2; as president, 158, 170, 171, 174, 213n21; Battle of New Orleans (1815) 95, 144; Hermitage, 157; inauguration, 1829, 170–171, *172*; on Monroe's southern tour, 146, 157–161; Seminole War, 140–142.; presidential candidate, 1824, 133, 168, 169, 172, 173; presidential tour of New England, 177, 212n173
Jay, John, 16, 38, 41, 45, 51, 188n7, 188n8, 189n17
Jay's Treaty, 75
Jefferson, Thomas, 3, 5, 7, 8, 38, 52 57, 59, 60, 61, 62, 64, 65, 66, *67*, 68, 69, 70, 71, 72, 73, 76, 83, 91, 96, 97, 100, 119, 127, 128, 132, 142, 169, 171, 173 194n112, 197n6, 197n7, 199n41, 200n61, 201n78; as minister to France, 66; as partisan leader, 64–65, 71, 73, 74–83, 127, 132; as president, 63, 84, 85, 86, 87, 88, 89, 90, 92, 124, 151, 153, 168, 175, 178, 216n109; as Washington's secretary of state, 65, 68, 69, 70, 72, 73, 81, 197n6, 199n35; as Adams's vice president, 60, 65, 74, 75, 76, 77, 78, 79, 80, 81, 82; attacks on Alexander Hamilton, 65–71; break with Alexander Hamilton, 201n85; correspondence, 56, 57, 68, 69, 77, 81; criticisms of George Washington, 76, 80–81, 201n86; death of, 177; inaugural address,1801, 84; inauguration, 1801, 3, 63, 83, 171; Jefferson-Burr ticket, 76, 82, 202n96; opposition to monarchy, 69–71; "Revolution of 1800," 83
Job seekers, 14, 39, 182n16
Judicial branch, 33, 43, 188n7

Kendall, Amos, 164, 216n90. See Jackson, Andrew
Kennedy, William, 147, 214n36. See Washington, North Carolina
Kentucky, 77, 78, 80, 137, 142, 161, 162, 163, 164, 166
Kentucky Gazette, 167, 168

Index

Kentucky Republican, 167
Kentucky Resolutions, 77, 78, 79, 201nn73–74, 201n78. See also Alien and Sedition Acts; Breckinridge, John C.; Jefferson, Thomas; Virginia Resolutions
King, Rufus, 114, 129, 130. See also Federalists
Kings, 12, 56, 57, 58, 59, 65, 84
Kosciuszko, Tadeusz, 77
Knox, Henry, 51, 72. See also War, Secretary of

Lafayette, Marquis de, 69, 176, 212n173, 217n25
Lang, John, 109, 112–113. See also *New York Daily Gazette*
Langdon, John, 16. See also president pro tempore
Latrobe, Benjamin, 85, 130. See also Capitol, U.S
Lear, Tobias, 48, 49. See also Washington, George; Presidential furnishings
Lee, Richard Henry, 30, 32
Lee, Thomas, 147, 214n37. See also Charleston, South Carolina
Legislative branch, 12, 14, 15, 63 64, 68, 73, 79
Legislatures, state, 77, 78, 80
Legitimacy, 10, 16, 17, 22, 25, 34, 37, 43, 73, 80
Lespendard, 61. See also Sedition Act
Lewis, William B., 158, 173, 215n78
Lexington, Georgia, 156. See also Crawford, William H
Lexington, Kentucky, 157, 161, 165, 177
Liberty, 63, 66, 68, 72, 76, 77, 141
Livingston, Robert R., 24, 25, 38, 40, 41, 43, 185n68, 188n9, 189n22. See also Chancellor, New York State
"Long live George Washington, President of the United States," 25, 41, 186n77. See also Washington Inauguration, 1789; Livingston, Robert R
"Long live the President," 11, 55
Louisville, Kentucky, 163, 164

Maclay, William, 12, 23, 27, 28, 30, 31, 33, 187n93
Madison, Dolley, 5, 86, 87, 88–89, 186n86. See also First lady; Balls, inaugural
Madison, James, 5, 8, 27, 28, 31–32, 38, 41, 44, 51, 57, 66, 68, 72 73, 75, 77, 78, 79, 81, 83, 86, 97, 127, 131, 132, 142, 169, 187n112, 189n18, 194n112, 216n109; as advisor to George Washington, 27, 38, 41, 44, 51; as president, 88–89, 95, 108, 143, 151, 153, 168, 175; Democratic-Republican opposition, 57, 66, 68, 72, 75, 77, 78; in house of representatives, 27, 28, 31–32, 68; inauguration, 1809, 89, 204n123; role of political parties, 131–32
Magistrate, 6, 32, 104, 105, 108, 150, 166. See also presidency
Maine, 118, 126
Manhattan, 15, 21, 109. See also New York City
Mann, Horace, 111
Manufacturers, American, 16, 29, 54, 57, 96, 106, 163, 165
Marshall, John, 83, 84
Maryland, 16, 50, 80
Mason, Jeremiah, 98, 99 (portrait), 114, 117, 129, 206n27. See also Federalists
Mason, John, Jr., 104, 207n46. See also Monroe's northern tour
Massachusetts, 29, 51, 75, 80, 82, 111, 115, 116, 118, 130, 134, 174
Mazzei, Philip, 76, 79, 81, 200nn65–66. See also Jefferson, Thomas
Merry, Anthony, 86, 87, 88. See also Jefferson, Thomas
Merry, Elizabeth, 86, 88. See also Jefferson, Thomas
Mexican-American War, 177
Michigan, 126
Military Academy, U.S. (West Point), 98, 108, 110, 208n76
Military Defenses: during Monroe's tours, 96, 100, 105, 107, 108, 109, 110, 138, 139–140, 148
Militias, 25, 51, 82, 84, 89, 96, 117, 148
Minerva, 76. See also Newspapers, Federalist

Index **239**

Mississippi River, 10
Missouri Controversy, 142, 212n1
Monarchical rituals, 4, 5, 11, 12, 19, 22, 25, 26, 32, 34, 37, 38, 41, 57, 58, 59, 62, 63, 64, 69, 70, 79, 81, 88, 89, 90, 127, 180n6
Monarchy, 4, 6, 8, 10, 11, 12, 13, 25, 26, 27, 28, 31, 33, 36, 37, 38, 41, 56, 59, 62, 64, 65, 69, 70, 71, 76, 79, 81, 82, 84, 113, 161, 171, 174
Monticello, 75. See also Jefferson, Thomas
Monroe, Elizabeth, 119, 209n118
Monroe, James, 5, 6, 7, 8, 77, 81, 90, 96, 98, 144, 202n15, 202n17, 211n157, 216n109; a president, 91–93, 94, 95, 96, 97, 99, 100, 101, 103, 104, 105, 106, 107, 108, 109, 110, 112, 113, 114, 115, 116, 117, 118, 119, *120*, 121, 122, 123, 124, 125, 126, 127, 128, 129, 130, 131, 132, 133, 134, 136, 141, 142, 143, 145, 146, 147, 148, 149, 150, 151, *152*, 153, 154, 155 156, 158, 159, 160, 161, 162, 163, 164, 165, 166, 167, 168, 171, 173, 175, 176, 178; as Virginia governor, 144; Chesapeake tour, 135, 138–140, 174; death of, 177; "Disappearance" during Southern tour, 137, 157; inaugural address, 1817, 92, 96, 137, 169; inauguration, 1817, 98, 111; non-partisan vision, 59, 91, 92, 94, 97, 134, 137, 153, 168, 169; Northern tour, 1817, 91–93, 93 (map), 98, 100, 103, 104, 105, 107, 108, 109, 110, 112, 113, 114, 115, 116, 117, 118, 119, 120, 121, 122, 123, 124, 125, 126, 127–39, 131, 133, 134, 135, 138, 146, 153, 165, 166, 167, 174, 175; outreach to Federalists, 97, 98, 100–101, 103, 115, 121, 129; Southern tour, 91, 92, 94, 107, 135, 136 (map), 137, 138, 142, 144, 145, 146, 147, 148, 149, 150, 151, 152, 153, 154, 155, 156, 157, 158, 159, 160, 161, 162, 163, 164, 165, 166, 167, 168, 173, 174, 212n3
Monroe, Lieutenant James, 134, 138 146, 150, 157, 174–175
Morris, Robert, 48. See also Presidential housing

Morse, Samuel F. B., 151, 152 (Monroe portrait)
Mount Vernon, 11, 14, 15, 16, 17, 43, 46, 47, 48, 49, 54, 56

Nashville, Tennessee, 157, 158, 160, 161, 173
Natchez, 144, 158
National Intelligencer, 85, 113, 125, 148, 157, 165. See also Gales, Joseph; Seaton, William
Nation's capital: New York City, 13, 15, 26, 19, 23, 24, 27, 39, 44, 48; Philadelphia, 48, 49, 54, 60, 61, 75, 76, 83; Washington, DC, 63, 66, 84, 85, 88, 89, 104, 113, 119, 126, 138, 141, 154, 157, 166, 170, 171
National Gazette, 68, 74. See also Freneau, Philip
Newark, New Jersey, 61
New Bern, North Carolina, 55, 147
New England, 16, 50, 51, 52, 54, 75, 82, 91, 95, 97, 98, 103, 114, 115, 122, 123, 126, 129, 177
New Hampshire, 16, 51, 52, 85, 98
New Hampshire Gazette, 104, 112
New Haven, Connecticut, 15, 110, 111
New Jersey, 15, 16, 19, 44, 50, 61, 104, 109
New Jersey Journal, 7
New Orleans, Louisiana, 137, 165. See also Clay, Henry
Newport, Rhode Island, 52, 54, 61
Newspapers, 4, 6, 7, 9, 15, 17, 22, 35, 45, 50, 54, 58, 59, 60, 61, 62, 63, 64, 65, 68, 70, 74, 76, 90, 101, 103, 105, 106, 112, 113, 114, 117, 121, 126, 128, 129, 133, 137, 157, 158, 161, 166, 167; Democratic- Republican, 74, 75, 77, 78, 80, 113; Federalist, 117, 126, 210n122
Newspapers' editors, 6, 9, 22, 57, 59, 78, 80, 92, 94, 101, 106, 109, 112, 137, 166, 171; Federalists, 92, 124; Democratic-Republican, 124, 125, 126
New York City, 11, 12, 13, 14, 15, 16, 17, 19, 22, 23, 24, 26, 27, 29, 37, 39, 44, 45, 46, 47, 48, 49, 50, 51, 52, 54, 55, 66, 104, 107, 109, 110, 114, 134

240   Index

New York Gazette, 6, 48, 109, 112–113, 207n66. See also Lang, John
New York Evening Post, 113
New York State, 24, 25, 38, 49, 50, 52, 70, 104, 118, 168, 175, 177, 182n14; 1804 gubenatorial campaign, 70
Niles' Weekly Register, 106, 114, 167
Norfolk, Virginia, 135, 139, 146
North Carolina, 10, 50, 54, 55, 80, 135, 143, 145, 146, 147, 148, 154, 182n14, 183n84

Oaths: congressional, 33; federal, 33; presidential, 24, 25, 26, 27, 58, 60, 83–84, 109, 170
Ohio, 118, 126, 163, 177
Ohio River, 163, 216n89
Otis, Harrison Gray, 97, 98, 101, 102 (portrait), 103, 115, 116, 121, 130, 131, 134, 206n23, 206n25. See also Federalists; Hartford Convention; Monroe's Northern tour

Page, John, 31, 80, 200n58. See also Democratic-Republicans
Pamphlets, 70, 75
Partisan organizations, 7, 8, 57, 59, 62, 63, 64, 69, 71, 74, 77, 82, 90, 119, 133, 135, 171, 172, 173
Partisan surrogates, 8, 64, 65, 69, 74, 76, 78, 154
Patronage, 77, 131
Peale, Angelica, 18. See also Washington's pre-inaugural tour
Peale, Charles Willson, 17, *18, 67,* 107, 184n47
Pendleton, Edmund, 75, 200nn57–58. See also Democratic-Republicans
Pennsylvania, 16, 23, 28, 49, 50, 73, 80, 126; Emancipation law, 49
Pennsylvania Avenue, 170
Pennsylvania Mercury, 21
Philadelphia, Pennsylvania, 17, 37, 44, 46, 47, 48, 49, 50, 54, 60, 61, 75, 76, 83, 101, 103, 104, 107, 110, 177, 191n61
Pinckney, Charles, 75, 200n60; as "South Carolina Planter," 75

Pinckney, Charles Cotesworth, 75, 76, 80, 153, 215n61. See also Adams-Pinckney ticket
Pinckney, Thomas, 75, 153, 215n61
Pintard, John, 111–112
Pittsburgh, Pennsylvania, 163
Planter class, 138, 143–144, 146, 147, 148, 149, 150, 153, 154, 156, 160, 161. See also Monroe's Southern tour
Plumer, William, 85
Poems, 6, 51
Political organizations, 5, 6, 59, 64, 65, 94
Political parties, 6, 7, 9, 76, 85, 94, 96, 97, 109, 112, 114, 121, 122, 125, 127, 128, 129, 131, 132, 133, 134, 153, 163, 168, 169, 170, 171, 178. See also Democratic-Republicans; Democratic Party; Federalists; Whig Party
Pomp, 6, 58, 89, 113, 129, 167
Pope, William, 163
Pope, Worden, 163
Popular sovereignty, 5, 6, 8, 12, 36, 105, 134; as "fiction," 6, 179n3, 180n12
Port Folio, 88
Portraits, presidential, 52, 55–56, 118–119, 120, 151, 152. See also Monroe, James; Washington, George
Portsmouth, New Hampshire, 50, 52, 103, 129
Postal Service, U.S., 6, 74, 77, 104, 128, 200n67
Postal Service Act of 1792, U.S., 74, 101, 207n38
President, 4, 5, 6, 8, 9, 11, 12, 13, 22, 24, 25, 26, 27, 28, 29, 30, 31, 32, 33, 34, 36, 37, 38, 39, 40, 41, 42, 43, 44, 45, 46, 47, 48, 50, 51, 55, 56, 59, 60, 61, 62, 63, 64, 73, 74, 77, 80, 81, 82, 83, 84, 85, 86, 89, 91, 97, 98, 100, 103, 104, 106, 111, 112, 113, 114, 115, 121, 125, 128, 130, 136, 163, 168, 169, 171, 173, 175, 176, 178
President-elect, 23, 36
Presidential accessibility, 35, 38, 40, 42, 44, 46, 47, 55, 59, 62, 84, 89, 104, 105, 106, 112, 171
Presidential ceremony, 6, 7, 8, 9, 15, 24, 30, 33, 34, 35, 36, 39, 40, 42, 43, 83, 94, 171, 175

Presidential clothing, 16, 29, 37, 45, 46, 60, 96, 106, 119; informality of Thomas Jefferson, 85, 86
Presidential conduct, 3, 6, 31, 34, 38, 40, 42, 43, 48, 100, 106, 112, 114, 167, 168; unrepublican, 47, 112, 125
Presidential court, 41, 112, 113
Presidential Dignity, 41, 42, 43, 44, 46, 47, 58, 59, 89, 100, 119
Presidential drawing rooms, 45, 46, 60
Presidential elections, of 1789, 4, 11, 13, 14, 15, 25, 36, 127; of 1792, 57, 70; of 1796, 59, 73, 77, 79, 81; of 1800, 59, 64, 74, 75, 77, 79–80, 81, 82, 202n96; of 1812, 175; of 1820, 161, 168; of 1824, 161, 168–169, 172–173, 175; of 1828, 173, 174; of 1832, 174; of 1836, 177; of 1840, 177
Presidential entertainments, 5, 35, 39, 42, 43, 44, 45, 47, 49, 55, 60, 85, 88; theater, 45
Presidential expenses, 27, 40, 47, 48
Presidential furnishings, 35, 37, 47, 48, 49, 170, 192n64
Presidential horseback rides, 45, 55, 62, 84, 100, 104, 117, 146, 170
Presidential invitations, 35, 42, 44, 45, 85, 89, 100, 103, 106, 109, 121
Presidential levees, 6, 36, 37, 42, 43, 45–46, 58, 59, 60, 62, 85, 89. See also Presidential entertainments
Presidential salary, 27, 33, 48. See also Washington, George
Presidential social calendar, 44, 45, 46, 47, 190n31
Presidential steward, 47, 48, 49
Presidential visiting hours, 35, 37, 39, 43, 45, 59, 62
Presidential visitors, 35, 39, 41, 42, 45, 46, 58, 84. See also job seekers
Presidential walks, 37, 45, 62
President pro tempore, 16. See also Langdon, John
Press, freedom of, 74, 78, 82, 84
Processions, 16, 21, 25, 51, 54, 55, 58, 60, 92, 105, 117, 125, 138, 149, 160, 165, 170

Progress: royal, 11, 17, 37, 56, 181n4; Republican, 16, 148, 167
Providence, Rhode Island, 54, 111, 116

Quincy, Eliza, 121
Quincy, Josiah, 121
Quincy, Massachusetts, 61, 121

Ramsay, Dennis, 17. See also Alexandria, Virginia
Randolph, Thomas Mann, 69, 71, 73, 80, 83, 198n20. See also Jefferson, Thomas
Receptions, 5, 6, 7, 8, 16, 36, 37, 50, 51, 54, 62, 83, 85, 89, 113, 117, 118, 147, 156, 157. See also Presidential entertainments
Refreshments, 45, 85, 125, 170
Regional tensions, 135, 136, 137, 138, 151, 166–167, 169, 195n121
Religion, freedom of, 82, 84
Republican government, 4, 5, 6, 7, 9, 10, 11, 12, 13, 14, 16, 17, 18, 22, 25, 26, 27, 28, 29, 32, 34, 36, 37, 38, 40, 41, 43, 49, 50, 56, 57, 58, 61, 62, 64, 65, 68, 76, 84, 90, 92, 96, 97, 104, 106, 109, 119, 127, 131, 132, 134, 135, 138, 153, 161, 169, 171, 173, 175, 178
Republican political culture, 4, 5, 6, 7, 8, 11, 13, 22, 25, 30, 33, 38, 43, 51, 60, 61, 68, 76, 80, 83, 84, 107, 109, 126, 167, 171, 191n60
Republican principles, 3, 4, 7, 8, 9, 17, 22, 29, 31, 32, 33, 36, 37, 38, 41, 44, 47, 49, 57, 59, 62, 72, 73, 81, 84, 92, 96, 97, 112, 114, 124, 125, 126, 133, 137, 140, 141, 143, 147, 150, 156, 161, 166, 168, 176
Rhetorical campaign, 5, 63, 65, 69, 76, 77, 78, 79, 80, 82, 83, 178; "Anglican" 76; "Anglomen" 76; "Monarchists, 71, 78, 79, 127; "Monocrats," 69, 70, 79, 80; "Papermen," 79; "War-party," 79. See also Democratic-Republicans; Jefferson, Thomas
Rhode Island, 10, 50, 54, 182n14, 193n83
Richmond Enquirer, 124, 125
Ritchie, Thomas, 124, 125. See also *Richmond Enquirer*

242   Index

Rituals, 3, 4, 6, 7, 8, 16, 19, 29, 33, 34, 36, 43, 54, 55, 59, 64, 70, 92, 104, 107, 111, 126, 127, 138, 144; Southern, 144, 154. See also monarchical rituals
Roads, 104, 146, 160, 195n120
Royal subjects, 22, 27, 56
Royalty, 12, 58, 62
Russell, Benjamin, 124–125, 126. See also *Columbian Centinel*; "Era of Good Feelings;" "Newspaper editors, Federalists."
Rutledge, Edward, 10

St. Paul's Church, 24, 27. See also New York City; Washington, George, Inauguration
Sackett's Harbor, New York, 104
Saltonstall, Leverett, 124
Savage, Edward, 52, 53. See also Harvard University
Schuykill River Bridge, 17. See also Charles Willson Peale
Savannah, Georgia, 55, 137, 154, 156, 157
Seaton, William, 112, 125. See also *National Intelligence*; Gales, Joseph
Second American Party System, 94, 133, 171, 173, 212n175. See also Democratic Party; Whig Party
Sedition Act, 61, 77, 78, 124. See also Alien and Sedition Acts; Kentucky Resolutions; Virginia Resolutions
Seminole War, 137, 140, 141, 142, 156, 158, 160, 161, 163. See also Florida; Jackson, Andrew; Monroe, James
Senate, U.S., 4, 13, 14, 15, 16, 23, 24, 25, 27, 28, 30, 31, 32, 33, 38, 58, 73, 83, 84, 98, 143
Senators, U.S., 14, 15, 19, 23, 24, 25, 28, 30, 39, 45, 85, 89, 98, 101, 115, 130, 134, 174
Servants, presidential household, 47, 48, 49
Simplicity, republican, 84, 85, 86, 110, 112, 114, 119, 127
Silsbee, Nathaniel, 134, 174
Slaves, 48, 49, 147, 149, 154, 157, 158, 164; George Washington's, 49; Martha Washington's, 44
Slavery, 135, 142, 143, 153, 193n82; Gabriel's Rebellion, 144

Smith, Margaret Bayard (Mrs. Samuel H. Smith), 86,
Smith, Samuel H., 85, 86
Society of Cincinnati, 72, 107
South Carolina, 31, 54, 55, 75, 76, 80, 135, 143, 145, 146, 148, 149, 150, 153, 156
Sovereign authority, 3, 4, 11, 13, 16, 17, 22, 34, 37, 50, 56, 61, 62, 64, 82, 84, 90, 91, 94, 111, 114, 134, 174
Spain, 140, 141. See also Florida
Speech, freedom of, 74, 78
Springfield Armory, 111
Springfield, Massachusetts, 111
State, U.S. Department of, 33
State, U.S. Secretary of, 52, 65, 66, 67, 71, 86, 96, 97, 115, 121, 129–130, 141, 142, 163, 173, 199n41, 216n109. See also Adams, John Quincy; Jefferson, Thomas
Steamboats, 104, 109, 110, 146
Stiles, George, 105, 113. See also Baltimore, Maryland
Story, Joseph, 116. See also Boston, Monroe's tour
Stuart, Archibald, 74, 81, 199–200n49. See also Jefferson, Thomas
Stuart, David, 58, 196n135. See also Washington, George
Stuart, Gilbert, 119, 120 (Monroe portrait), 151, 209n118
Sullivan, George, 122. See also Webster, Daniel
Supreme Court, U.S., 38, 124
Swift, Joseph Gardner, 98, 99, 104, 107, 116. See also Monroe's Northern tour
Symbols, 3, 4, 7, 8, 29, 34, 36, 55, 61, 62, 109; classical, 16, 17; monarchical, 16, 17

Tariffs, 96, 160, 165. See also American System
Taylor, John, 78. See also Virginia Resolutions
Tennessee, 80, 136, 142, 146, 157, 158, 159, 161, 163 173. See also Jackson, Andrew
Thomson, Charles, 15

Titles, presidential, 24, 28, 30–33, 41, 59, 188n5
Toasts, 16, 17, 51, 55, 58, 138, 144, 147, 151, 156, 160, 161, 164, 165, 167, 183n39, 214n26. See also regional disagreements
Tompkins, Daniel D., 109, 168
Transylvania University, 165
Treasury, U.S. Department of, 33, 68, 69
Treasury, U.S. Secretary of, 38, 65, 66, 68, 69, 71, 129, 137, 141, 154. See also Crawford, William H.; Gallatin, Albert; Hamilton, Alexander
Trenton, New Jersey, 18, 20, 107, 108
Triumphal Arches, 6, 11, 17, 18, *19*, *20*, 51, 111, 122, 126, 167, 181n4, 184n45; criticisms of, 122, 167
Trumbull, John, 55
Tucker, Thomas, 31–32. See also Titles, presidential

Vice president, 13, 14, 15, 16, 25, 28, 33, 42, 43, 59, 73, 74, 79, 80, 82, 83, 84, 109, 142, 170, 175, 216n109, 217n5
Virginia, 16, 17, 30, 31, 38, 50, 54, 76, 78, 80, 81, 90, 95, 115, 118, 130, 132, 135, 143, 144, 145, 154, 168
Virginia Herald, 113
Virginia Resolutions, 77, 201n73. See also Kentucky Resolutions; Madison, James; Taylor, John

War of 1812, 89, 91, 94–95, 96, 105, 108, 139, 140, 143, 146, 147, 158, 160, 207n65; Battle of New Orleans, 95, 144; Treaty of Ghent, 95
War, U.S. Department of, 33
War, U.S. Secretary of, 72, 136, 138, 141, 145 146
Warville, Brissot de, 69
Washington, DC, 63, 66, 84, 85, 88, 89, 104, 113, 119, 126, 138, 141, 154, 157, 166, 170, 171; as permanent nation's capital, 66, 190n61
Washington, George: as president, 3, 4, 5, 6, 7, 8, 10, 14, 15, 19, 31, 39, 41, 44, 45, 46, 47, 48, 50, 51, 57, 61, 63, 64, 65, 66, 67, 68, 69, 70, 72, 73, 74, 84, 85, 89, 90, 91, 92, 96, 100, 104, 107, 108, 109, 111, 118, 119, 126, 127, 150, 151, 153, 17, 175, 176, 178, 186–187n92, 188n7, 190nn32–33, 194n114, 199n42, 210n85; Eastern Tour, 7, 11, 16, 37, 50, 51, 52, *53*, 54, 56, 118, 193n83; inaugural address, 1789, 25, 27, 186n87; inauguration, 1789, 5, 11, 12, 13, 23, 24–27, 28, 29, 30, 33, 34, 35, 36, 38, 51, 55, 58, 60, 62, 171, 183n28, 186n79; inauguration, 1793, 58, 69; Jefferson's criticisms of, 76, 80–81, 201n86; pre-inaugural tour, 6, 11, 12, 16, 17, *20*, 21, 22, *23*, 29, 50, 51, 55; Rhode Island tour, 52–54; query on presidential conduct, 35, 36, 37, 38, 39, 40, 42, 43, 45, 49, 56; Southern tour, 11, 16, 37, 50, 51, 52, 54, 55, 56, 135, 150, 193n83, 194n114; tours' impact, 96, 105, 127, 138, 166, 169, 175, 177
Washington, Martha, 37, 43, 44, 45, 46, 47, 48, 49, 55, 190n32, 190n33, 190n34, 196n135; "Lady Washington," 44; "Marquise Washington," 44
Washington, North Carolina, 147
Watson, John F., 46
Wayne, James M., 156. See also Savannah, Georgia
Webster, Daniel, 94, 98, 122, *123*, 124, 130, 134, 174, 176, 177, 206n27; as Whig, 174, 177; Bunker Hill Monument, 176, 217n24; Plymouth Rock Commemoration, 176, 217n24; role in Monroe's northern tour, 121–122, 130, 174; tour of 1833, 177, 212n173
Western Monitor, 157
Western territory, 10, 91
Whig party, 97, 133, 134, 173, 174, 175, 177
Whiskey Rebellion, 71, 72, 73. See also Democratic-Republican Societies
Wilmington, North Carolina, 148
Wirt, William, 97, 128, 130, 211n157
Wise, John, 79
Wise's Tavern, 17
Worcester, Massachusetts, 15
Wythe, George, 73. See Jefferson, Thomas; Yale University, 111

E 176.1 .M73 2010
Moats, Sandra.
Celebrating the Republic

JAN 1 8 2010